FLOWERING LOTUS

FLOWERING LOTUS

A View of Java in the 1950s

HAROLD FORSTER

SINGAPORE
OXFORD UNIVERSITY PRESS
OXFORD NEW YORK
1989

Oxford University Press

Oxford New York Toronto
Delhi Bombay Calcutta Madras Karachi
Petaling Jaya Singapore Hong Kong Tokyo
Nairobi Dar es Salaam Cape Town
Melbourne Auckland
and associated companies in
Berlin Ibadan

Oxford is a trade mark of Oxford University Press

First published by Longmans, Green and Co. Ltd.,
London 1958

First issued as an Oxford University Press paperback 1989

This edition of Flowering Lotus: A View of Java, First Edition,
is published by arrangement with
Longman Group UK Limited, London

ISBN 0 19 588946 0

Printed in Malaysia by Peter Chong Printers Sdn. Bhd.
Published by Oxford University Press Pte. Ltd.,
Unit 221, Ubi Avenue 4, Singapore 1440

For

CORAL

who shared in the
making of this book

PREFACE

WHEN I was posted to Java in 1952, I made a hasty round of the London bookshops to search for information about my future home—and came back almost empty-handed. Books in English about the Dutch East Indies seemed pitifully scarce and out-of-date, while the new-born Republic of Indonesia was still so young that there was practically nothing available on the subject except scattered reports and occasional articles. My mind therefore was open—one might almost say blank—when I arrived in the island and my impressions were formed at first hand on the spot. The four years I was there nearly doubled the life of the Republic, and though the heroic phase of the War of Independence was over, I saw something of the equally vital struggle to consolidate the victory of the Revolution. More-over, since my post was in the interior, at the new university in Jogjakarta, I saw a rather different side of Javanese life from most —less hectic than the political merry-go-round of the capital, less hackneyed than the beaten path of tourism. These are my excuses for writing this book.

I want to emphasise that it is a book about Java, not Indonesia as a whole. I have written only of the places and people I saw for myself. Though Java is the most important of the thousands of islands that make up the Indonesian archipelago, it is by no means the only important one nor typical of all the rest. Stretching over 3,000 miles along the Equator between Malaya and Australia, these islands display a rich variety of races, religions, languages, civilisations. There is Sumatra, dwarfing Java in size and natural wealth, with such varied peoples as the warlike Moslems of Atjeh, the Christian Bataks and the matriarchal Menangkabaus; the still huger bulk of Borneo with its fringe of isolated ports and its vast untouched jungle, inhabited by pagan Dayaks; the orchid-shaped Celebes whose people range from the educated Menadonese to the primitive Toradjas; and the Spice Islands and the Lesser Sundas and the still Hindu isle of Bali. One of the most urgent problems of the Republic of Indonesia is to weld all these diverse elements into a genuine unity without excessive centralism—or separatism.

Yet Java, though comparatively small, occupies a dominant position among its giant neighbours. History has made it the most highly developed and civilised of the islands and its population has multiplied till the Javanese now far outnumber all the other Indonesians together—fifty millions in this one thin island and some thirty in all the rest. Java has always been the head and heart of Indonesia, the core of every major island-empire since the decline of Sumatra's Shrividjaya a thousand years ago; and Shrividjaya is not much more than a name. The first monumental evidence of the high civilisation achieved by the Indian colonial kingdoms, which probably imposed themselves on the Malay population in the first centuries A.D., is to be found in Java, in the eighth-century Hindu temples of the Dieng plateau, in the colossal assertion of ninth-century Buddhism at Borobudur, in the soaring Shivaite rejoinder of tenth-century Prambanan. It was in Java that the Hindu civilisation of the archipelago reached its climax in the medieval empire of Modjopahit, which spread its authority almost to the bounds of modern Indonesia. Islam came first to Sumatra, but it was the Javanese successor states that rose to international fame after the overthrow of Modjopahit (traditionally 1478)—Bantam crowded with Elizabethan sails and Mataram whose dynasty still survives in the splinter princedoms of Mid Java. When the Dutch East India Company decided to set up a permanent fortified base in 1619, they chose Jacatra (Djakarta) in West Java, renaming it Batavia and making it the capital of an ever-expanding commercial empire that was eventually taken over by the government as the Netherlands East Indies. Java was the scene of the British invasion in Napoleon's time and the five years' rule of Raffles; of the great rebellion of Prince Diponegoro in 1825–30; of the first nationalist movements at the beginning of our own century; of the Dutch surrender to the Japanese in 1942; and, after the Japanese surrender three years later, of the Declaration of Independence by President Sukarno. And in the four years' struggle that followed it was Jogjakarta, the historic centre of pure Javanism, that served as the capital of the besieged Republic and the symbol of the new spirit of Indonesia.

The sketch of a head necessarily leaves out many important aspects of the body, but it may still give a good idea of the subject's character. Perhaps this book, though confined to Java, may throw a little incidental light on the larger question of Indonesia.

It would be impossible to thank by name all those who helped me with information and explanation, suggestions and guidance, hospitality and transport. I trust they will be content with a general acknowledgment: to my students of Gadjah Mada University; to my colleagues on the staff and their wives, the members of the Saturday Club; to the leaders of the Jogja dance groups and the ASRI art school; to princes and to peasants, not forgetting our servants' old mother. But there are two persons that I would like to thank individually for special contributions to my enquiries: H.H. Sultan Hamengku Buwono IX of Jogjakarta for the private interview which provided the basis of Chapter 7; and Professor Bernet Kempers, who supplied most of the technical information about Java's antiquities in Chapter 10.

NOTE ON THE SPELLING

Indonesian spelling is phonetic, but in one or two cases I have taken certain small liberties with it in order to make the pronunciation more obvious to English readers. Thus:

(*a*) *j* by itself indicates the sound of English *y*, which has been used instead, e.g. Surabaya;

(*b*) *k* at the end of words indicates a glottal stop and has been omitted in the commonly heard words like *betja* (betjak);

(*c*) in Mid-Java the long *a* is pronounced *o* and normally spelt so, e.g. the Premier's name was written Sastroamidjojo, though really Sastraamidjaja; for consistency I have applied this to historical names too, so that King Djajabaja becomes Djoyoboyo—as pronounced;

(*d*) the Dutch form *oe*, representing the *u* sound, is still retained by most people in their personal names, though officially abolished otherwise; thus the city of Bandung is now spelt so, not Bandoeng, but President Sukarno still signs himself Soekarno. I have, however, used *u* throughout.

With these modifications I think the reader who, like myself, likes to feel at home with the pronunciation can go ahead without worrying over the names and incidental Indonesian words. In only one case have I used a dubious spelling—in the name that occurs most frequently of all, Jogjakarta. Phonetically it should be, and sometimes is, written Djokjakarta; but having read and written the more familiar, though less correct, form every day for four years, I found I just could not use the other in my book.

CONTENTS

ILLUSTRATIONS

xiii

Photographs not otherwise acknowledged were taken by the author.

Part One

THE STUBBORN CITY

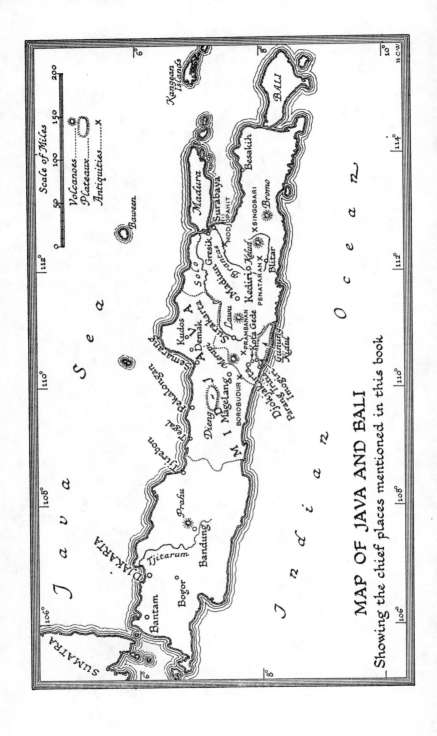

MAP OF JAVA AND BALI

Showing the chief places mentioned in this book

I

ANCIENT AND MODERN

A T last, through the heavy tropic darkness, our train came gasping into Jogja. That was how the name of our destination was spelt on the outside of the carriage, and that was what it was always called, though the correct form was Jogjakarta, or Djokjakarta, or even, in the full Javanese version, Ngajogjakarta, while Raffles in his *History of Java* (1817) spelt it Yug'ya Kerta. The popular abbreviation, informal and universal, was a sign of the place it held in the affections of the people—Jogja, the stubborn city of the Sultans, the sanctuary of Java's ancient traditions, the cradle of Indonesia's freedom.

At that moment, however, our main feeling was relief rather than romance, our interests practical rather than historical. All we wanted, as we climbed stiffly down to the station platform, was a good wash and a good meal. There were excuses for our somewhat mundane attitude. For one thing we were not tourists; we were to live and work in Jogja for at least three years. The amusing discomforts, the almost desirable difficulties that add a chiaroscuro to the tourist's memories, assume different proportions for the resident—there is no comfort in an infinite prospect of sweat and tepid rice. Then, again, we felt that we had been packed off with inconsiderate haste (through no fault of the Indonesians, it is true) on an unnecessarily risky journey. When we arrived at the port of Djakarta the previous morning, I had expected a few days in the capital for consultation and acclimatisation, and then an easy two-hour flight to my post. The railways, our Dutch shipmates had assured us, were quite impossible, being

3

regularly attacked by the bandits and not infrequently cut. It was a shock to be met at the dock with two tickets for the 6.40 train next morning.

In the circumstances we had not slept well. The heat of Djakarta is oppressive and our bungaloid hotel, built round a courtyard full of washing and only too near an odoriferous canal, was a sad contrast to the spotless spickness of our Dutch liner. As with most Indonesian hotel rooms there was a small open terrace attached, on which we sat as long as we could, watching the little house-lizards crawling up the walls and over the lamp-bowl, a situation which assured them of plenty of prey but also made their digestive processes transparent. At last we were driven inside by the mosquitoes and the droppings of the lizards. Five empty iron bedsteads, gloomily shrouded in dirty beige nets, crowded our bedroom but only emphasised our sense of abandonment. An inadequate electric fan buzzed and creaked on the washstand. It was almost a relief to be called before dawn, which took place about 6 a.m. with monotonous regularity all the year round.

The sun came up quickly and it was broad daylight as we drove through the shabby streets to the railway station. The streets were already crowded but even more so was the canal that divided them, a sluggish yellow ditch that dismally failed to remind one of the gracious waterways of Amsterdam. Wherever they settled the Dutch traders and colonists seem to have expressed their nostalgia in the creation of canals, a whim peculiarly unsuited to malarial climates. The death-rate in old Batavia (as the capital was called in the Dutch days) was daunting. The Indonesians, however, found the canals convenient and indeed indispensable, since there was no other water supply in their seething slums. They were addicted to washing; as a doctor remarked, they had a strong sense of personal cleanliness but very little of hygiene. The thick water was being churned up by a pack of slim brown bodies in every stage of dishabille—naked splashing children, boys draped tentlike in their checkered *sarongs*, women in soaked but modest underwear—and engaged in every kind of ablution from bathing and tooth-cleaning to laundry and the less savoury forms of morning toilet. It was fortunate that the water was quite opaque.

Then came our train journey, nearly thirteen hours of it. The first-class carriages were spacious, comfortable, and at the start, clean. As soon as we began to move, however, the snag appeared. The engine ran on wood, its tender stacked high with logs like a timberyard; if we left the windows open, we were soon smutted with soft, unbrushable clots of wood-ash; if we shut the windows, we were boiled alive. This dilemma rather diminished our powers of appreciation as we rattled across the lush and steaming plains of the north coast to Tjirebon. It was all new to us, the flooded rice-fields glittering like broken mirrors, the stooping lines of coolie hats and the moon-shaped horns of the buffaloes, the coconut palms shooting skyward to burst into leaves like green rockets, the tattered banana groves and all the other trees whose names we did not know. But inside our moving oven thirst competed with sleep for our first interest. There was a restaurant service on the train, but we had been warned against this and supplied with a packet of inadequate sandwiches. Where the Dutch had stressed the danger of bandits, the Americans had impressed on us the perils of ice.

"You must never drink water in Indonesia unless it's been boiled," they warned us earnestly, "and never, never touch their ice or you'll get dysentery for sure."

At last our thirst became intolerable. We found we could order beer, bottled and so presumably safe. The bottle was warm when it came but in each glass stood a large lump of ice! It was too much—we decided to risk dysentery; and after that we drank water and ice freely all over Java without ill effects.

After the ice the bandits. . . . As we turned up into the hills after some six hours' journey in order to cross to the south coast, we were joined by an armed guard of soldiers. I am not particularly bandit-conscious; seven years in Greece just after the war taught me to regard them as a natural hazard of travel, a stroke of bad luck like a tyre-burst. But I always felt more anxious when provided with military protection. The Communists of the Greek hills were more likely to go for government troops and arms than to indulge in mere highway robbery: in Java the bandits were political too, though not of the same persuasion. The *Darul Islam* was a movement of fanatical Moslems who wished to set up an Islamic theocratic state in Indonesia; their leader, Kartosuwiryo, broke away from the Republic with its policy of religious toleration in March 1948, when the Renville Agreement forced the Republican army to withdraw from West Java, leaving the guerilla struggle against the Dutch to the fanatics, who set up their own independent and still unsuppressed 'government' in the hills around Bandung. Our guard therefore increased my anxiety rather than allayed it, but on the whole the comparative cool of the hills more than compensated for such worries. As we climbed up over the backbone of Java, a long chain of volcanoes, the scenery became more varied and abrupt, yet essentially the same —everywhere a luxuriant green to the tops of the surrounding slopes. At Purwokerto we had reached the south side of the mountains and were safely through the worst bandit country. Everyone got out of the train to stretch and relax and smoke, and it was here that we first consciously noticed that clinging perfumed air that is so typical of places where a number of Javanese are gathered together. Soon we traced it to the fumes of the blunt cigarettes on every side; even little boys of six or seven were smoking happily and unrebuked as they squatted on the platform's edge. Surely it could not be opium? Fortunately we found an English-speaking fellow-passenger who informed us that these were the famous *kretek* cigarettes, in which the tobacco is mixed with cloves; their crackling gives the cigarettes their name.

The last stretch of two or three more hours through flat country seemed endless, leaving us as empty of romance as a squeezed lemon. It was well after dark again (dusk was as regular as dawn, between 6.30 and 7 p.m.) when we finally emerged from our carriage, stained and hungry, to be greeted by a smart young University official with a fine green Plymouth. Our troubles, we felt, were over as we swept into the wide front court of the Garuda

Hotel with its sunken garden and its lily pond and the canopies over the stairways glowing with multi-coloured glass. A first-class room had long been booked for us, perhaps one of those upstairs with a balcony. The manager soon shattered our dreams. Unusually solid and podgy for an Indonesian, with a round cropped head, he complacently denied all knowledge of our booking. Documents, entreaties, threats left him unmoved—all the first-class rooms were occupied by important visitors for the celebrations and he could only offer us a second-class one at the back. At last we allowed ourselves to be led, still feebly protesting, to a kind of slum opposite the kitchen, an ill-lit cell with a vast plank bed and no bathing facilities. There was a bathroom nearby, reached by a corridor open to the public gaze; but it was a poor specimen of the 'Dutch bathroom', the only type to be found in Java and even at its best unsatisfactory to English prejudices. It consisted of a narrow tiled chamber with a stone tank of water in one corner, a small aluminium can with a handle across the top and sometimes a cold shower. This one had a shower, but it was rusty and cobwebbed and all the taps were waterless. I gazed with horror into the stagnant and slimy depths of the tank, which had obviously not been drained out for months, but at last I took the plunge—or rather (for we had been warned not to try to squeeze ourselves inside) I plunged the can into it and hurled the water desperately over myself. Feeling refreshed but not clean, we changed and went across to the dining-room.

We were to get to know this room only too well in the next ten months and slowly the service and even the quality of the food improved. But at the time of our first encounter it was at a very low ebb. A large gloomy hall with dark brown panelling, stained glass windows, and a peeling yellow ceiling chilled our anticipations. We wandered from table to table trying to find a cloth that was not stained and patched; a waiter, whose only uniform was a black sidecap of the sort that had become the symbol of nationalism, padded up in bare feet and dingy vest and planked down before us the whole meal together, complete from soup to fruit and all already cold—cold and watery consommé, cold and stodgy white rice, cold and damp brown vegetables, and the inevitable bananas.

Coral, who had faced so much that day, could not face this and burst into despairing tears.

Next day was our wedding anniversary and we rose as late and lazily as we could. Even so it was only 8.20 when we came out of breakfast, for a long lie-in was not really pleasant in such a climate. The heat roused you soon after dawn and though it lay heavily upon your eyelids and your will-power, the dank sweat of the pillow and the Nessus-touch of the mattress soon forced you to drag yourself to the shower. As we tackled the manager about a change of rooms, our University friend suddenly re-appeared with his car.

"Are you ready?" he asked gaily.

"Ready for what?" I answered with some bewilderment.

"For the Commencement celebrations; they start at 8.30."

In our flurry the previous night we had not thought to enquire about the celebrations mentioned by the manager nor imagined it possible they might concern us. But now it appeared that all those important visitors had come to attend a University function and I was expected to make my first appearance there. With blasphemous haste I changed from shorts into unseasonable *sub fusc*. and the green car ploughed its way through seas of bicycles down a long straight street to the Sultan's palace. Through a white conventional gateway we came upon a wide and grassy square, across which we sped to the high-roofed forecourts of the *Kraton* with its slender pillars and elaborately decorated pediment of flowers and bees and snakes. Up a wide flight of stairs we hurried to a second pillared hall, crowded with dignitaries and students of both sexes. But I was diverted to a smaller building on the right, just in time to join a crocodile of learned persons, the leading figures swathed in black robes heavy with velvet. Their heads were crowned with tasselled academic caps in the shape of a lotus blossom, the emblem of the University but not, one must hope, symbolic of its spirit; thick silver chains made the Professors look even more like mayors in mourning. Ought I to have worn my own Cambridge robes? I had not thought to bring them to this tropic land where even the Jesuits wear white. Yet on second thoughts why should not the trappings of learning be just as important as the trappings of an army in creating the requisite spirit of pride and emulation? Gadjah Mada University might be only three years old, but it was determined to rival the solemn splendours of those Dutch foundations at which most of its Indonesian professors had graduated.

The crocodile wound through the packed hall and up onto a low marble dais, where a smaller roof below the main roof, both richly carved and gilded, formed a canopy over a polished grey plaque. Here the Sultan used to sit in state three times a year. Our procession divided respectfully on either side of it and settled in serried lecture-room chairs facing one another and the speaker's rostrum. The proceedings began.

For the next two hours I was able to sit back and take stock of the place and people among whom I was to work as a lecturer in English. Luckily I found myself sitting next to the only other Englishman present, a young archaeologist from the London School of Oriental Studies, who was revisiting the rich relics of Central Java's Hindu civilisation. He explained to me who was who and what was what and interpreted the programme, a duplicated document whose surprisingly minute and unoriental time-table bore a creditable relation to actuality. It was obvious that the name 'commencement' was a literal and logical description of the ceremony, not used in the topsy-turvy Anglo-American sense of the final conferment of degrees; it was in fact the opening ceremony of the new academic year (which, despite the Equator, corresponded to our own) and consisted mainly of long speeches in Indonesian, a language as yet quite unintelligible to me.

First came the annual report by Dr. Sardjito, the President of the University. This post corresponded roughly to an English University's Vice-Chancellor, the man who wields the real executive power. The honorary head, corresponding to the Chancellor, was Prince Paku Alam, head of Jogja's secondary royal house, who was seated in an elaborately carved chair in front of us; at a still higher and remoter level was the Sultan himself as a sort of patron. Dr. Sardjito looked a typical Professor, white-haired and wispy with a mild and piping voice that seemed miles removed from the harsh and violent realities of the outside world. Yet this shy little figure was reciting a series of highly practical statistics and facts which showed how, under his leadership and organisation, a University of over 5,000 students had sprung into being in three years. He was one of Indonesia's most noted medical men and during the Revolution the Dutch had sent 200 men to arrest him. He only escaped by an epic bicycle ride through the ricefields.

My eyes wandered to the sea of eager brown faces on my right, the students of the new Indonesia. They were dressed in Western fashion, the boys in open white shirts and trousers, the girls in simple cotton frocks—the price of modernism is the rejection of the picturesque. In the streets of Jogja we had seen plenty of both men and women clad in Javanese dress, but they looked to be mainly of the uneducated class; in this hall the only men to be seen in turbans and skirts were elderly officials of the Sultan's household. In the case of the married ladies, however, national costume was still in favour and the front rows, where the wives sat, were like a herbaceous border of sombre brown skirts and brightly flowered blouses. As I studied the students' features, in which the common denominators seemed to be straight jet-black hair, large and liquid black eyes, flat noses and wide, toothy and charming smiles, one of my cherished preconceptions about the Far East was exploded: here at least were no inscrutable and impassive Orientals but young people full of gaiety and restlessness, whose free and open expressions presented no mask to the world—a world where a mask was no longer needed. Their complexions varied from a rich brown, sometimes with a delicate bluish bloom like a plum, to a lovely golden tan, such as our pallid socialites vainly pursue in long and expensive sojourns on the Riviera; but with normal human cussedness they in their turn admired and strove after our enviable Northern pallor.

Dr. Sardjito sat down and his place at the rostrum was taken by the speaker of the annual oration. This was Dr. Johannes, Dean of the Technical Faculty, a youngish man with piercing dark eyes and a lurking smile on features gaunter than usual. He came from Timor, the most south-easterly island of the Indonesian archipelago, in half of which the Portuguese still maintain a relic of their imperial glory. The Johannes family had produced several men distinguished in academic and public life, and he himself had been Minister of Public Works in the first Cabinet after the establishment of the unitary Republic that replaced the federal United States of Indonesia in August 1950. His subject was the development of atomic science and it is exceedingly unlikely that I should have understood much more if he had spoken in English. As it was, I could catch nothing except the occasional name of some Greek philosopher and the continually recurrent words *atoom-atoom*. This I realised from my rudimentary studies of the Indonesian language was the plural of the word *atoom*, an atom; for their delightfully simple way of forming the plural was just to repeat the word twice. In writing, however, this would be too clumsy in the case of long words, so they merely wrote *atoom2*—a system which gave a formidably mathematical look to their literature. In other ways too their grammar was engagingly uncomplicated—no declensions, no conjugations, no genders, no articles, not even a verb 'to be'! At first sight Indonesian looked like the language learner's dream. But very soon it became apparent that this simplicity, like the alleged simplicity of English grammar, was deceptive; that the very lack of obvious rules made it more difficult to speak correctly and express oneself in a natural way. Nor was the language without its complexities as soon as one progressed beyond the pidgin stage; a wilderness of prefixes and suffixes with consequent consonantal changes made the dictionary into a labyrinth.

Indonesian is a new language, a political creation of the nationalist movement. It is the national but not yet the native language of the various peoples of the scattered and diverse islands that were united by Dutch conquest to form the Netherlands East Indies and inherited as a unit (New Guinea excepted) by the Republic of Indonesia. In Central Java the people's mother tongue was Javanese, in West Java they spoke Sundanese, in the eastern districts you might hear Madurese; and in the myriad other islands there was a similar multiplicity of tongues. Even Javanese had three varieties, the high language, the middle and the low, to be used according to the status of your interlocutor, higher, equal or lower than yourself—with the paradoxical result that the Sultan always had to use the low language and servants the high. But in the early days of the nationalist movement it was seen that there could be no national feeling without a national language, and at that time the only lingua franca was Dutch, which was clearly unacceptable in a struggle against the Dutch. At the critical Youth Congress of 1928 a resolution was passed demanding ' One country, one nation, one language', and wisely, despite the preponderance of Java both in population and leadership, the language chosen was not Javanese. The other islands, jealous of their individual cultures and ready to suspect Javanese imperialism, might well have held aloof from uniting their efforts under such auspices. So the Congress chose Malay, for centuries the common medium of intercourse between the traders and pilgrims of the archipelago and thus a good basis for a national language, especially as the various peoples of Indonesia are ultimately of Malayan origin. But *Bahasa Indonesia*, the Indonesian language, is not identical with the language of Malaya. Based on a Sumatran dialect, it had to be rapidly developed and extended to apply to all the higher requirements, technical, abstract, literary, of a fully modernised civilisation, and in this sudden expansion it adopted words from every available source, Sanskrit of the old Hindu Empires, Arabic of the Moslem missionary conquerors, Portuguese and Dutch of the Western colonisers, English the modern world-language and the universal Greco-scientific terms like *atoom*. To me, unacquainted before with Malay, it was the simplest basic words of *Bahasa Indonesia* that continually slipped through the meshes of my memory, leaving me floundering in dumb unintelligence. Only where I could relate the sounds to some previous linguistic experience—a Latin root like *Minggu,* Sunday, from the Portuguese *Domingo,* or *medja,* table, from *mensa*; a Middle Eastern loan like *pasar,* a market or bazaar, or *dewan,* a divan or council—did the words stick readily; but on the rarefied level of *paedagogik* or *reorganisasi* or *ber-air-condition* I was much more at home. Nor was I the only one to find such difficulties—the Indonesians themselves were still learning their own national tongue and used it with some effort. In the towns the intellectuals still thought in Dutch and, privately and un-officially, preferred to converse and express their ideas in that language. In the villages the elders still knew no tongue but their own, Javanese or Sundanese or whatever it might be. Tony, the archaeologist, told me that on his visits to the villages the head-man would call as interpreter one of the school-children since they were the only ones who knew any Indonesian! We were watching the birth-pangs not only of a nation but of a language too.

At the end of the atomic oration we rose and trooped down the broad steps from the plateau of *Siti-hinggil,* the upper hall, to the ground level of *Pagelaran,* where the verandahs had been par-titioned off to form offices and lecture-rooms. In a large lecture-room refreshments awaited us and I could hardly wait to pass along a line of handshaking officials. Damp and sticky from long contact with my chair, I had been dreaming of iced beer—but had forgotten that Indonesia is a Moslem country. We were handed fizzing glasses of orange crush, which we came to know as the inevitable, truly national beverage. *Oranje Krus* was so sweet that it left you thirstier than before, but at least it was pre-ferable in colour (the taste was indistinguishable) to the alternative concoctions of viridian or magenta or jaundice-yellow.

Back at the hotel we were brought a bottle of warm Heine-kens, for the refrigerator was out of order. But we had had a long morning and at least it was beer.

Meeting Tony was agreeable, but it was not restful. He was no dry-as-dust archaeologian living in a monumental vacuum but a man who saw history as a continuous process and took as much interest in the affairs of the modern Indonesians as in the daily life of *Pithecanthropus soloensis* or the builders of Borobudur. He ranged mentally (and physically as far as possible) over the whole of South-east Asia and over the whole of recorded time. He was stimulating, intolerant, humorous and overwhelmingly informative about every aspect of our new world, and he swept us under his very active wing. After an appalling lunch he helped us to beard the manager and, though we were still denied the upstairs room that had been booked for us, we achieved a move into the first-class area of the front court, cleaner, more spacious and provided with its own bathroom. The disadvantage was that, being on the ground floor, the open verandah was haunted by relays of whining and irrepressible beggars and equally persistent but much more amusing hawkers of gilded leather lampshades. We got no siesta that day.

By now our only idea for an anniversary celebration was an early bed. But Tony had other ideas.

"I'll take you out to a Chinese restaurant for a really good meal. Then I'm meeting a man from the Ministry of Culture who's going to take me to a Wayang Kulit show and I'll get him to take you too."

"Wayang Kulit?"

"A shadow-play—it means leather puppets. You mustn't miss a chance like this."

We had no energy left to stand up against his energy, not enough strength of mind to be blasé on our very first day. He led us along the swarming street, scorning the glitter of an Ice Cream Palace, and turned into a small open shop with four or five tables separated by low screens. The tablecloth was reasonably clean, but the low room was thick with heat and flies and the dust that drifted in from the host of passing wheels. A heavy smell of frying and coconut oil did not dismay us as we let Tony pick out specialities from the exciting-looking menu; the triple-barrelled dishes, the fantasy of Chinese characters, promised revelations of delicate titillation. I do not remember what we had, but I know it was a disappointment, tasting chiefly of frying and coconut oil. I felt a little sick. We found the cultural official waiting for us on our return, and he looked all that his title suggested. A high brow, fastidious nostrils and fingers of amazing length and subtlety of gesture were combined with grave courtesy and a little English. Of course we must accompany them, but there was no hurry, the performance lasted all night! Our consternation was relieved by Tony, who told us we need not stay till the end, and we pressed them to set out soon—that way we might get to bed sooner. Reluctantly they rose and drove with us to a private house in the suburbs, only half an hour after the supposed time of starting. Of course we were too early. As we passed through the dark garden, we saw a small crowd of neighbours and children quietly staring at a blank screen in one of the windows. But we were ushered indoors and given seats of honour on the operational side of the screen, where we could see the actual puppets, not merely shadows, with the manipulator and the *gamelan* orchestra at our feet.

I had seen the *Karaghiozi* shadow-plays of Greece with their fantastic caricatures and satire of the affairs of the day under the traditional surface. I knew these originated, as the name indicates, from Turkey, but I had not realized that their ultimate origin was much farther East in the shadow-plays of Java. But though the technique was the same, the spirit was very different—the Greeks gay and satirical with an inevitable political slant, the Javanese serious and conservative with an underlying religious feeling. The religion, however, was not Islam. The basis of Java's culture was the older Hindu civilisation that preceded Islam, reaching its apogee in the fourteenth-century Javanese empire of Modjopahit under the mighty Prime Minister Gadjah Mada. This was the period that had given the Javanese their legends and heroes, their customs and ceremonies, their arts and monuments. The puppets and the dancers performed the myths of the Indian epics, the *Ramayana* and the *Mahabharata*; the modern politicians named their national university, their only battleship and innumerable streets after the empire builder of

Modjopahit. Even the national emblem of this, the biggest Moslem state in the world, was a figure of Hindu mythology, the Garuda-bird, the winged mount of Vishnu—the same, incidentally, as the emblem of Buddhist Siam!

In Java Islam did not have time to strike deep roots before the coming of the Christians: the traditional date of the Moslem conquest of Modjopahit was 1478 and the Portuguese fleet first appeared in Malacca in 1509. Obediently the people adopted the religion of their new or converted rulers, but the customs and beliefs of over a thousand years of Hindu domination could not be so easily eradicated and a curious dualism became characteristic of their religious practices. However, this did not worry them any more than it worries the readers of English poetry that their hero, King Arthur, died in a struggle against the English. "We are not fanatical," my students assured me—and what a relief it was to hear such civilised words in our modern world and doubly so in a newborn state just emergent from a fight for freedom.

In front of us under a brilliant electric light sat the *dalang*, the story-teller and manipulator of the puppets, and on either side of him, stuck in the soft trunk of a banana tree, were ranged the leather figures. They were stiff flat cut-outs, up to two feet high, looking at first sight quite solid; yet when you saw the shadows, you found that they were a mass of delicate perforations, giving an impression of filigree or lace. They were gilded and painted in conventional colours, the heroes with black or blue or green faces to symbolise honesty and coolness and patience, the giants red with passion and greed, the ladies usually a vacillating yellow and the clowns white. The shapes were even more stylised and fantastic. The heroic characters had thin straight noses like test-tubes pointing earthward from bent heads on stalklike necks; their eyes were long and narrow, their heads adorned with elaborate crowns or helms; from wide distorted shoulders the thin, mobile, jointed arms hung down to their feet, but below the shoulders the body narrowed like a vase to the waist, widening again for the stumpy, skirted legs. The evil or comic characters were just the opposite of the slender and straight-nosed aristo-

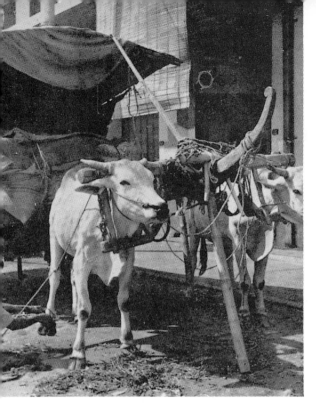

Street scenes, Jogja

Bullock cart

Five in a tricycle, or *betja*

A Javanese village market

Packing quinine, Bandung

crats. Snub noses and round bulging eyes with coarse-fanged mouths and stout clumsy bodies marked them out for hate or ridicule.

What was the origin of these strange conventions? Raffles reported a tradition that they dated from the early days of Islam when the ingenious casuistry of a Moslem missionary contrived to reconcile the Puritanical demands of the new religion, with its ban on the representation of the human form, and the people's pleasure in the *Wayang* plays by so distorting the figures that they could no longer be classed as human. But the distinguishing features of each character, colour, dress, expression, were still preserved so that the audience could identify them in their new shapes. "By these means," said the Susunan Moria, "while the world in general will not imagine the figures to be human, the Javans from recollecting their history, will yet be able to comprehend the characters they are intended to represent, and enjoy in secret their national amusements. Or if, in time, they should forget the originals, and confound them with the distorted resemblance, they will be impressed with the idea that it was only after conversion to the faith of the Prophet that their ancestors assumed the present shape of man." Unfortunately this pleasing fable is not supported by the other evidence, such as ancient coins and the similarity of the puppets used in still-Hindu Bali.

Meanwhile the *gamelan* was playing quietly and we gazed at the unfamiliar instruments, drums and gongs, metallophones and one lone viol. The players squatted cross-legged on straw-matting, dressed in dark skirts, striped jackets and close-fitting turbans. The music was gentle and mournful, a soft and monotonous tune agreeable to Western ears, with none of the shock and clash of the Chinese assault on one's sensibilities. Behind the low ramparts of the metallophones the musicians seemed to be dreaming as they stroked their instruments with padded hammers, evoking slow bell-tones—the Western xylophone, though wooden, is far more strident and staccato than these brass keys with their bamboo sound-chambers. The tubular drums, resting across the drummer's knees, combined both lead and syncopation

c

under the tattoo of his long agile fingers. The medieval-looking viol gave out a plaintive but faint moan from its two strings. Sometimes a woman singer, seated like the rest, would raise her voice in a nasal wail, like a crooner in real pain.

The inner room by now was uncomfortably crowded, most of the guests doffing their shoes at the door and settling on the straw mats. The *dalang* set up what looked like a large, pointed leaf in the middle of the screen, lit some incense and began to intone a prayer. Then removing the 'leaf'—in reality a representation of the mountain of life—he began to take one figure after another from the racks and parade or plant them with formal movements before the screen, all the while telling the story in a monotonous sing-song. Variations of tone indicated the passages of dramatic dialogue, but to us the easiest way of identifying the speaker was to watch the movement of the puppets' arms, manipulated by sticks of horn attached to their hands—if they stretched out their arms, they were speaking; if their arms hung down, they were silent. Nothing very exciting happened for a long time though many characters entered and left the stage. We were glad of the appearance of refreshments, glasses of tepid tea and small sausage-shaped packages wrapped in banana leaves, which turned out to contain damp coagulations of the inevitable rice. Suddenly the tempo of the music increased and grew animated; at last, after prolonged and wordy defiance, the heroes were preparing to fight. Amid much rattling and clashing they flew at each other and the battle raged with as many knockdowns and comebacks as a Hollywood fistfight. But, as in Hollywood, the good guy won in the end, and the story quietened down till the next challenger appeared. There was comic relief, too, when the fat pop-eyed servants waddled on, but the scenes dragged on interminably for us, who could not follow a single word, as the language used was Javanese.

There was one figure, however, that held my attention. His bullet head, rolling eyes and bulky white shape somehow looked familiar.

"Who is that character?" I asked.

"That is Bagong," replied our companion. "He is one of the clowns."

"Surely we've seen him somewhere before," I murmured to Coral, pointing him out. She studied him for a moment. "Of course—behind the desk at the hotel!"

The thought of the hotel, of bed, became urgent. Our eyes were glazed, our minds refused to register any more impressions. Soon after midnight, after some three hours of the show, there was an interval. The introduction was over, Tony told us; now the real action would start, the interesting part; it would only last another three hours and then the last three hours, the conclusion, was not so important. The whole show would end about 6 a.m.

This time we really did insist on going home at once, whatever we might be missing. After all, we had years of Jogja ahead of us, and it was still only our first day.

2

STREET CORNER OVERTURE

THEN Tony left, and the pace of life dropped abruptly. Whether from reaction or the cumulative oppression of the heat, lassitude set in quickly and I found myself, after only a few days in the glamorous East, deep in ennui. This sudden spiritual and physical inertia was a recurrent feature of the next ten months, for it was not till we escaped from the hotel that I began to feel that I was getting nearer to the real life of Java. It was a malaise compounded of exhaustion, frustration, loneliness, discomfort, lack of vitamins and a kind of pervasive hysteria that magnified each petty irritation into a grievance and made life mountainous with molehills. The Hotel Garuda—formerly Grand Hotel de Djokja—had already got me down.

It was not entirely the fault, one must admit, of Bagong. His European guests were a difficult lot, riddled with complexes that might have puzzled an expert psychiatrist. But even elementary Western psychology seemed to be beyond him. His manner, sometimes offhand and indifferent, sometimes jocular and familiar, was calculated to redouble the annoyance of those who approached him with some well-founded complaint about the food or the laundry, the service or the water-supply. He was one of the few Indonesians we met who did not display a natural and delicate courtesy—and the state of the hotel at that time demanded the highest tact on his part. As it was we suspected the worst: we saw deliberate malice in his failure to improve the conditions; we denounced him as a secret anti-white; we were goaded to fury by his ultimate, desperate evasions.

"I am sorry," he would smile when we came with some cast-iron complaint, "but I am only the under-manager. You must ask the manager about that."

"Then please send for the manager."

"He is not here; he lives in the town."

"Well, get him on the telephone, then."

"I am afraid he is away in Djakarta just now."

"When will he be back?"

"I do not know."

He had all the technique of the Orient in dealing with Western importunity, except its polish.

The hotel was the Quartier Latin of Jogja—an involuntary and disgruntled Quartier Latin. Owing to the housing shortage most of the rooms were occupied by foreign experts, who formed a hard core of unwillingly permanent residents. Dutch, German, French, Italians, Austrians, Hungarians, Yugoslavs, Russians, Indians, South Africans, English—one or two of each, plus three or four Americans; doctors, technicians, teachers, business men, musicians, anthropologists, chemists: these formed a group incoherent both in interests and in means of expression. Too various in origin to form a genuine community, too different from our surroundings to escape into local society, we found common ground only in our grievances and frustrations. At our daily forays in the dining-room or seeking a breeze in the garden court at dusk we swopped atrocities, adding fuel to each other's fires and denouncing Indonesia with all the vehemence of thwarted love.

We were impatient, and the East demands patience. It was a period of painful readjustment, and unfortunately some of our Western friends did not stay long enough to readjust. At best, hotel life is unnatural, and we were living a life that belonged neither to East nor to West. Though the stream of Javanese life roared past our windows day and night, we were somehow isolated and apart on an artificial island, in a far-from-ivory tower. Cut off from the restraints of normal society, eccentricities flourished and passions flared till we became as odd as the inmates of any Grand Hotel in fiction. It only needed a shaping imagination and a dramatic climax to become a ready-made novel; but the climax always failed, the expected bangs subsided to whimpers, and our stories ended as a collection of disjointed anecdotes.

The Americans, of course, were the most impatient and it was they who consequently lost their balance most quickly in the slow-motion world of Indonesian bureaucracy. The turnover in United States personnel during our stay was tremendous in proportion to their numbers. They came eagerly, overflowing with goodwill, were shocked to be met with reserve and distrust, grew disillusioned and begged for instant withdrawal. Their desire for escape took different forms—Homer took to misanthropy, Hank to indiscriminate love; Al took to the bottle and bombarded the fountain with the empties, Wilbur to pills and potions for his thirty-seven allergies. The Europeans on the whole were less extreme but more pathetic. Theirs was a long-term despair, the gradual disintegration of the exile, for many had no home to return to, no country to own them. They were the gloomy drinkers, the vacant starers, the whisperers, the suspicious and touchy cadgers. The Dutch covered up their bitterness with a dour stolidity or a loud and beery heartiness.

Only the old Austrian, still as ramrod-straight as in his days in the Imperial Hussars, seemed to have found the answer in Yoga and the films of Fred Astaire. Every dawn we could see his legs waving above his balcony wall as he stood religiously on his head; and most evenings he would urge upon us the wonders of the latest American musical—ach! the precision of the dance-movements, the beauty of the breath-control! We found his detachment enviable but not imitable. The next slug in the salad or lost letter or scorched shirt would set our nerves jangling again like the bells in the street outside.

Those bells! They formed the dominant theme of our street-corner overture and persisted till it became a nocturne. Across the open side of the hotel quadrangle ran the main artery of Jogja and the walls seemed to act as a sounding board. A T-junction and a level-crossing a few yards from the gates ensured the maximum of traffic noise. Actually the Javanese are a quiet people, and no form of traffic is more silent than a bicycle; but both in the mass can produce an oppressive volume of disturbing sound. The people, obliged to raise their voices, became shrill and harsh of tone, while the jerkiness of the language with its plethora of glottal stops did nothing to add to its music. The surging flood of cycles led inevitably to a continuous and discordant tinkling, while the few but spacious motorcars had to blast their way with the horn through the wobbling mass. Hawkers with hand-bells and the jingling harness of horse-cabs added their variations to the theme, and every now and then came a louder ringing, which I took at first to be the chapel bell of some enthusiastic mission. But the nearest church was away at the far end of the street beside the colonnaded palace that passed with the Revolution from the Dutch Resident to the Indonesian President, and this ringing proved to be the warning for the descent of the tall black-and-white girders that swung down to guard the level-crossing. The last straw was added by the train, which began from far away to wail like a fogbound trawler and put an end to our struggle to hear and be heard above the bells, chatter, klaxons, hooves, auxiliary motors, rattles, squeakers, and what not. All conversation, indeed all thought, was suspended till it passed.

It was intolerable, but at least it was real. Clutching my head in the effort to concentrate on morpho-phonemics or the Romantic Revival, I would find my attention more and more distracted by the pulsating life of the street outside. Stretching absolutely straight for more than a mile from the palace gates to the pillar set up by the seventh Sultan at the northern cross-roads, it changed its name as often as if it were an English street—and in fact the name of the central section, by which it was generally known, *was* English. *Malioboro*, I was assured, was a corruption of Marlborough, an unexpected reminder of the brief British occupation of Java under Raffles, from 1811 to 1816. Architecturally it was not distinguished, a mixture of low, tiled shacks and neon-bright modern boxes with one or two Dutch gables for variety. Most of the public buildings, the Post Office, the banks, the ex-Residential ex-Presidential National Hall, were concentrated at the southern end; only the provincial chamber of deputies, once the parliament of the embattled Republic, stood halfway down Malioboro in a small park studded with grey andesite statues.

The central statue represented General Sudirman, the Republic's first Commander-in-Chief; but the sculptor, Hendra, did not show us some idealised sword-waving hero but a gaunt figure with burning eyes, leaning on a stick and wrapped in an old greatcoat—a strange sight in such a climate. For Sudirman was a dying man when he led the guerilla resistance after the Dutch capture of Jogja on 19 December 1948, when practically the whole revolutionary government was caught and interned. In the chilly damp of the mountains this dauntless consumptive continued to lead and inspire Indonesia's first national army, even when his men had to carry him from front to front in a primitive sedan-chair. He lay buried in the Heroes' Field at Jogja, to which he returned, wasted but triumphant, in July 1949, only to die a few months later. Another sort of memorial of that sudden Dutch onslaught (usually referred to, with typical politeness, as the 'Second Clash') was provided by the bombed and burnt-out shells of shops and homes in Tugu, the northern stretch of the street, which in consequence was still shabbier than the rest of it.

Yet, shabby or not, Malioboro had an air about it, an atmosphere lacking in the more pretentious city-centres of Bandung or Surabaya or Semarang. It was not the buildings, it was not even the all-pervading odour of coconut oil that made the difference: it was the people. There was still a prevailing Dutchiness about the bigger cities—Dutch businesses, Dutch notices, Dutch names, Dutch gutturals and, above all, mountainous Dutch bodies—that made them seem rather less exotic than Soho. In Jogja, however, Europeans were the exception and our first appearance caused stares and speculation and even an occasional bicycle-crash. Malioboro belonged unfeignedly to the East. *Sarong* and *surdjan*, *kain batik* and *kebaya*, Shanghai dresses and pyjamas were still common street wear despite the Westernising tendency of the students and officials.

To one brought up in the grand old traditions of Hollywood and Miss Lamour it was a shock to learn that the *sarong* was exclusively a male garment. It was in fact a wide tube of checkered cloth that could be gathered up and tucked round the waist to form a loose skirt with the folds hanging in front. In the heat of the day a worker might sling it like a sash over one shoulder, revealing a very brief pair of shorts, or in the cool of the evening it might serve as an all-enveloping shawl. It was an informal sort of dress, cool and simple, originating not from Java but Sumatra. Formal Javanese wear, for gentlemen as for ladies, was the *kain batik*. This was a simple length of cotton cloth, decorated with an elaborate pattern, mainly dark brown or blue in Central Java, where such subdued and unprovocative colours were regarded as more in keeping with their reserved and serious character than the frivolous pinks and greens of Pekalongan or Bandung. The trouble was that the prevalent brown was a very difficult shade to match, so that my eye was often disappointed by chromatic discords between the ladies' skirts and their *kebayas*, long-sleeved jackets for which they favoured brightly variegated flower patterns. High clicking slippers of carved and painted wood, a stole of silk or *batik* draped over one shoulder and an incongruous plastic handbag, completed the fashionable lady's outfit. I longed for plain colours in the blouses, yellow or dark green or wine-red, to harmonise with the *batik*; and I wondered where and when the failure of taste arose, for the traditional costumes of the dance were most striking in their colour schemes.

As for the Javanese male, his *batik* skirt was similar to the female, but his striped jacket was oddly reminiscent of an old-school or club blazer. A band of *gamelan*-players in their uniforms of green-and-white or purple-and-chocolate might almost be a cricket team waiting in the pavilion. But the blazer effect was spoilt by the stripes of the sleeves, which went round the arm instead of lengthwise, and by the cut with its high collar and drooping front; while in full dress the back was hitched up over the polished wooden hilt of a *kris*, stuck in a broad embroidered waistband. To crown their costume they had a kind of turban of *batik*, usually readymade, the shape of which varied with each district; that of Jogja stretched over the skull in tight flat folds from a point low on the forehead to a small bun at the nape of the neck, giving the wearer an unflattering lowbrow appearance. The women's dark oiled tresses were likewise drawn back smooth and tight to a large coil at the neck, where they were netted, skewered with long combs of silver or tortoiseshell and often plumped with false hair; but the ladies were careful to shave the peak of their brows, thus gaining an effect of considerable intellectual superiority over their husbands.

For the poor the essentials of their costume were the same, but the *batik* stole served a very practical purpose as a shopping bag or sling to support any kind of load from a baby to a bundle of faggots. The infants, seated astride the mother's hip, looked comfortable enough; but the other loads were borne on the back, great baskets of coconuts or mangoes, sacks of potatoes or cassava, so heavy that the bearer had to lean forward at an angle of nearly 45 degrees. Many of the women must have walked miles from their villages, but they padded steadily forward down Malioboro to the big *pasar*, the covered market where they would squat on low concrete platforms and spread out a colourful selection of wares, golden bananas and scarlet chilis, prickly green soursop and pink star-apples, hairy crimson rambutan and purple avocado, together with still more brilliant confections of their own in mauve or vermilion. The older women's mouths were often distorted with big loose gobs of tobacco protruding from the corner and the scarlet splashes of their spitting were startling until I realised that the cause was not tuberculosis but betel-juice. To chew betel was once the indispensable pleasure of all classes, so that a golden spittoon was one of the regular attributes of royalty. But though the so-called 'nut' (really a composition containing lime) strengthens the teeth, the accompanying betel-leaves stain them so badly that the aristocracy used to cover them deliberately with black varnish. We only saw one or two elderly

persons, like Prince Widjil, with black teeth. The modern generation preferred to use the crimson juice for the modest reddening
of the lips (Western lipstick, greasy and flaunting, was not
approved), while for face-powder they used a compound of rice-
flour and roots which gave them a ghastly and unconvincing
pallor.

Not all the market women went all the way down to the *pasar*.
Many settled down on the pavement before the shopfronts of
Malioboro, laying out rolls of *batik* or baskets of fruit or pale
green eggs in the spaces between the wooden racks of the bicycle-
stands, making congestion worse congested. Near the park the
vendors specialised in flowers; near the railway station in white
straw matting and the abominable *duryan*, a knobbly fruit whose
overpowering smell has been vividly summed up as 'sweet
drains'. Drab strings of second-hand clothing hung next to racks
of gaudy pin-ups, where the President and the Sultan rubbed
shoulders with the blondes of Hollywood. Nor were these the
only obstacles to the pedestrian's progress. The cigarette pedlars
set up little box-like stalls whose open lids were packed with a
disingenuous array of 'Kansas' and 'Silver Dollars' and 'White
House' packets. Other wayside stalls displayed an astonishing
variety of fountain-pens, sun-glasses and the more detachable
bicycle accessories, among which it was sometimes possible to
recognise and repurchase one's own missing possessions. Here
and there a permanent kiosk like those on the street corners of
Paris made a bottleneck, but instead of lurid magazines, the windows glowed with lurid bottles, orange and magenta, emerald
and ochre, saffron and rose. A rough table and bamboo benches
nestled alongside, never unoccupied day or night.

After dark the booths and blockages multiplied. Dark-faced
Indians from Malabar cooked pallid flapjacks by the flare of pressure lamps; small groups surrounded the fortune-tellers whose
inspired sparrows would pick, or rather peck, your lucky cards;
a bigger ring pressed round a story-teller expounding some crude
but lively strip cartoon, now a Javanese Superman, now a blunter
variety of the B.O. story, in the hope of luring or driving the

listeners into the clutches of his partner, who lurked in the background with pills for the body or pincers for the teeth. But of all the street traders, day or night, those that impressed themselves most sharply on the attention were the itinerant food-hawkers with their primitive mobile canteens, contraptions of boxes or cans or drawers suspended from either end of a bamboo yoke that bounced up and down with every step despite the coolie's mincing, hip-swinging gait. Collision with one of these creaking affairs might bring on you a shower of glowing charcoals or iced water or broken glass. A walk down Malioboro could be full of excitement.

Alternatively you might try to cross Malioboro. At any hour between 6 a.m. and 9 p.m. this was a hazardous attempt, even at the official crossings. Cycles are less lethal than cars but more unpredictable, and the overwhelming majority of Malioboro's traffic consisted of bicycles—or tricycles. This was one legacy of Dutch culture at least that was unlikely to be cast out in a hurry. Nearly everyone seemed to boast a bicycle, down to the raggedest worker, and nearly every bicycle seemed to boast a passenger. But, though popular, cycling had not become vulgar in Indonesia. It was still an affair of high handlebars and upright figure, a dignified gliding, and there was no sign yet of the strenuous crouch and bulging buttocks that disfigure the English week-end countryside. Even passenger-riding was a refined art. The carrier-borne female sat side-saddle, balancing herself at an elegant incline, her hands modestly restraining her billowing skirt and never, under any circumstances, clinging to her escort. To touch a member of the opposite sex, even a husband, in public was considered shocking, or as they termed it themselves, ridiculous. Many a raised eyebrow, many an embarrassed giggle, was caused by our walking down the street arm in arm.

The tricycle is the taxi of the Far East. The Indonesian type, known as *betja*, differs from its cousins in Singapore and Bangkok, for the passengers ride in front and the driver behind. Some said that the Japanese insisted on this arrangement during their occupation, as their fastidious noses were offended by the wafts from the sweating coolie in front. Whatever the reason, there were other advantages of this system that more than outweighed the perils of head-on collision. The passengers enjoyed more privacy than in Singapore, where the driver sits alongside, and a wider view than in Siam, where the foreground is filled with the coolie's background. Though in bad weather the cramped seat, the low folding hood and the dank and dingy rain-curtain flapping against your knees were apt to induce claustrophobia, on a warm evening and a smooth road the *betja* provided a rare combination of pleasures, coolness, speed, colour, and even a kind of music.

The padded seat, slung between the front wheels, was gaily upholstered in red or green or blue leather and the mudguards decorated with flowery patterns and still more flowery names. Sometimes the wooden back-panel displayed a primitive willow-pattern landscape or a volcano à la Hokusai. But in Jogja we never saw the wild efflorescence of uninhibited folk-art that was common in Surabaya, where the rash of decoration spread even behind the wheels and the seat itself was a riot of popular mythology: dragons and cowboys, elephants and aeroplanes, tigers and lovebirds, Mickey Mice and, not least, girls—girls at the mirror, girls on motorbikes, girls in swimsuits, girls retiring behind the bed-curtains with a coy 'Goodnight!' *Betja* music, however, was as delicate as *betja* art was crude. A shrill and ghostly humming, like the song of the wind in the pines, rose and fell with the speed of the machine. Only after many months did I trace the source of this unearthly accompaniment, a rubber band stretched tightly between two small bars under the seat and working on the principle of the Aeolian harp.

Yet for all its charms many visitors were shy of the *betja* because of the repute of the driver. A sinister myth had grown up around the *betja*-boy: he had become a symbol. For some he was the eternal victim, haggard and consumptive, pedalling his heart out for his rich exploiters; for others he symbolised the mob, wild and unstable, ready to gang up on lonely and unwary strangers;

for both he represented the raw material of revolution, discontented and dangerous. No doubt a community of thousands of tough and ill-rewarded workers (30,000 in Djakarta) is always potentially inflammable; and tipsy or quarrelsome passengers are always likely to find trouble. But to us the drivers generally seemed as cheerful as their machines and their worst fault was their ignorance of local geography. Unfortunately they would never confess it till, after twenty minutes of bumping along, we put the direct question:

"Do you know the address we asked for?"

"Not yet," the *betja*-boy would reply, as he pedalled blithely on.

The alternative form of public transport was the horse-drawn cab, the four-wheeled *andong* or the two-wheeled *dokar*, both equally shabby and decrepit, with dark square canopies overhead and black leather blinds that could be rolled down against the rain. The scraggy little ponies trotted tinkling along much slower than a *betja*, but they could draw amazing loads. Half a dozen adults, a sprinkling of children and several sacks of rice or vegetables might be crowded into a single four-wheeler; once in a convoy of six on their way to a wedding I counted a total of forty guests. The two-wheeler was less accommodating than these skeletal carriages, as it had closed sides like an old-fashioned trap. *Dokar* was in fact a corruption of the English dog-cart—one of those relics of the British way of life that have survived in odd corners of the world and throw such a peculiar light on our contribution to civilisation. In Normandy I have come across porridge and the prefectorial system, in Corfu cricket and ginger-beer, and now in Java I met the dog-cart and the garden-party, metamorphosed into *garudopati*.

So through the seething crowds and the swirling wheels we would penetrate at last to the shops and plunge into a strangely contrasting atmosphere of stagnation. Ninety per cent of the stores were owned by the Chinese, whose names painted over the doorways in ornate and complex characters gave a promise of glamour and mystery that was sadly disappointed by the dingy and commonplace interiors. Nor was their famed commercial acumen and devotion to profit at all obvious to the casual shopper. I had expected to be subjected to all the aggression of high-pressure salesmanship, but in fact the pressure could hardly have been lower. Lolling behind his cash desk, the shopkeeper would show utter apathy as I poked inquisitively about his shelves. To any inquiry for a particular article there were two standard answers that soon became only too familiar:

"Tida' ada."

"Sudah habis."

As these phrases mean respectively "There isn't any," and "Finished," they saved the salesman the trouble of getting up and having a look. But there was no need to be discouraged. If the article wanted was not in the appropriate shop—and it might be, despite the shopkeeper's indifference—I could just try the shop next door and the next and the next. It did not matter what the store's speciality might appear to be; each one was an adventure, a treasure hunt, in which the most incongruous goods mixed as readily as in a village general store. I have combed the iron-mongers for a hammer and run it to earth in a grocer's; there were paintings for sale in a fruit shop; shoes and bicycle spares crowded the counters of a bookshop; and Jogja silver could be found in them all. Only the dark and sad-eyed Indians in their Bombay Silk Palaces eschewed all sidelines, while the few surviving Indonesian enterprises were mainly devoted to the more artistic and less profitable branches of business.

The government's policy for the Indonesianisation of commerce had not proved a lasting success and most of the expropriated concerns had already returned to the control of the patient Chinese, who were willing to pinch and scrape and live squalidly behind their shops, building up their capital and buying up their neighbours. The Javanese had a more lordly attitude towards money as something to be spent if you had it, borrowed if you hadn't, but never slavishly pursued for its own sake. This induced a certain fecklessness over money matters, a readiness to incur debts, defer payments and misappropriate funds in hand, that was unfortunate in administration and fatal in business. Sharp practice was far from their intentions, but the resulting entanglements were apt to give that impression. They were money-conscious only on the lowest level, in tens of rupiahs but not in ten thousands. In trade we found them as hawkers and stall-holders but seldom as big operators, and in the higher spheres of society they would practise minute economies, pursue marginal bargains and collect endless little subscriptions with an enthusiasm that perhaps owed something to the parsimonious Dutch. (Departing Dutchmen held successful auctions of their household goods down to the smallest item; I remember one where a buyer was found, at half-price, for a part-worn rubber.) But the larger the sum involved, the larger the latitude in credit and time—and time has no urgency in the East. The idea that time is money, or that either of these is among the prime factors of life, is quite alien to the Indonesian mentality and thus forms a ready source of misunderstanding with the preconceptions of the Americans.

The chief specialities of Jogja, to be found in shops of all descriptions, were silver ware and *batik* cloth. These were real local industries, traditional and living crafts still carried on in the age-old way. To walk down the narrow streets of Kota Gede, the 'silvertown' two or three miles outside Jogja, and listen to the tinkling of innumerable hammers behind the labyrinthine walls was to be transported back to an earlier age and a lost magic. One expected to see a troop of Walt Disney gnomes at work in the dark sheds; and indeed in the flickering light of their braziers the slight and shadowy figures of the craftsmen, as they squatted brown and glistening over miniature anvils, hammering and cutting, welding and embossing, clad only in a *sarong*, did give the impression of beings from another world. It was a mistake, however, to expect unworldly innocence when it came to bargaining for some richly-chased dish or a set of florid spoons. It was the tourist who was the sucker; the same article cost more at the source in Kota Gede than it did retail in Malioboro. The pre-

Rice fields in Western Java

Descendants of headhunters have a more peaceful occupation today, making grotesque masks from coconut shells

Javanese worker with his lunch

A Kampong girl

valent style was heavily decorative in the Victorian manner, with flowery mouldings and symbolic garuda-birds picked out by a black stain in the outlines and hollows; it looked more like a reflection of Dutch taste of the last century than any genuine native inspiration. Nevertheless the silversmiths were proud and sensitive about the Jogja style and refused to imitate anything modern or European. When we wanted mustard-pots to match our salts and peppers, they protested their inability to copy such models—until they learned that ours were Indian work. This changed the case at once, and now we have a beautifully matching set.

Batik was a more uncommon craft, peculiar to the country, though even this was said to have originated, like almost every other art except the shadow-play, from India. But for seven centuries at least it had been practised and developed at the courts of Java's princes and it could be truly called national in every sense of the word. A Javanese technique with Javanese designs, by Javanese producers for Javanese consumers, it formed the basis of the national dress of rich and poor alike, and was practised by rich and poor alike, the pastime of aristocratic ladies and the livelihood of ragged workers. There were two types of *batik*, hand-painted (*tulis*) and stamped (*tjap*). But the word 'painted' was misleading, since the colours were obtained by the method of dyeing white cotton cloth and the painting consisted in covering over with wax the parts that were *not* to be coloured. *Batik*-making was thus a somewhat laborious process, as every colour demanded a fresh dyeing and every dyeing demanded the waxing on both sides of all the parts not to be dyed that colour; so a pattern of four colours had to be painted over with wax four times, dipped four times into the different dyes, dried again after each dip, scraped free of the unwanted wax, and so to the beginning again.

Considering the amount of labour involved, it was amazing that the printed factory-made *batiks* could be produced so cheaply, for the equivalent of £2 or so. In any other country the printing would be regarded as a handicraft, for it was all carried out by

D

skilled craftsmen, not by machines. Each colour-pattern had its appropriate stamp, a mould of intricate metalwork like a large iron, which the worker dipped in hot wax and then laid skilfully down on the cloth, so that the pattern fitted exactly without overlap or break. Yet the printed product was considered distinctly inferior, the hand-painted length being four or five times more costly although the material and the size were just the same, and the work was indistinguishable to all but the expert eye. In the painted *batik* the pattern was first drawn in pencil, then traced in wax with a selection of peculiar instruments, called *tjantings*, that might be compared to a rudimentary form of fountain-pen. They consisted of short sticks of bamboo with a tiny copper bowl fixed at the end, from which projected a minute taplike spout; the size of the spout varied according to the thickness required for the lines. When dipped in the pan of liquid wax that was kept boiling on a brazier, the bowl was filled like the reservoir of a pen and the painter could draw several lines at a time.

The patterns, however, were not left to the inspiration of the artist. They were traditional, changeless and exact, each with its own name and its own meaning, which any of the older Javanese could tell you at a glance. There was, for instance, the V-shaped *Parang Rusak* (broken *kris*), which used to be the prerogative of royalty, or the *Sido Mukti* (for happiness), worn by bride and bridegroom, or a hundred others. Most of the motifs were set in diagonal lines, which were considered less harsh than the vertical or horizontal and known by the expressive title of 'soft rain'. Each district had its own designs and colour-schemes, but those of the old principalities, Jogja and Solo, were the most conservative, being mainly confined to indigo and dark brown, the hues of dignity. Lightness of colour went with lightness of mind; mauve, for example, was unsuitable for any but young unmarried girls.

A handmade *batik* might take three months to complete, but, though it demanded great care and patience, it was a restful occupation for the painter, seated on a low stool with the cloth hanging over a sort of bamboo towel horse, ready to her hand. It was in fact the Javanese equivalent of knitting, and many highborn ladies still practised it for a hobby, as well as poor women for a ridiculous wage. In the old days, when the wives and daughters of the aristocracy were not allowed to leave the confines of their homes after the age of puberty, this slow and delicate pursuit must have been a godsend—perhaps the unseasonably voluminous *batiks* worn by royalty owed something to the boredom of their womenfolk! But Coral never found time to finish even her first *batik tulis*.

At 9 p.m. the shops put up their thick wooden shutters and Malioboro began to quieten down, for the shops were its life. There were no bars and no night-clubs in puritan Jogja. Drinking strong liquor and dancing in the Western style were considered immoral, and the only attempt to organise such a dance at the hotel, in honour of a visiting Austrian football team, had to be cancelled at the last moment as a sinister band of youths was prowling round, ready to hurl stones through the windows. At Oen's restaurant or the Tip-Top Ice Cream Palace the waiters became fidgety if we lingered on as the clock approached 10 p.m. But in any case, once our meal was finished, there was really nothing to keep us in these empty and cheerless halls with their cold strip lighting and crackling radios. To me even the food was no attraction—except as a relief from the hotel's eternal "rice or potatoes?" Though my friends would rhapsodise over the rare and sophisticated delights of the Chinese kitchen, the birds' nest soup and the bamboo shoots, the noodles and the fried rice, the frogs' legs and the 'shrimp beefsteak', I still found the dominant flavour in every dish was coconut oil. A perfumed ice-cream would round off an over-rich meal, for in this land of luxuriant fruits dessert was apparently unknown.

So for an evening's entertainment there only remained the cinema, and the film habit grew on us like a drug. Yet what else was one to do? Writing and reading both require light, and light generates heat. In the fanless stuffiness of our rooms the mere effort of mental concentration, let alone the physical exercise of writing, was sufficient to send the sweat coursing down our sides. In the comparative cool of the garden court the perpetual gossip and grousing soon palled. The cinemas, it is true, were stuffy too, since the uncertainty of the weather did not permit the double delight of the open-air theatre. But there was no effort involved, nothing but a passive receptivity. In fact the more vapid the film, the more perfect the relaxation; and in such a climate maximum relaxation was the ideal. The programmes were chaotic, depending entirely on day-to-day box-office returns, so that many of the films we set out to see—particularly the allusive and understated British type—had already vanished. Then came a crawl from cinema to cinema in a desperate search for the evening's narcotic. Once by a comedy of errors we found ourselves watching the same Western two nights running. But our mania was by no means singular; night after night we would meet other members of the foreign intelligentsia at one or other of the 'bioscopes'. Even there, however, the professors and doctors and UNO experts could not wholly divest themselves of seriousness, and we became involved in many an argument of Teutonic depth and obscurity over the rival merits of cutlass, six-shooter and sub-machine gun or the psychology of Bomba the Apeman.

More interesting than our own reactions, however, were those of the Indonesian audience. For them Hollywood portrayed a way of life and a code of behaviour that was quite extraordinary. The speed, the violence, the noise, the brashness, the naked display of passions—and of legs—shocked and at the same time thrilled. Above all, the climax, the inevitable and long-drawn-out kiss, never failed to call forth excited catcalls and embarrassed titters. The Western kiss, that sensual and unhygienic mouthing, was not practised among the Indonesians. They preferred the more refined olfactory sense and indulged in what has been unromantically termed the 'sniff-kiss', hence rating a fragrant skin high among the physical charms. For them our kind of kiss was the grossest form of public contact, and though it proved impracticable to cut them out of American films altogether, the

Indonesian censors could, and did, cut them down considerably in duration. On the hoardings of Malioboro the censorship was still stricter than inside the theatre (which after all no one needed to enter if they didn't like it), and it was common to see the more lurid advertisements patched with prudish strips of brown paper where the gigantic lips were meeting or the silken thighs tossed too high.

To the young, however, there was an undoubted attraction in the zest, freedom and feeling of modernity that came of imitating American ways. Jazz was popular and, behind closed doors, jive; even kissing might sometimes be secretly ventured on—by engaged couples. Most of the audience, though, found the epic simplicities of the Wild West or the Spanish Main more familiar and attractive, whereas the complex and shadowy slaughters of the gangsters were apt to elicit giggles rather than gasps. In humour the custard pie prevailed rather than the comedy of manners (the manners, after all, were Western); and the record run of Reinhardt's venerable *Midsummer Night's Dream* was evidence not so much of the highbrow tastes of Jogja as of Shakespeare's universality.

Purring back in our *betja* after the show, we would make better speed in the deserted roadway. But the pavements would still be alive with vendors and villagers who had failed to get rid of their stock. Settling down on doorsteps or in recesses, they continued gaily chattering and laughing throughout the night; sometimes one would strike up a plaintive and endless tune on a bamboo flute; and the itinerant masseur passed and re-passed, rattling a tin as a call-sign.

Some of them wrapped themselves in their thin *sarongs* and stretched out on the hard concrete in peaceful slumber—unlike the nerve-wracked inhabitants of the hotel. Slowly, despite the chatter from Malioboro, despite the flute, despite the rattling tin, despite the chorus of frogs from the lily-pond, we would sink into exhausted and uneasy sleep, only to be roused again in the small hours by the raucous coughing and clanging from the bathroom as the water-supply came on. Soon after, or so it seemed, the quiet was shattered anew by the blasts from the neighbouring engine-sheds; then the boom of loudspeakers from the new mosque announced the start of another day.

The bicycles began to pour down Malioboro.

3

THE FACE OF THE FUTURE

On the Monday after our arrival the Dean of the Faculty of Literature, Pedagogy and Philosophy called with the car to take me down to the Faculty building and introduce me to my colleagues and students of the Western Literature Department. I was a little surprised to hear about the students. I knew that my appointment was the first Lectureship in English in the history of the University and had imagined that my first job would be planning and organising an English syllabus. But Professor Sigit informed me that the Department had already been in existence for over a year, so that two generations of students were anxiously awaiting my arrival. Theoretically the Department was a modern languages school; but the absence of the requisite teachers made it in effect a Department of English with a series of Dutch, Chinese and Eurasians holding the fort till my arrival. My task therefore would be one of reorganisation rather than organisation, revising instead of devising.

Professor Sigit himself was an educationist and had been thrown into prison by the Japanese for refusing to bow to his classroom door at the beginning of each class as a sign of obeisance to the Son of Heaven. The professed liberators of Asia did not stop at imprisoning the recalcitrant Professor himself; they also arrested his eldest son and daughter. Yet he could not be accused of sympathy for the rival colonialism of the Dutch. True, he had received his higher education in Holland. The few Indonesians who achieved University training during the Dutch regime *had* to go to Holland, for there were no universities in the

Indies. The Dutch, in fact, recognised the danger of education for a colonial people, leading inevitably to demands for responsibility and eventually release from even the most paternal tutelage. Ninety per cent of the people were illiterate. Only a small élite, the aristocrats who acted as middlemen between the government and the peasantry and a few students of special promise, were given the advantage of a European education in the delusive belief, common among colonial powers, that to know us is inevitably to love us, that admiration spells allegiance, that Western thought induces Western feelings. Doctorandus Abdullah Sigit did not cease to be a true Javanese or a devout Moslem because of his Dutch degree. He had been a deputy of the Masjumi Moslem party in the revolutionary parliament and among the Professors of the national University he was notable for persisting in wearing Javanese dress.

The car turned left on reaching the palace square and threaded its way down a narrow street and into a high arched gateway. This was Widjilan, one of the many once-stately homes of the Sultan's innumerable relatives that lay hidden behind the high walls and stout wooden doors of the *Kraton* area. The Faculty of Literature was then the youngest of the University's seven schools and there was not room for it in the main buildings; so, until the new campus should be completed (and at that time it consisted of a foundation stone and nothing more), Prince Widjil lent them the forecourt of his home. The arrangement was by no means ideal from the practical point of view, but for me it had a certain charm, an air of tradition and continuity that was lacking in the efficient but characterless classrooms to which we moved later. Our accommodation consisted of the *pendopo* or open hall with the surrounding courtyard. These halls, which are used for ceremonial occasions and dance performances, have no walls, just a raised floor and a wide pyramidal roof supported by rows of pillars, as they are designed for maximum coolness. In Widjilan the outer colonnades had been screened off with partitions of plaited bamboo to form long narrow lecture-rooms, while the reception rooms at the back were used as offices. The central floor was a no-man's-land of cupboards, blackboards and notice-boards, behind which, during the breaks, the staff lurked in dim discomfort. The courtyard stretched on three sides with a variety of shabby buildings of wood or plastered brick, some used as bicycle-sheds, some as store-rooms, some still inhabited by the Widjil retainers. Tall trees shaded and obstructed the entrance and on the left a row of poles almost as tall supported some wicker birdcages. Ropes and pulleys enabled the cages to be hoisted to the top during the day, but at night or in the rain the birds were lowered and brought under cover. Such poles could be seen everywhere in the old streets and villages; birdsong was an important element in the pleasures of Javanese home life.

We entered the *pendopo*, skirted the piled desks and reached the 'common room'. A formidable lady rose and Professor Sigit introduced me to Mevrouw van H., my only colleague in the English Department. The severity of her expression was heightened by the long nose and pale blue eyes that often give the Dutch a peculiarly cold expression; her grey hair was drawn back tight from her brow and her grey dress completed the impression of chill.

"I suppose you've come to turn us out," she said abruptly.

This greeting left me dumb. It was no use my protesting that the job had been offered me out of the blue, that I had had no previous designs, and indeed very few ideas, on Indonesia. She was echoing the widespread and bitter delusion among the Indies Dutch that the revolution was deliberately and treacherously fostered by the British in order to deprive Holland of her richest colony and replace her influence by ours.

The origin of this unfortunate belief lies in the history of the first days of the revolution, when it fell to British forces to undertake the re-occupation of the Netherlands East Indies. The Dutch point to the delay of six weeks between the Japanese surrender and the arrival of allied forces in Java, a delay which enabled the Republicans to establish their authority throughout the land. Such facts as that the Indies had only just been transferred from MacArthur to Mountbatten, that SEAC was poised to push over-

land and had few ships available, that the Japanese collapse suddenly faced it with the occupation of vast areas of South-East
Asia—these arguments cannot shake their myopic concentration
on their own problem. Why were there no Dutch troops in the
area? Why were the Dutch ships not immediately despatched to
Batavia? A few ships, a few troops, they still believe, could have
rallied the loyal masses against the terroristic repression of the
quisling Sukarno gang. (Yet the mere rumour that Dutch troop-
ships were waiting beyond the horizon, when the British were
disembarking at Surabaya, was sufficient to touch off the bloodiest
battle of the revolution.) They point to General Christison's
broadcast from Singapore on 29th September 1945, when he
spoke of the 'existing Indonesian authorities' and asked for their
help and hospitality. Was not this *de facto* recognition, a free
hand to go ahead? Volumes of political perfidy have been read
into these practical words of a soldier, whose orders were to pro-
tect and evacuate prisoners of war and internees, disarm the
Japanese, and maintain law and order; and whose earnest hope
was to avoid meddling in Indonesian internal politics. For those
who remember the pre-war days when the Indies were a 'paradise', it seems impossible to conceive that the 'happy, childlike
natives' were in fact neither the one nor the other; and the humi-
liation of being forcibly expelled by 'the softest people on earth'
makes them seek for scapegoats, of whom the handiest are the
British. This made conversation with them very tricky, particularly as they insisted on reverting to the subject, like a sore
place that one cannot resist scratching.

The Indonesians' decision in 1950 that the country's second
language should be English instead of Dutch only served to confirm suspicion of British motives. The world-wide currency of
the English language (so strikingly demonstrated by the Bandung
Conference of April 1955, when the representatives of twenty-
nine nations of Asia and Africa made their speeches directly in
English without recourse to interpreters) was not accepted as
sufficient justification for the change. But the cup of bitterness
overflowed when the use of Dutch as a teaching medium was

forbidden even to Dutch teachers. No wonder my own appearance was greeted by Mevrouw with hostility, even though she did her own teaching in excellent English; I was the agent of Albion's perfidy, the thin end of another anti-Dutch wedge.

Three months after my arrival, on 19th December, the university celebrated its third *Dies Natalis*. According to this calculation Gadjah Mada was only set up in 1949. But that was the date of its official charter as a national institution of full university status. Its real beginnings dated from the first days of the revolution, for the Indonesian leaders recognised from the start the urgent need for trained personnel, in which they were almost completely lacking. Under the Dutch regime there was no university, only a few scattered technical colleges. All other academic education had to be obtained abroad. During the Japanese occupation even these inadequate facilities closed down, though Batavia's Faculty of Medicine and Surabaya's school of dentistry managed to reopen and carry on in spite of the necessity of learning and using Japanese. Then Japan collapsed and all was in suspense again.

The new Republican government immediately ordered the reopening of the two medical colleges. But the battle of Surabaya and the arrival of Dutch troops forced the evacuation of the Dental School to Malang in the hills of East Java and the Medical Faculty to Klaten in Mid-Java. Meanwhile new Faculties of Law and Arts had been set up in Jogja with the help of the Sultan and Ki Hadjar Dewantoro, Indonesia's first Minister of Education, who, twenty-four years before, had founded the first of the *Taman Siswa* schools to ensure that Eastern culture and values should not be lost in the schooling of young Indonesians. Now came the vision of an Indonesian university, and the students and teachers, short of books, apparatus, staff and indeed everything except determination, laboured and improvised to give it reality.

There were worse difficulties to follow. In July 1947 the Dutch launched their first 'police action' and Malang was occupied. The dental students were dispersed, some to join the

Student Army, some to Klaten with what equipment they could salvage. But still their odyssey was not finished. On 19th December 1948 came the 'Second Clash', when the Dutch forces seized Jogjakarta, the Republican capital itself. Automatically all the faculties closed their doors and the students, girls as well as boys, vanished to the countryside to join the guerilla struggle.

But this time the Dutch had shocked world opinion and in May, under pressure from the United Nations, they agreed to retire. Only the immediate area of Jogja, however, was handed over at once, and Klaten was not in that area. Dr. Sardjito, the head of the Medical Faculty, had remained through the months of the occupation in a nearby village, in spite of two raids on his house; and now he organised the students, staff and employees to pack all the precious equipment they could on their bicycles or their backs and smuggle them along the muddy tracks and rutted back roads till they reached sanctuary at the great Hindu temples of Prambanan. There they were in Jogja territory and could complete the last few miles in the comparative safety and comfort of ox-carts. The Medical Faculty had arrived at its haven at last.

The Faculties of Law and Arts had been set up in the forecourts of the Sultan's palace and now the Sultan again came to the rescue of the university. He offered the Crown Prince's palace, Mangkubumen, to house the medical departments, and extraordinary changes and ingenious adaptations made it possible to open the Faculty by 1st November 1949. Now the main *pendopo* with its famous green and gold carved roof and its crystal chandeliers was filled with scribbling students instead of swaying *serimpi* dancers and echoed to the microphone instead of the *gamelan*. A screen separated a pile of gilded beds and ceremonial umbrellas from the work benches of the physiology and optics department; the long carriage shed became a free polyclinic and the *gamelan* store a dispensary. Nowhere was the contrast between the old Java and the new more striking, and at the same time the continuity.

Thus the various branches of the embryo university became concentrated in Jogja; and on 19th December 1949—exactly one year after the Dutch capture of the city—Gadjah Mada National

University was formally established by charter. Dr. Sardjito, the frail but dauntless leader of the peripatetic Faculty of Medicine, was appointed President. In 1951 the old Faculty of Arts was expanded to include Western literature and moved to separate quarters in Widjilan. And eighteen months later, in time for the University's third birthday, I came upon the scene myself.

It was hardly to be expected in the circumstances that everything would be running smoothly. The lack of trained and experienced administrative staff in particular was glaring, as it was in every branch of Indonesian government. The serried desks of the offices on the verandahs of Pagelaran were a wilderness of bureaucracy; urgent papers would take weeks to pass down a single line of In and Out trays. It was ten months before my appointment was officially confirmed by the Ministry, and until then they could only offer me an 'advance of pay'! In the strained atmosphere of mutual commiseration at the hotel, without pay, without housing, without books or equipment, without vitamins, and without apparent prospects of ever getting any of these, the little band of Westerners swore again and again that they would quit. Yet somehow most of us carried on, for there was one important item of which we all had a plentiful supply— students. They had conquered so many difficulties to get where they were; it was up to us to face a few ourselves for their sake.

The mere physical problem of finding decent quarters for such a rapidly growing flood (463 in November 1949; 3,439 at the time of my coming in 1952; and 8,570 when I left in 1956) was formidable enough. Accommodation was the biggest headache and first priority. Thanks to the Sultan the various Faculties at least had roofs (often very ornate ones) over their heads, and classes could be carried on, albeit in a somewhat amateurish manner. But with the target figure of 10,000 undergraduates being rapidly approached, Jogja was bursting at the seams. Somehow, somewhere they were all fitted in; packed into bungalows, servants' compounds, garages, cubicled *pendopos*, or when approved, *kampongs*. But it could not go on like that.

The Sultan was President of a foundation for constructing full-scale students' hostels, and two of these were completed before any of the ambitious Faculty buildings on the campus-to-be. The first was opened on 19th September 1954, the day of the annual 'Commencement'. The day's oration was technical but appropriate, an engineering professor expatiating on the use of metals in building. We then trooped across the town to a glaring, barrack-like new block, which illustrated his words; steel, concrete and prefabrication had banished the fear of collapse in earthquakes, which was responsible for the bungaloid squatness of the Dutch Tropical style, and its three storeys towered above the surrounding houses. In a big cool recreation hall we settled down to a new bout of oratory from the orchid-festooned stage. First came the architect, who handed over the keys to the Sultan; the Sultan in his turn handed them to the Minister of Public Works, who handed them to the Minister of Education, who handed them to Professor Sardjito for the University. The best orator was the Minister of Education, Muhammad Yamin, who looked like a genial gorilla but was a poet and pioneer of the nationalist literary movement. He made the audience laugh wryly by remarking that the building had been begun three governments ago! It was only too true—we had seen student demonstrations against the delays, when muddles in planning and procurement, too little of this material and far too much of that, had caused the allocations to run out and the work to be suspended.

But now the hostel was at last completed and 400 boys were housed in more comfort than many perhaps enjoyed in their overcrowded homes. We walked round the dormitories, where six or eight students had room for a bed, folding cupboard and desk each. Boys from all parts of Indonesia mixed here, learning to live together and understand each other's differences; the energetic and aggressive Sumatrans with the shy but stubborn Javanese, Moslems with Christians, students of letters with students of science. It was a microcosm of Indonesia's future. That evening another aspect of the synthesis that is essential if Indonesia is to achieve true identity as a nation was illustrated when that same ferro-concrete hall was the scene of a celebration in the form of a leather-puppet show.

Only three months later the second hostel was opened, for girls this time, but the atmosphere was less happy. The building itself was even better equipped, even luxurious by Indonesian standards; only three girls per room and a bathroom attached to each. The opening was honoured by President Sukarno himself. It was the 19th of December, the University's fifth *Dies Natalis*, and the second time I had seen the President at the birthday celebrations. As before, his coming filled the courts of the *kraton* with excited cheering students, but this year there was a noticeable lack of girls in the great hall of *Sitinggil*. Their absence was still more conspicuous when we moved to the new hostel. Here, at the opening of their own future home, there was not a girl to be seen except for a few appointed to act as ushers. A wide array of empty seats faced the platform and the President's expression darkened as he observed this obvious boycott. It was a feminist protest against his second marriage, which had only lately been revealed and had caused intense indignation among the women's leaders, who were fighting for the establishment of monogamy despite Islam's allowance of four wives. The President's example had struck a bitter blow at their hopes, but it also struck at his own immense popularity. There had even been talk of strikes and demonstrations, but the authorities vetoed such ideas and the protest thus took a negative but effective form. Feminism was a force to be reckoned with in modern Indonesia.

One of the points that had surprised me, when I came to meet my students, was the strength of the feminine contingent. In the English Department the girls actually outnumbered the boys, and in the university as a whole they formed nearly 15 per cent of the total, with representatives in even the least humane of the Faculties. These figures were remarkable when considered in their Indonesian context. In a Moslem country, where the right to literacy had only just been won, women shared complete equality in education. The very fact that the men of Indonesia were denied their rights till feminism had become an accepted feature of modernism, enabled the Indonesian woman to spring, like Minerva, fully-armed into the world. Their rights were conceded not by grudging male masters but by partners in the same struggle. There was no denial of a full degree as at Cambridge; no fight against the Suffragettes or the 'Flapper Vote'. In Indonesia there was universal suffrage at the age of eighteen.

The heroine of the Indonesian feminist movement was not, therefore, a fighting leader like Mrs. Pankhurst or Mrs. Doria Shafik of the Daughters of the Nile, but a gentle-faced woman who spent her life in the seclusion of her father's or husband's home. Raden Adjeng Kartini was born on 21st April 1879, the daughter of the regent of Japara on the north coast of Java. Her father was a man of liberal ideas for his time and sent his little daughter to primary school, where she developed a deep thirst for learning. But even a progressive parent could not leave his daughter to go out in the world after the age of puberty, and at about twelve poor Kartini was taken from school and kept, as was customary with aristocratic girls, within the walls of her father's residence. From there she wrote the letters that made her into a national figure—after her death. They were addressed to a liberal Dutch couple and expressed her longing for higher education and more emancipation for women and her revulsion against the humiliating conditions of their life, especially the lack of freedom in marriage. Yet in due course she herself obediently married her father's choice, the Regent of Rembang, who was much older than she was and a widower with several children. And the marriage turned out a success, thanks to her own gentleness and her husband's sympathy with her ideas. In her new home she continued the girls' school that she had opened at her father's with her sisters. But a year later, in 1904, Kartini died in her first childbirth.

Her Dutch friends collected her letters under the title *From Darkness to Light* and, thanks to the power and spirit with which they were written, they had an extraordinary influence on the Javanese leaders. Published just at the time when the Indonesian nationalist pioneers were themselves building up their educational movements such as the *Budi Utomo*, Kartini's letters led to the acceptance in their minds of the equal right of women to freedom and education. She was adopted by the budding feminist movement as their symbol and spiritual guide. In 1912 the Independent Women's organisation (*Puteri Merdeka*) was founded and one of their first enterprises was the establishment of 'Kartini Schools' for girls, concerned with such domestic sciences as cooking, sewing, embroidery, and so on. But these were not the only fruits of her ideas. Moved by her spirit, Javanese parents began to send their daughters to school, then to high school along with the boys and finally even to college. The first Indonesian woman physician graduated in the early 1920s and women teachers and office workers soon became quite common. After the Revolution they might aspire to any height—already one had held Cabinet rank as Minister of Social Affairs and another was president of the national electoral committee.

No wonder the girl students held special celebrations on 'Kartini Day', 21st April, the anniversary of her birth. On that day they would appear for their lectures in national dress, looking strangely metamorphosed and grown-up in their *kains* and *kebayas*, their normal film-star hair styles demurely disguised with supplementary plaits.

Another surprise was the apparent prevalence of aristocracy among my pupils. The popular initial R, I found, did not stand for a name (for the Javanese had no surnames, only a single personal name), but for the title *Raden*. Had Gadjah Mada University, the product of revolutionary democracy, already become the preserve of privilege? Whence this plethora of titles? The fact was that, though *Raden* implied some relationship to a princely family, it might be extremely distant. It was carried down, I was told, to the thirty-second generation; and when I recollected that there were four princedoms in central Java and that royal families often numbered several dozen children, it was easy to understand how titles had become rather widespread in this area—

E

in fact, even more so than might appear, for some of my students, in conformity with the democratic and egalitarian spirit of the new Indonesia, had dropped the use of their titles.

Even so, there seemed a large proportion of them. But it was not privilege but biology that filled the ranks of the students with so many boys and girls of good family. Admission to the University depended on passing a certain standard in the final examinations of the senior secondary schools and the government was generous with scholarships; birth or wealth in themselves therefore were of minor importance. But even in the most determinedly egalitarian society (and the Sultan's heir was ploughed in his secondary school entrance) one cannot provide genuine equality of opportunity. The child of educated and intelligent parents will always have a comparative advantage.

I found the students much more easy to get on with than their elders, my colleagues and contemporaries. Kindly and courteous as the older generation was, I never felt that I had really got close to them. It was not merely their natural reserve—and Jogja was noted even among the Javanese for the aloofness of its people— but the sense of a lingering, perhaps unconscious, but irradicable mistrust of the European that stood between us. This made me hesitant to assert my ideas and cautious over such mild reforms as introducing some written examinations; for they were almost morbidly sensitive to the least suggestion of a 'colonial' attitude. With the younger generation, however, I felt no such inhibitions. Independence had come to them young enough to be natural, before they could be conditioned to an inferiority complex. They had sufficient self-confidence to accept guidance. As one of them wrote in the University magazine, complaining of the lack of foreign professors:

'At present a common disease seems to prevail in Indonesia, the fear of foreign influence. . . . This attitude gives rise to an exaggerated prejudice against Westerners in general and the Dutch in particular. In our opinion such a fear is unfounded. It will only make us feel inferior to them. . . . Our students are old enough not to adopt the bad influences. We always like to say "We are not a weak nation." A strong nation is not so easily persuaded to give up its principles.'

With my students I felt free to express my views and give advice frankly, dispensing with the extra wrappings of tact and patience that made dealing with my colleagues so laborious and frustrating. I like to believe they knew I was on their side.

Of course in this relationship I had the advantage of the traditional oriental respect for the teacher. This was reflected in their habit of addressing teachers as *Bapak* or *Pa'* for short, meaning (as you might guess) 'Father'. But it should be noted, lest we attribute too weighty a significance to this mode of address, that mere age in itself was equally worthy of respect, so that the elderly chauffeur who fetched us each morning was as much a 'Pa' as his passengers. One unfortunate consequence of this old-world equation of age and wisdom was that it was difficult for a young man, however brilliant, to obtain an appointment as a university lecturer, since some of the students might be older than their teacher. This stumbling-block hindered the recruitment of English staff, as the salary offered was too little to attract any but the young and adventurous—or the failures. So, despite the annually swelling numbers, I remained on my own till the end of my time.

But after all the most important effect of their university years would probably be the mutual influence of the students on each other. If Gadjah Mada could, by bringing together the best of Indonesia's youth from all over the country, foster their sense both of community and of individuality, of national and personal values, it would be well justified, even if the academic standard might leave much to be desired. The Indonesians were proud of their community spirit, *gotong-royong*, but this was really a small-scale local feeling, the limited loyalty of mutual dependence; while individual personality traditionally counts for little in the East. The future of the new nation demanded wider loyalties and the full development of personal potentialities, and the university might achieve just this.

It was not all plain sailing, though. The grouping of students from different islands in their own *ad hoc* hostels was natural, but not always fortunate. Once indeed it led to tragedy. The freer manners of a Menadonese colony offended the local *kampong* and an open feud broke out when a Menadonese boy took a Javanese girl to the cinema alone. In the subsequent hostilities a night foray by the students resulted in the accidental death of an old villager. Next night a mob of *kampong*-dwellers, bent on revenge, set out to storm the hostel but found it guarded by a cordon of police. So with horrible unreason they made for another Menadonese hostel, some way distant and quite separate, dragged an innocent boy from his flimsy garage-room and lynched him mercilessly. The one encouraging feature of this dreadful story was the highly responsible reaction of the authorities on both sides, who promptly took steps by word and example to prevent a deplorable incident from growing into an outbreak of communal strife. But it showed how thin was the veneer of national consciousness over the ancient rifts of regionalism.

As for individuality, the Ministry of Education's expressed ideal was not only the dissemination of knowledge but 'spiritual cultivation' or, as we would say, character-building, so that 'the necessary sense for independence, activity, initiative and responsibility may be developed'. But the age-old tradition of submission to one's elders and one's community made it slow work encouraging the spirit of self-reliance and self-expression in the young. Most of the students were shy of active responsibility and preferred the background, leaving it to the enterprising few (usually Sumatrans) to organise such societies as there were. At first these were mostly large-scale student welfare organisations, university-wide or even country-wide, with a mainly passive membership. But gradually the spirit of individuality began to manifest itself in private groups and celebrations and rags. My own students, for instance, formed a literary society; the medicos ran a boisterous end-of-term carnival; and each Faculty had its own initiation rites.

One evening I suddenly met an alarming mob advancing down

Malioboro with banners and flaming torches, howling, whirling like dervishes and hideous with masks and green dunce's caps.

"What is happening, a demonstration or a riot or what?" I asked a student who was luckily at hand to reassure me.

"They are the Greenhorns of the Law Faculty, sir," came the proudly self-conscious reply. "It is one of the traditions of our University. Do you have such a custom at Cambridge, too?"

I commended the spirit that was already creating traditions for a three-year-old institution.

Gadjah Mada University was only one aspect of the immense effort of the Indonesian government to raise the people from 90 per cent illiteracy to modern educational standards, with a ten-year plan for universal elementary education by 1960. Ambitious and probably impracticable as this plan was, it nevertheless made for one of the most impressive and successful undertakings of the young state. For the whole people was behind it. The thirst for learning, so long denied them, was intense, as notable in the adults as in the streams of tiny brown dolls to be seen in every village, padding happily along the muddy pathways between the bamboo groves and the canals, proudly clutching their exercise books or slates.

But the first essential for schooling is a sufficiency of teachers, and so every possible candidate was quickly given employment in the schools. As English was now the second language of Indonesia, taught for a total of six years in the Junior and Senior secondary schools, there was an urgent call for anyone with knowledge of the language and many of my students, as soon as they passed their first-year examination, were engaged to pass on their inadequate knowledge in the local schools. It was a desperate position, for owing to their school duties they could not give full time to their university studies; engaged in examining others, they had no chance to prepare for their own examinations. Before long they and their pupils were fellow-undergraduates, and it was amusing to observe how quick was the return on my work, as my teaching was reproduced to me at second hand. Yet gradually the standard was rising and gradually the senior students managed to pass out, the first B.A. in English being granted in October 1954.

The difficult years were far from being ended, the standard was far from satisfactory, the syllabus far from perfect, and the staff still utterly inadequate—consisting as it did of myself alone. But something was being achieved, and it was a privilege to have a share in it.

4

THE LIVING PAST

WHILE I was fully occupied with my lectures, poor Coral found time hanging heavy on her hands in the hotel. No household chores, no meals, no shopping to worry about, these are perhaps bearable deprivations; but with no friends and no diversions to fill the empty hours, the lack can become trying. In the oppressive heat, as the dry season threatened to break, even her Greek vivacity began to wilt. Clearly she must find some outside interest to occupy her time and mind.

She decided to study the art of Javanese dancing, for which the courts of Jogjakarta and Surakarta were justly famed. Mrs. Sigit, whose motherly kindness was by no means exhausted by her own brood of eleven children, took her to meet Prince Tedjokusumo, an uncle of the Sultan, whose school of dancing was the best-known of the three in Jogja. The idea of a royal dancing-master seemed strange at first, but in Java it was an honourable and aristocratic art and the court dances used to be forbidden to any but relatives of the monarch. These solemn and graceful rituals with their spiritual and religious significance formed an important part of the education of a prince or princess: it was an honour to be chosen to perform at one of the numerous celebrations. The performances were not, of course, public, but in these democratic days the audience was less exclusive than of old and invitations could generally be obtained in return for a contribution to the society or committee organising the show. More than once we saw the Sultan's brothers take part in the dance-dramas.

Tedjokusuman, the home of Pangeran Tedjokusumo, was a

55

typical princely residence with its great gate, walled court, trees and *pendopo* jutting out into the centre. This cool and shady hall with its highly polished marble tiles and glittering chandeliers was the dance-school. Coral took private lessons in the evening, but the regular practices took place every Sunday morning; and it was on one of these occasions that I paid my first visit to her school.

The pupils were practising for a performance due in a few weeks and I watched the teachers checking and polishing their movements, concentrating on the hands and head, for these were the most important and expressive motions. We are apt to think of dancing as an art primarily of the legs, but the Oriental gives pride of place to the arms. In Jogja the girls' feet were almost invisible under the long *kain*, which was so arranged that a fold fell between them like a tail. All one could see was a slow and dignified dipping and bending of the knees or occasionally a rapid tiptoe walk that represented flying. Nevertheless the leg movements were as exactingly practised and controlled as the rest, as Coral soon found at her classes. She would come home exhausted from practising walking (each foot placed heel to toe at an almost Chaplinesque angle) or turning (an intricate combination of foot and knee work) or sitting and rising, all carried out with the enormous deliberation of a slow march, the precision of a drill manoeuvre. The gestures came later; but even if she could remember the complex arrangement of each separate finger, it was impossible for any normal European to bend them and the wrist and the elbow back into the fantastic curves that seemed so easy to the supple Javanese. Still harder was the head movement, for it seemed against nature, jerking from side to side horizontally, as if detached from the neck. Weeks of intensive practice were needed to get beyond a ridiculous wagging of the chin or shoulders. Coral was not by any means the first Western woman to be trained by the Pangeran, but he would only grant that one ever approached the requisite standard for a public performance—and she was a famous ballet dancer.

Coral's lessons had their reward not so much in her own

achievement as in the enhanced appreciation of the expert's skill. As we watched the teachers moving springily around on their broad flat soles, quietly correcting and demonstrating, we began to realise the severity of the training for the *Wayang Orang*, or 'human puppets', as the performers in the dance-dramas were called. That day it was not a dress rehearsal and the young men were dressed informally in *sarongs*, singlets and anachronistic wristwatches instead of flowered breeches, wings and gilded armlets. Occasionally, when the timing or footwork of the incredibly complex fighting sequences went astray, they allowed themselves a brief and rueful smile. But this was strictly unofficial. Complete impassivity of expression was the rule, while the dialogue was intoned with ecclesiastical monotony except for a stylised falsetto giggle of mockery or a sudden bay of anger. It was the hands, not the face or voice, that expressed their emotions in a conventional code of gestures, a code so seldom representational that it remained a mystery to me. The result was an atmosphere strangely remote and unworldly, well suited to the legends of gods and heroes that they were portraying, and the actors' sudden relapses into smiling humanity came as quite a shock. The teachers put them right without fuss but with firm insistence on precision, for the essence of the male style is the snap with which the motions, however slow, are carried out.

There were several instructors disposed around the hall and we noticed that they rather differed in type from the common Indonesian. They were taller than the average, which made them look thinner, especially in their high-necked vertically-striped jackets and long *kains*; there was a high incidence of moustaches, which the normal Indonesian cannot achieve; and their features were distinctive, particularly the long, narrow and even aquiline noses which contrasted with the broad snubness of the generality. Prince Tedjokusumo himself was the most striking example, immensely thin with features of almost Byzantine length and pale blue eyes behind his steel-rimmed spectacles. The aristocratic distinction of the '*Kraton* type' of Jogja has been noted by several travellers and makes it easier to believe in a genealogy

that traces the royal line back to the legendary Indian founders
of the Hindu-Javanese empire.

A month later we attended our first full-dress performance of
Javanese dance-drama. The occasion was the thirty-fourth
anniversary of the foundation of the Krida-Beksa-Wirama Dance
Group, an organisation for teaching and preserving the art of
Jogja dancing, founded by Prince Tedjokusumo. His purpose
was to spread the knowledge and practice of the classical court
style to wider circles and to revivify the art with new creations on
the traditional lines; in this way the spiritual heritage and national
consciousness of the Javanese would be fostered and reinforced
against the pressure of Western modernism and materialism. It
was not an antiquarian revival like the folk-dance groups in
England, nor a reactionary attempt to put the clock back. In
Central Java, the Princes' Lands, the dance was still very much
alive, not only as a hothouse bloom of the courts but as a popular
entertainment in every village and on every occasion. The found-
ing of the K.B.W. group was an assertion of faith in the past and
the future, in the spiritual values of Java's ancient culture and its
continued liveliness and usefulness to the people. No longer was
the practice of the court dances confined to the palace; commoners
might learn even the sacred *Serimpi*, once the exclusive right of
princesses. The Group, though it remained largely aristocratic
and strictly amateur, brought the general public into closer contact with the higher standards and conceptions of skill and
aesthetics that had been developed in the *Kraton*, helping to raise
the level of popular performance and spread the sense of unity
among all classes.

That the public appreciated this initiative was obvious when
we looked around the hall on the evening of the anniversary celebration. We had had great difficulty in obtaining tickets and now
we had still more difficulty in finding seats, even though the dance
was held in a more spacious *pendopo* with close-packed chairs
serried on three sides of the floor, like an Elizabethan apron stage.
An elaborate twelve-page programme showed that we were to see

a 'Fragment' from the *Mahabharata*, which with its companion epic, the *Ramayana*, supplied the material for endless dance-dramas. This particular fragment lasted only five and a half hours and concerned the birth of Gatotkatja. He is one of the favourite heroes of the Javanese, who have adapted the Indian legends to local scenery and adopted certain characters, notably Ardjuna, as their ideal figures and indeed their ancestors. The programme told in detail the story of the four acts: how the giant Sekipu came and demanded the hand of the goddess Wilutama for his king; how the gods refused and were defeated in the consequent warfare; how Gatotkatja, the baby son of Bima, was plunged in a volcano and emerged full-grown and endowed with magic strength; and how he finally conquered the army of the giants. But besides that the programme gave numbered diagrams of the positions of the dancers and technical details of the tunes and combinations of instruments. It was clear that this was as highly organised and scientific an art as the ballet.

In due time the *gamelan*, which had been strumming softly in the background amid the gilded baskets of bouquets and faded photographs of royalty, struck up a more vigorous rhythm and the splendid procession of gods and goddesses strutted or glided in. There were two distinctive styles of movement, the *gagah* or vigorous and the *alus* or gentle. The ladies were invariably gentle and the men usually vigorous, but certain male characters were distinguished by their gentle and modest demeanour; a smooth and rather slinky walk, in fact, was the sign of a true gentleman like Ardjuna. Nothing could have been less like the accepted Western vision of Oriental dancing-girls than the stately and deliberate progress of the Javanese vestals. Moving with almost inhuman slowness and detachment, bodies erect and unbending, and eyes fixed modestly downwards, clad in floor-length *kains* and high-necked jackets with a feathered tiara to complete the effect of aristocratic dignity, they were the embodiment of chastity—a vision that even the loosest imagination in the spectator and the slenderest beauty in the dancer could hardly make provocative. Beautiful indeed they looked, in spite of their sickly yellow face powder, with their large dark eyes and full lips and their slim and graceful figures; and the costumes added to their charms. The tunics of wine-dark velvet fringed with gold and the long red-and-white sash clasped with a broad gold belt set off the dark brown and white of their *batik* skirts without clashing. Necklets and armlets and winged coronets of gilded leather added to the rich effect, while their black hair glittered with starlike flowers at the back.

The sash was an essential and vital part of the costume, being continually flicked back or delicately fluttered or twirled over the dancer's hand according to some principle which I never fathomed. The males were likewise sashed and equally adept at their manipulation. But their *kains* were tucked up high above figured cloth knee-breeches, for they needed their legs free. The vigorous types moved with high wide steps, balancing gymnastically on one foot with the other stretched straight out to the side, a feat demanding the utmost muscle control. Their torsos were bare, though gods wore a pair of conventional leather wings like a spaceman's oxygen pack; their heads were decorated with double-decker crowns or black curly helms; and their lips sported neat cavalry moustaches of burnt cork, suggestive of their Indian origin. The giants, like the Demon King in a pantomime, were at once figures of horror and fun with frightful scarlet masks, popping eyes, huge fangs and long matted hair, while strings of bells jingled mockingly round their ankles. It is strange that, whereas in India this tinkling accompaniment is regarded as a refined and essential part of the music, in Java it is reserved for giants, clowns, monkeys and suchlike undignified characters.

The play slowly unwound its leisurely story with tireless detail of every conference, embassy, message, challenge of the opposing sides. It seemed as though the Cold War would never end; even when the champions at last faced each other, they spent long minutes in mutual defiance and Homeric boasting before they started to circle round like angry dogs. Then a sudden whirl of stabbing arms and leaping legs realistically mimed the duel, yet with every movement so carefully controlled and co-ordinated that they never actually hit each other. Chivalry demanded that you should not hit your opponent when he was down, kneeling dazed after an athletic roll across the floor, nor even when his back was turned, as often happened in the convolutions of the dance. But there seemed to be no inhibitions about the use of unsporting weapons. Heroes in trouble resorted without compunction to a wicked-looking magic club that my informants aptly called the Atom Bomb; and Gatotkatja, after his volcanic ordeal, enjoyed the unfair advantage of complete command of the air. His triumph, we were told, symbolised the powers of youth, when inspired by true gallantry. The Javanese like to draw a moral from every tale.

This first performance was typical of the many other *Wayang Orang* shows that we saw in the following years. The resemblance to the *Wayang Kulit* in theme and action was obvious to us even then. The orchestra was the same and the *dalang* led and controlled the performance in the same way, setting the time with his hammer, reciting the necessary commentary and generally acting as director, conductor, compère and prompter all at once. But what we did not immediately realise was that the shadow-play came first, that it was not a case of puppets imitating men but of men imitating puppets. The name—'human puppets'—was perfectly accurate.

Actually the word *wayang* originally means 'shadow' and, as so often with the Oriental mind, a whole mystique is implicit in it. A *wayang* performance is the shadow of human life and numberless fine-drawn parallels and edifying lessons are discovered in every story. The white screen is the world; the lamp is the sun, the token of life; the puppets are the people; the *gamelan* is the rhythm of their life; and the *dalang*, whose hands move the puppets and can play with them as he likes, represents the power of God. The play symbolises not only the obvious struggle between the good and bad principles (and the bad, though frustrated, must never be finally wiped out, as that would upset the eternal balance and harmony of the world) but also the triple development of life itself in the father, mother and the world. The smallest details are as full of mystic symbolism as the major conceptions. The leaf-like 'Mountain of Life', set up in the centre of the screen after a period of blank nothingness, represents by its perforated images of men, animals, things and earth the unity of all sides of life, while its pointed top stands for the climax of life, which is death. The clowns, far from being mere comic relief, are symbols of major importance, following the hero and representing the qualities that guide him. The obese and pendulous Semar with his rolling eyes symbolises the motherly quality of tender-hearted wisdom combined with ambition; Petruk of the long nose and perpetual grin represents intellectual power plus cheerfulness; and the lame, deformed and squinting Gareng somehow indicates firmness of will, care, honesty, concentration and contentment. The love of allegory pervades every *wayang* performance, and each story, whatever the source, is turned to a moral point. However obscure and far-fetched the symbolism might seem, the educational and moral value of the *wayang* was stressed to me by all and they assured me that this aspect of the show was as fully appreciated in the villages as at court.

The *wayang* is said to be an original Javanese art, for once not imported from India, despite the predominance of the Hindu epics in its repertoire. It is supposed that the performances were originally held in honour of deceased ancestors and that on such occasions the souls of the dead descended and entered into the puppets. The *dalang*, as the medium, was regarded as a holy man: and he still begins the evening with an offering and a prayer. The cult of the ancestors never ceased, but the ancient stories were overlaid by the grandeur of the epics brought by the Indian colonisers. Yet even now Semar as the incarnation of the ancestral spirit talks down to the Hindu gods in the low language. Later the *wayang* techniques were used for more modern themes such as local legends and history, not to mention propaganda, and topical additions to the canon have continued to this day. But the ancient Hindu stories, however performed, have always remained the most respected and popular of all. This was the type we generally saw, though in very various surroundings; sometimes in the dim green depths of the *kampong* that huddled under the bamboos a few hundred yards behind our smug suburban street; sometimes in the prefabricated modernity of the students' hostel; sometimes in a private house or *pendopo*. The *wayang* is part of the texture of Javanese life and still holds its own among the competing attractions of modernism, thanks to its spiritual affinity with the mysticism that lies at the heart of that life.

Of all the occasions when we watched these shows, the one that somehow appealed to me most was that held in our *kampong*. There were no invitations, no rows of chairs, no electric light. It was the annual celebration of this little community to which we belonged and contributed for administrative convenience, though far apart in all ways except physical distance. When we heard the *gamelan* ringing through the still, soft darkness, we walked down the well-brushed earthen paths through the palms and bamboos, following the sound of the music and the murmur of many voices. Suddenly we came upon a clearing, dimly lit by the flickering oil-lamps of tiny stalls. All round a throng of villagers jostled quietly and good-humouredly, with children nipping in and out and babies slung on nearly every hip. Over their heads I could see a white sheet stretched on a frame between the pillars of a large hut and an elaborate brass lamp hanging before it to throw the shadows on the screen. This was a humble entertainment with only a three-piece *gamelan*, but the *dalang* was as skilled as ever in manipulating over a hundred puppets. Courteously the crowd made way for us and we were conducted to a sort of box, where the headman sat in his black cap and Western clothes. Seats and cups of tea were rapidly forthcoming, and from there we were able to watch the shadow side of the screen, flickering with the life that only an oil-lamp can give. We also watched the audience, for here under the shelter of the roof sat the men, the masters. Cross-legged on the mats they looked most dignified in their sober Javanese costumes. The scene reminded me of an old-fashioned club with its male exclusiveness, its gravity and its cards. Very few were paying any attention to

the screen as they sat in small circles, gambling away their hard-
earned and easily-lost rupiahs with what looked like paper
dominoes. A few lucky women and children lined the edge of the
floor and contrasted with their lords by their chatter and their
thrilled absorption in the shadow-play.

Another time we saw a *Wayang Orang* there with a full caste of
more than a dozen dancers. This was a special effort for *Lebaran*,
the end of the Fast and the biggest feast of the year. A pavilion
had been specially built, with a real stage. Once more we were
pressed to official seats with tables and tea and vases of paper
flowers, and through the festive greenery and the intrusive fringe
of children we watched the heroes and clowns, dressed up in full
fig, go through the usual evolutions. These were professionals; but
all their skill could not entirely overcome the conditions. The creaky
boards, covered with coconut matting, wobbled and unbalanced
them as they strode forward; the narrow platform would hardly
hold them all; and the patriotic red-and-white streamers, looped
from the roof, caught in their high crowns and entangled their
slashing arms. The performance had not the polish of Tedjokusuman, but there was no doubt about the enthusiasm of the
audience. Indeed their excited chatter grew so loud that often,
close as we were, we could not hear the words of the performers
—and for once there was no microphone. But what did it matter
when everyone already knew the story as well as we know that
of a pantomime? No one can be expected to sit in a state of
reverent hush for nine whole hours. I doubt if the first audiences
of Aeschylus or Euripides listened to every word of their trilogies.

The professional dancers mostly came from Solo, for Jogja
jealously preserved its amateur status. Sometimes a single per-
former would be engaged for, say, a wedding, sometimes a whole
troupe for bigger celebrations. The Solo style showed certain
differences from Jogja; for instance, the dancing-girls had their
shoulders bare as in old-fashioned court dress, and used a long
scarf instead of a sash. But basically the movements were the
same, as slow and decorous as those of any princess. In Jogja

Performance of a Wayang shadow play

Shadow puppets

Hero and giant fighting

President Sukarno dancing the
Handkerchief Dance with students

Solo dancer

full-scale professional plays could be seen at the fairs, known as *Pasar Malam* (evening bazaar), that were often held on the great grassy square in front of the palace.

At these times the whole green would sprout a mushroom growth of bamboo shacks, ranging from mere booths to large theatres. In between were neon-lit stalls of cheap goods and dim little restaurants where we sometimes risked a beer or fried rice; hawkers offered jazzy clay horses or fantastic cocks, ingeniously made up of red and blue balloons, or grotesque papier-mâché dragons with concertina-like bodies; horrific sideshows boasted such wonders as human-headed snakes. Everywhere there was a bedlam of loudspeakers blaring the discordant voices of Indonesian barkers and American crooners; and the jostling crowds seemed happy simply to jostle.

The 'Reconstruction Fair' of April 1954 lasted a whole month and the major attractions were enclosed in a high fence with a grand triple-roofed entrance. The amusement park contained not only the usual swings, roundabouts and rickety Great Wheel, but a kidney-shaped artificial lake. There were exhibitions of police work, agriculture and fishery, and a working model of what appeared to be the industrial Jogja of the Sultan's dreams. There were smart little shops and restaurants, and a gaming-hall where the winning numbers were decided with darts. But the main attractions were still the theatres of various kinds, *Wayang Orang, Ketoprak* and *Sandiwara*. The most elaborate and expensive was the traditional *Wayang* with its large cast, full *gamelan*, rich costumes and masks, and lurid succession of backcloths. Every night it presented a different play from the classic series of the wars between the Pendawas and the Kurawas. The *Sandiwara*, on the other hand, was a modern development with naturalistic acting, dialogue in Indonesian and stories taken from all sources. Their repertoire for the month, for instance, included historical plays on national heroes like Suropati and Diponegoro, romances of Baghdad, the French Revolution, and the 'Revolution of Surabaya'. I particularly wanted to see this last, as I suppose it dealt with the battle against the British in 1945; but a

F

cloudburst washed it out and I never discovered whether the Javanese stage now has its own version of Colonel Blimp.

The *Ketoprak* was also a development of the last twenty or thirty years, but it formed a popular compromise between the classical and modern styles. Originally a village entertainment, it grew in splendour as it grew in popularity and soon rivalled the *Wayang Orang* in costume, staging and music. It remained, however, a lower form of art with less polished dancing, extempore songs, everyday language and crude sentiments—such as open love-making! The singing and dancing were growing more and more perfunctory, but the *gamelan* and the Javanese language still distinguished it from mere *Sandiwara*. The stories were mostly based on Javanese history and ballads; their programme at the fair included such favourites as the Pandji love-tales, the wooing of the Queen of Modjopahit and the fall of the rebel prince Arya Penangsang. But there was no fixed canon and the one we visited was set in Stamboul with red-fezzed officers and—to Coral's indignation—a comic couple of cringing Greeks.

To complain, as foreigners in Djakarta do, that there is no regular theatre even in the capital, is to give a misleading idea of the liveliness of dramatic activity in Indonesia. Experiment and expansion have been continuous down the years. Sometimes the impulse came from the courts, as with the *Langendriya*, a highly refined combination of dance and song that approaches opera, invented by the poet-prince Mangkunegoro IV of Solo; sometimes from the villages, like the *Ketoprak*; sometimes from abroad, like the *Sandiwara*. Students would experiment with Ibsen and Shakespeare (we saw a Javanised version of *Macbeth*—without the Lady!), and the infant film industry strove, with increasing success, to master the technique of this modern form of shadow-play. The Cultural Department of the Ministry of Education was solicitous to encourage every form of dramatic expression, old or new, to serve both tradition and progress. These aims were not necessarily contradictory. The *Wayang Golek*, with wooden doll puppets, was a popular feature on Jogja Radio; the *Wayang Bébér*, a primitive painted scroll, proved more useful than loudspeakers in explaining government measures to the peasantry; the *Wayang Pantja Sila* was a new variation on the old themes, personifying the mystique of the new democracy; and the *Wayang Suluh*, using highly realistic cut-outs, actually sought to portray current events such as the Bandung Conference. Even in the classical dance-dramas the clowns were apt to gag about the questions of the day—we once heard one break into comic English! The *Wayang* was by no means out of date.

Separation of the dance from the drama resulted in the creation of performances that were not part of any ancient story but simply represented some emotion or activity in ballet form. They were usually attributed to some legendary character but not very consistently or insistently. The holy *Serimpi* might be interpreted as a competition between two Hindu heroines to rescue a handsome prince or as the mystic struggle to preserve the cosmic equilibrium, while some assigned its origin to a pre-Hindu religious dance. It made no difference to the choreography with four dancers representing the two characters to give it more balance. Their movements were so very dignified and slow that some exalted Middle Eastern guests fell asleep during the performance in their honour. The *Kelono* dance, which mimed a young man in love, dressing up, trimming his moustache and embracing empty air in an ecstasy of imagination, was generally assigned to Prince Pandji, whose separations and reunions with his beloved were the theme of a whole cycle. The feminine counterpart was the *Golek*, or 'Doll', showing a girl busy with her make-up, and it was particularly popular because of its suitability for small celebrations with only one dancing girl. We saw it on such varied occasions as a University party, the anniversary of the Treasury Clerks' Union, and a village wedding. Another popular solo was the *Bondan*, a highly representational mime of a mother bathing her baby in the river, which ended with her balancing on her waterpot and dancing there with twirling parasol till a kick broke it and proved it was an ordinary, empty clay jar. The first time we watched the *Bondan* was at a May Day party held in the Garuda by the Hotel-workers' Union, a branch of SOBSI, the Indonesian TUC. Our room boys welcomed their exploiters with true Javanese courtesy and were embarrassed when I found a copy of the official programme, which revealed only too clearly the controlling hand behind the celebrations. I could not make out much of this thick document, but a poem, 'From the Death Cell', by Ethel Rosenberg, was plain enough. Our next *Bondan* was at an ancient sacrificial ceremony of the limestone workers. It was, perhaps, a rather proletarian dance.

Whatever the occasion, religious or political, social or commemorative, traditional or modern, dancing and the *gamelan* were the inevitable accompaniment. Rooted in the heroic past, attributed to the hero-king Erlangga, the art of the dance had never ossified or lost touch with the people. It was natural for them to express themselves in this way. When the first Sultan of Jogja wished to train his soldiers in spearmanship, the exercises he devised took the form of the *Lawung* dance, where four soldiers and two clowns go through competitive manoeuvres under the eye of rival sergeant-majors. The science of self-defence developed into a combination of ju-jitsu, dance and mysticism called *Pentjak*, which was a popular sport all over Indonesia. When K. H. Dewantoro set up his nationalist *Taman Siswa* schools in 1922, the curriculum naturally included the art of Javanese dancing.

Nor had the classical dance societies been content with a Byzantine conservatism, but had created new subjects and new ways of expressing them. The thirty-fifth anniversary of the Krida-Beksa-Wirama was marked by a *Bedoyo* performance that symbolised the history of the revolution, from the last days of Dutch rule to the final triumph of the Republic. The *Bedoyo* was a classic dance by nine girls, and I found it hard, in spite of detailed diagrams, to follow their changes of identity and interpret their formal movements in modern terms. The only easily recognisable event was the bombing of Jogja, when three of the girls circled their crouching companions with the flying motion and the biggest gong tolled out the crash of the bombs. Not to be outdone in choreographic progressiveness, the Communists organised their own dance society, LEKRA (The People's Cultural Club); and in 1955 they took part with their aristocratic rivals in a performance in honour of the Chinese cultural mission, presenting such suitably democratic themes as the 'Peasants' Dance' and the 'Workers' Dance'. Yet somehow even LEKRA failed to escape entirely from the time-hallowed prejudices of tradition. The simple motions of the peasants, as they sowed and cut the rice, had a natural dignity; but there was no doubt that the workers were comic. Their movements, as they carried loads, sawed wood, laid bricks, and so on, were in the jiggly clownish style of the lower classes in the classic plays, and comedy broke out unashamed when they counted their pay and immediately staged a sit-down strike.

The Chinese Commissar's face preserved perfect inscrutability during this display.

The strange thing was that in Central Java, despite their devotion to the art of dancing, there were no folk-dances in our sense of the word; dances, that is, where the people actively participate. Their role was always the passive one of spectators. What they translated as folk-dances were in fact popular dances, as opposed to the court-dances—dances which in the old days were permitted outside the palace, but only in a kneeling position or, if standing, in masks. Thus arose the *Wayang Topeng* (mask dance), an inferior form of *Wayang Orang*, dealing with humbler subjects such as local history. I was amazed when, in a piece concerning the foundation of the glorious Modjopahit empire, the founder, Prince Widjoyo, appeared in a foolishly grinning, pop-eyed mask. It was not satire, but respect for the higher beings of the classic drama, that led them to portray a mere human so. But that did not make it a folk-dance; it was still ballet.

Even the rough *Djatilan*, the dance of the Bamboo Horse, was normally performed by professional entertainers, though it used to be played by villagers when an epidemic or crop-failure threatened. Another name for it was *Reyog Ponorogo*, from the remote little town near Mount Lawu where it originated. The people of Ponorogo were as mysterious as their dance; both seemed more primitive than usual, and their customs were so idiosyncratic that it was believed that they belonged to the original stock of Java, somehow surviving unabsorbed in this backwater. The *Djatilan* was certainly a contrast to the sophistication of the Javanese dances. At the evening fair some ragged musicians would start banging gongs and drums with a monotonous hypnotic rhythm, while two dancers pranced around on flat bamboo hobby-horses, emitting weird shrieks. When the drumming had drawn a crowd round their hut, a terrifying new figure emerged in a tiger's-head mask crowned with tall peacock feathers. There was no stage, no enclosure for this show. Slowly, with the tiger jigging menacingly forward or suddenly lunging at the wildly circling horses, the troupe made the round of the whole fair, followed by a ring of awed spectators. It was really a trance-dance, where the dancers were supposed to become the animals they represented. But the blare of canned music drowned the throb of the drum and the glare of neon lights wiped out the mystery of the shadows. It was not conducive to trance and we soon gave up waiting for it. Nor was I convinced when one Sunday I found a troupe performing at the street corner outside our house. There was no tiger; but the hobby-horse galloped and rolled about, ate dry grass, and was whipped across the back without flinching. Then a more indefinite beast took his place. From its shape it might have been a pig and it stamped about in a mush of grain and water that it had been gobbling greedily. But the way it jumped sharply around was hardly porcine. Finally it walked blindly through a hedge, returning with a cassava bush in its mouth. Whatever it was supposed to be, when the music stopped and the leader tapped him with the whip, the player recovered far too quickly.

In Jogja, what with students from the other islands and cultural missions from China and India, we were able to compare the Javanese style of dancing with those of its neighbours and its sources. Such a comparison left no doubt as to the major influence of India on the civilisation of Indonesia. When Prithvi Raj Kapoor brought a goodwill mission in 1956, the movements and gestures were demonstrably in the same idiom as the Javanese, though to us, inured to the delicate impersonality of the latter, the leaping vigour, rolling eyes and expressive grimaces of the Indians appeared a little theatrical and undignified, a trifle vulgar. For all their differences these dances obviously belonged to the same world; in fact the prima ballerina had once studied under Prince Tedjokusumo and publicly paid him homage.

But the Peking Opera took us into a world utterly strange. The mission sent by Communist China in July 1955 was formidable in size and efficiency. The varied and expert programme proceeded with unnatural slickness; but the banality of the modern items—jaunty propaganda songs and pretty-pretty lotus ballets—only served to set off the brilliance of the classic drama. Basically perhaps, in the formality of the gestures, the monotonous whine of the songs, the fantasy of the masks, the Peking Opera might display a common heritage with its oriental neighbours. But it had developed quite differently with emphasis on the spectacular rather than the graceful. Heavy with robes of gorgeous brocade, the actors stumped and the actresses tripped around—except in the fighting dances, where more lightly clad acrobats twirled swords and turned somersaults and kicked spears to and fro with miraculous skill and speed. Above all, the music bore no relation to the slow melodiousness of Java's gongs and metallophones. The strange-shaped medieval instruments gave out a maddening succession of discords, all clashing cymbals and sudden gongs and grating strings, so that I ended a fascinating evening with a bad headache.

Of Indonesian dances those of Bali and South Borneo were closest to the Javanese; nor was this surprising, since Bali was and still is the last refuge of Hinduism, while South Borneo was colonised by Modjopahit. But while the Borneo style seemed merely a provincial imitation, Bali had developed something quite distinct, gayer and livelier, uninhibited by the puritanism of Islam. The dances from the other parts of Borneo, however, showed up the fact that the area of Javanese civilisation was only a fringe upon the dark and savage interior of that vast island. Feathered warriors leaping and whirling, covered in gold bangles and paint and flourishing narrow snaky-patterned shields; girls with fanlike plumes between their fingers, sinuously undulating, their ear-lobes stretched down to their shoulders with the weight of dozens of silver rings; primitive elongated guitars monotonously strumming and the rhythmical rattling of bamboo tubes—these came from the untamed jungle, not the marble-paved court. The same eerie wildness was suggested by a dance from Atjeh, that tameless stronghold of independence at the northern tip of Sumatra, which defied the Dutch for thirty years (1873–1904) and was now defying the Indonesian Republic. Nevertheless there were plenty of Atjenese studying in Jogja and the display we saw was given by some art students. They filed on in a long line, led by a chief in a high turban and a purple cloak; next came a man and woman with enormous crests of red, white and green feathers; then a dozen youths in white carrying tiny hard cushions fringed with bells, and last the musicians with gongs and a tubular drum. They sat in a semi-circle, singing and swaying in chorus and beating the rhythm on their tinkling cushions, while the leader swooped around them, finally sinking down before the feathered couple and raising them to dance in a trance-like way with bowed heads. It was all rather sinister.

This was the only time we watched a dance from Atjeh; but on many occasions we saw examples from other parts of Sumatra. The most popular were the Umbrella Dance and the Handkerchief Dance, and their popularity was surely due to the fact that they were folk-dances in the true sense of the word, dances in which anyone could join for the fun of the thing. Both were performed by couples, boy and girl, as in the West—though of course they did not go so far as to touch each other. Both were primarily dances of the feet. And when we add that the music was played on Western instruments with the catchy rhythm of European folk-dances (Coral recognised a melody from a Corfu tune in one of them), it was obvious that they owed much to the influence of the Portuguese. Although in point of time the Portuguese did not hold sway in the archipelago for very long— only about a century, and that four hundred years ago—their impact as the first bearers of European civilisation seems to have left surprisingly deep traces. Sumatra, stretching along the straits opposite their main base of Malacca, was more affected than Java, and perhaps the Sumatrans, with their more lively and demonstrative nature, were more open to the spirit of the West.

At any rate these Sumatran folk-dances, whether naturalised or native, satisfied the normal human urge to take part in informal and preferably mixed dancing; and in Jogja, where the modern western style was disapproved of (except behind closed doors), the Handkerchief Dance came to be one of the most popular features of any celebration. After a demonstration the girls in their shapeless mantles and the boys with *sarongs* wrapped kiltwise over loose trousers would turn to the audience and urge or drag new partners onto the floor. Roars of friendly laughter greeted the clumsy efforts of novices such as myself. Other victims were more skilful—for example President Sukarno himself, who was induced to take the floor at the University's fourth birthday celebrations. But the students were not satisfied till they had drawn his wife into it too. Shedding her shoes, Mme. Fatmawati joined in the fun, and before long the dance floor boasted not only the President and First Lady of the Republic, but also the Prime Minister and his wife, the Sultan, Prince Paku Alam, the Vice-Premier, the Minister of Information and the Chief of the General Staff.

It was a triumph of democracy and the dance.

In Java's dancing and music the past lived on. Thanks to the continuity of their tradition and practice these arts had preserved their Javanese character intact, free from the problems of Western influence that beset the sister arts of painting and writing. The

Indonesians, naturally musical, readily accepted the contribution of the West, but it remained something separate and apart. In 1952 the government set up a school of Western music in Jogja, but it did not seem to have taken root. It was teaching as it were a foreign language—not only because the teachers were in fact all foreigners, led by a morose Russian exile and enlivened by a Hungarian who had met a Flying Saucer on his way from Djakarta; nor because the music taught was all European, from Beethoven to César Cui; but because there was a great gulf fixed between the Western and the Javanese tone-systems, the diatonic and the pentatonic, so that any attempt to synthesise their technique and spirit was more or less impossible. For the people the five-tone system of the *gamelan* remained the true reflection of their deepest feelings. The idea of composing serious music in the Western mode, an Indonesian symphony, would be unnatural, spiritually if not technically out of tune.

The Western scale was used for lighter compositions such as the popular sentimental ballads known as *kerontjong* (an onomatopoeic name suggestive of the plucking of the accompanying guitar) or for stirring marches like the 'General Election' signature tune. Only one composer's name was remembered, and that was because he wrote the national anthem, *Indonesia Raya*. The remarkable thing about this rousing march was that it was adopted as the anthem of a nation that did not yet exist, and it actually made a great contribution to the realisation of the dream of nationhood. It was first sung by its composer, W. R. Supratman, at the All-Indonesia Youth Congress in Djakarta in 1928, when the country was still a Dutch colony and Djakarta itself was called Batavia. The song expressed in simple and stirring words and music the spirit of the historic resolution of that Congress that they all belonged to one people, the Indonesians, with one fatherland, Indonesia, and one language, Indonesian. Nowadays perhaps the words sound repetitious and banal with their insistent 'Indonesia our country, our nation, our people' and so forth, but at the time they were written every one of them was revolutionary. For there was no such country as Indonesia; it could only become a nation by overthrowing the colonial power; and the differences between the many peoples of the archipelago were emphasised and exploited by their rulers. The chorus, 'Indonesia the great, independent and free', was sheer treason and the song (like the red-and-white flag adopted at the same congress) was banned. But its swinging catchy tune was as irrepressible as 'Lillibulero' and spread the consciousness of nationality throughout the Dutch dominions in a way that political resolutions in the faraway capital could never have done.

The composer never saw the triumph of his song. Born in 1903, Supratman lived a restless, rebellious life, scraping a living with his violin, now as a teacher, now in a fashionable hotel orchestra, now at the street corner. On 17th August 1938 he died, aged only 35, leaving no family or fortune except the work that, exactly seven years later, was to become the anthem of the nation he had helped to make.

The situation in the other arts was just the opposite. Here the native tradition had broken down and a new start had to be made with inspiration coming from the West. The problem was how to express the Eastern spirit through Western media. The ASRI (Indonesian Academy of Plastic Arts), set up in Jogja in 1950, was a much more lively institution than the music school; indeed it was the centre of a budding renaissance in painting and sculpture. As we walked round the galleries at their annual exhibition, it was hard to believe that twenty years before there had been virtually no Indonesian painters at all—except in Bali. The exception gives the clue to the explanation; for Bali is still Hindu. It was the Moslem ban on the representation of living forms that had confined Java's artists to the stylised decoration of distorted *wayang* figures and limited the descendants of the sculptors of Borobudur to the craft of woodcarving.

It was not till 1938 that any concerted movement arose in defiance of religious obscurantism. One lonely pioneer, Raden Saleh, appeared in the age of Victoria, but, though patronised by the Sultan of Jogja (and in Europe by the Prince Consort), his example led nowhere. For fifty years after his death painting in Java was represented by soothing landscapes or romanticised scenes from life aimed at the tourist trade, the work of mediocre Dutchmen with one or two local imitators. But in 1938 the first group of modern painters was formed under revolutionary spirits like Sudjoyono and Affandi, who stressed the importance of personality and independence, the free expression of themselves as artists and as Indonesians, instead of the profitable platitudes of 'ricefields being ploughed, ricefields under water, pure and calm, or mountains painted the bluest of blues'. Under the Japanese these nationalist artists were encouraged and organised in the hope of propaganda assistance, but though they eagerly accepted the practical opportunities offered, they did not sell their souls. The Art department of *Putera*, the Jap-sponsored organisation for the 'concentration of the people's forces', was as clever as its political leaders in using it to foster Indonesian nationalism rather than Jap propaganda.

When the Dutch reoccupied Djakarta soon after the revolution, most of the artists followed the President to Jogja, which became a hive of busy art clubs. The leaders formed the nucleus of the ASRI, and we came to know them well when Coral took up the study of painting at the academy. Their teaching was hardly academic, for most of them were self-taught, like Affandi. who seldom used brushes, preferring to squeeze the tube directly onto the canvas or sit on the floor and spread the colours with his thumb. But it was undoubtedly stimulating, as masters and pupils alike experimented in the search for a style that should combine the modern techniques of the West with the inherent spirit of the East. Some were promising, some were not; but as we went round the bamboo huts and concrete garages where hollow-cheeked young men, vainly cultivating conventional beards and almost as conventional Communism, laboured and argued and sang, there was a feeling of ferment in the atmosphere, a feeling that something worth while might soon emerge.

Indeed something had already emerged. Affandi's work had been acclaimed in Europe. His two exhibitions in London in

1952 had impressed the critics with the tropical violence of his swirling primary colours and received the final accolade of a purchase by Sir Kenneth Clark. He went on to the Hague, Brussels, Paris, Rome, repeating his success, and he represented his country at the Venice Biennale. And there was Eddy Sunarso, still a student, whose entry for the international competition for a sculpture on the Unknown Political Prisoner—a gaunt and elongated figure lying face downwards in chained and exhausted despair—not only won a regional prize but, in the furore that followed the exhibition of the prize-winning pieces in the Tate Gallery, was actually voted by the public the second prize for the whole world. The judges' award had to stand, however, and I, as Britain's sole representative in Jogja, had the invidious task of presenting and explaining the disappointingly meagre cheque—a task made doubly embarrassing by the counterstroke of the Iron Curtain, a six-months' scholarship abroad. The Communists were assiduous in their wooing of Asia's intellectuals and Coral's comrades were for ever hastening off to such improbable art centres as Poland or Bulgaria. Eddy left the next day for Bucharest.

The revival of sculpture was even more recent than that of painting. The first experiments in carving in stone were made by Hendra, another of the ASRI teachers, in 1948. He had several striking statues and memorials to his credit, like that of General Sudirman, and he was an original painter, too. The *wayang*-like flatness of his figures achieved an essentially Oriental touch that made his work, like Affandi's, something more than a mere imitation of the West. Unfortunately the desiccating influence of Communist theory was beginning to affect him and others who took their politics too seriously. His plan for a national monument was a monstrous essay in the Stalinesque, while the brilliant leader of the artistic revival, Sudjoyono, had become so involved in the Party's activities that his painting was almost stifled.

But though the Indonesians might stray down many a blind alley in their search for self-expression, it was already safe to say that their artistic powers, so long repressed, had not been atrophied during the four centuries of Islam and now, with liberation, they were bursting out like some long-smouldering volcano in an impressive explosion of creativeness.

In literature it was not so much a case of renaissance as of completely new birth. For most of the Indonesians their new national language was alien and to attempt anything higher than textbooks or journalism was beyond them. The natural vehicle for their literary feelings was their own local tongue, and the Javanese in particular had a rich and recent tradition of poetry. The nineteenth-century courts, politically impotent, had devoted their leisure to music and literature with such success that scholars spoke of the period as the Javanese Renaissance. But it came too late. Now the young poets were writing in a different language as well as a different style.

As Indonesian was taken from a Sumatran dialect of Malay, it was not surprising that most of the pioneers of Indonesian literature were Sumatrans. But though they had the advantage of familiarity with the language of the future, they still had to discover a modern style. The traditional style of Malay poetry and prose was formal, long-winded and far removed from life, like our own pre-Renaissance romances, and the influence of the West was hardly felt till the present century, when journalism, with its demand for more concise and less flowery expression, forced Malay writers to break with the obsolete manner. Then the Dutch adopted their 'Ethical Policy', under which in 1918, tardily recognising their educational obligations, they set up a government printing house, the *Balai Pustaka* (Book Institute), to publish books in Malay-Indonesian as well as the regional languages. This opened the gates to a flood of novels, in which the dominant theme was the conflict of old and new, East and West, in the souls of the modern generation—not least in the writers themselves. As novelists they were *per se* adherents of Western techniques, but as nationalists they were in revolt against the West; as writers of Indonesian they were forward-looking and opposed to narrow local patriotism, but as heralds of national feeling they must seek inspiration in their own native background.

Open political discussion of course was banned; but the problems of nationalism were implicit in the tales of personal crisis, free choice against forced marriage, independence against parental authority, modern education against tradition.

The second and more deliberate phase of Indonesian literature began in 1933 with the foundation of a periodical called *Pudjangga Baru* (The New Writer), whose editors, Takdir Alisjahbana and Armyn Pane, sought by conscious critical discussion to work out the formula of the future. In their novels and plays they pointed out the impossibility of an absolute choice between acceptance and rejection of the West. Their western-educated heroes with Dutch or Eurasian wives found themselves rootless and lost; the new career-women discovered that intellect was not a substitute for the feminine virtues of simpler women; yet the modern free spirit could not be chained to outworn customs and obsolete conceptions. Armyn's brother, Sanusi Pane, himself a poet and playwright, neatly summed up the contrasting elements as seen by Oriental eyes: 'The new culture will be a mixture of East and West, part Faust and part Ardjuna, a combination of materialism, individualism and intellectualism with spirituality, feeling and collectivism.'

Yet when freedom came, it was not greeted with any carefully thought-out compromise, but by an outburst of poetry whose harsh realism and jerky rhythms owed nothing to the tradition of the East. Irregular, free and impressionistic, the verses of the 'Generation of '45' reflected the experience of young men who had grown up in the atmosphere of war and revolution, suffering and cruelty, misery and exaltation. No longer were the titles of poetic collections sentimentally pretty, like the *Jasmine Buds* of Muhammad Yamin or the *Cloud Blossoms* of Sanusi Pane; the two slim volumes that made up the work of their leader, Chairil Anwar, whose flaming spirit burned itself out in 1949 at the age of twenty-seven, were entitled *Sharp Gravel* and *A Melée of Noise and Dust*. Though they were in revolt against the tyranny of the West, they were full of a sudden self-confidence and no longer feared it. They took what they wanted and made it theirs.

By the time we arrived the first spontaneous outflowing of the eruption of '45 had worked itself out and the condition of literature was less exciting and prolific. Many of the older writers, such as Takdir, were concentrating on educational work, urged on both by the nation's needs and their own. Textbooks were far more profitable than literature; the reading public of Indonesia was not yet large enough to support even the most popular novelist. Yet the supply of new talent had not dried up. Among the newest was one of my own students, a boy from Solo named W. S. Rendra, who was widely regarded as the most promising poet of the younger generation. But he modestly disclaimed any original merit.

"They say I write a new kind of poetry," he told me, "but I don't really. It's just that I write Javanese poetry in Indonesian."

The artists of Indonesia were very conscious of their opportunities and responsibilities. They were in at the birth of a new age and a new language too, a Renaissance in which they must reconcile the rival claims of nationalism and internationalism. Asrul Sani, in a manifesto of the new school of writers issued in February 1950, just after the final recognition of Indonesia's independence, expressed their credo: 'We are the rightful heirs of the culture of the whole world, which we will develop in our own way. . . . Our Indonesianness does not lie in our brown skins, black hair and high cheek bones, but rather in the expression of our hearts and minds. When we speak of Indonesian culture, we are not thinking of polishing up and boasting of our past, but of a new healthy culture. It will be determined by all the voices sounding from all parts of the world, expressed with our own voice, in our own language, in our own forms. . . . We may not always be original, but the result will be stamped with our own character.'

...gja bride and bridegroom by the bridal bed

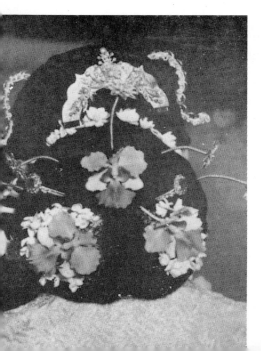

A bride's hair decoration

Giant guardian of the palace, Jogja

Sentinel at the Sultans' gate, Jogja

5

THE ROUND OF LIFE

WHEN we were settled in our house, we looked forward to a fuller social life than hitherto. In the hotel it had been difficult for us to entertain, and we had hardly seen the inside of a Javanese home. The trouble was not that the people were unfriendly; on the contrary, they were always extremely kind and courteous—when we met them. The difficulty was to meet them. In my work I came across only my immediate colleagues of the Faculty, and as Widjilan was separate from the main concentrations of the University, I seldom saw, let alone made contact with, the bulk of the staff. At first I faithfully attended the occasional public lectures, despite their length and unintelligibility, in the hope of meeting more colleagues. But the habit of introduction seemed unknown. The climax came with a farewell reception for one of the University's chief officials. Though I had never met him, I duly contributed to a parting presentation and supposed there would be some getting together. But we just sat in the big lecture hall, listened to several speeches, watched the presentation, then queued up to shake hands with him—for the first and last time in my case—and departed. I was none the wiser.

The ladies, as might be expected, were more socially minded and active in forming groups for all sorts of purposes, social, political, charitable, and so on. The biggest was the University Women's Family Association, of which Coral automatically became a member, but their meetings were too thronged for her to make more than a passing acquaintance with the other wives, a confused memory of large smiles and long names. Some of them, however, asked her to organise and lead a regular group for English conversation; and, after our establishment in the house, a small circle was formed, meeting each Saturday in a different home, the members of which gradually lost their timid stiffness under the influence of familiarity and Coral's emphasis on femininity rather than grammar. The Saturday Club was our social salvation. But for this we might never have achieved that degree of friendly intimacy with our Javanese environment that enabled us in the end to perceive a little of the reality behind the veil of shyness and formality.

At the best of times the Javanese are not effusive, but even the other Javanese complained of the reserve of the people of Jogja. We awaited calls from our new neighbours, but none came. Later we learnt that the newcomers should do the calling. But even so, a formal call broke very little ice, and those that we did make were almost painful in their stiffness. First we would sit and wait for ten or twenty minutes before the host appeared; far from being rudeness, this was an honour, for it meant that he was changing into his best clothes. It was incumbent on the host to receive callers and entertain them as long as they wished to stay, however busy and urgently required elsewhere he might be. We found the words, "We had guests", constituted a completely acceptable excuse for any degree of lateness. When the host or hostess finally appeared, we spent ten minutes or so in chat about indifferent topics (a courteous person should not rush at once into the purpose of his visit) before refreshments were brought in, glasses of weak hay-like tea or fizzy orangeade or a mauve coconut shake. Then a further pause ensued, as it was most impolite to start drinking before the hostess invited one to begin. When the tea was well cooled, the sign would be given; but even then it was correct to drink slowly and to leave part of the accompanying cake, so as to avoid any appearance of greed. A call was not to be lightly undertaken.

The Javanese were very self-conscious about good manners. They themselves had an elaborate code of delicacy, as noticeable in the villagers as in the educated. A peasant eating rice with his fingers from a banana leaf would use only the right hand, the hand of honour. They would only hand things with the right hand, too, bowing and supporting the elbow with their left; and it was rude to point with anything but the upturned right thumb. Bowing and bending to pass in front of another was *de rigueur*. Once at a crowded dance performance I sat down on a step in the gangway. There was plenty of room to pass, but as it was impossible for anyone to bend lower than me, even with the squatting walk, a complete traffic block resulted till Coral called my attention from the dance to the situation behind me. Old people were particularly respected, whether rich or poor, and in mixed company formal etiquette demanded a positively Victorian atmosphere of soft voices, lowered eyes and folded hands. Loud laughter was rather coarse but smiling was essential, with the result that nervous and futile giggles filled each pause of chat. Forms of address were also carefully laid down; but I never ceased to feel slightly at a loss, as if my personality had split, when my students addressed me in the Third Person in English.

The consequence of all this formality was that they were very anxious to learn about others' manners and nervous of behaving ignorantly in the presence of foreigners, who might laugh at them. We were often asked to give talks on European manners, and it was in vain that we pointed out that civility, though variable, is always recognisable and that their own forms of politeness were as good as any. (The courteous Middle Eastern belch does not, perhaps, bear out this theory, but fortunately it was not practised by the Javanese.) But nothing would reassure them. Students heading for Holland or Italy or even Japan would come to us for practice in the use of knives and forks. Too conscious of outward forms, these naturally mannerly people have developed an inferiority complex over manners.

After a month of two we decided to entertain some of our Indonesian friends to a buffet supper, which was the normal form of evening hospitality and one that avoided the difficulties of a formal dinner. By now Coral knew the wives well enough and she felt it was time for the husbands to meet. Invitations were sent out several days in advance; but since the custom was to reply only if one could not accept, we heard nothing further until one friend approached Coral with the anxious question:

"What are you holding the party for?"

"We just want to see you all and return some of your kindness."

"But is it some special occasion?"

"No, we just thought we'd like to entertain you in our home."

"Oh..."

The lady withdrew, obviously unconvinced; and a day or two later another sought to probe the mystery, which was deepened by the early despatch of the invitations. Javanese invitations generally arrived a few hours before the event—or sometimes after.

"Do tell us what your party is for," she begged, and Coral once more tried to explain our idea of hospitality.

By the day of our supper-party we were almost as worried as the guests, for it was obvious that they were uneasy about the whole affair and unlikely to enjoy themselves. Clearly we had to find some excuse for our party. I racked my brains and at last had a desperate inspiration.

"Now you really must tell us what your party is for," pleaded our friends when they were assembled that evening.

"Tomorrow," I announced, "is my mother's birthday."

"Ahhh. . . ."

Shining with relief, they all rose and shook my hand in congratulation. The party was saved, for it was justified.

When we considered this experience, we realised that in fact every time we had been invited out it had been in celebration of something or other—a wedding, a safe return, a visitor, a house-warming, a circumcision. The idea of holding a party for party's sake, of hospitality without due cause, was puzzling to them. This accounted for the quietness of our social life hitherto, for the cause was generally some family occasion. Slowly we found out about the continual round of entertaining that went on, and when our eager interest had dispelled their polite fears that we should be bored, we were invited to all sorts of occasions that they had been too shy to mention before. Javanese life turned out to be a series of *selamatans*, as they called the feasts which marked each stage of man's passage through life—birth, naming, circumcision, puberty, marriage, death and memorials, plus all the annual religious feasts. With families apt to run to a dozen members it can be imagined that they were kept fairly busy, apart from all the ramifications of cousinhood. Nor was the expense of all these celebrations, however simple, a negligible burden.

The biggest of these occasions was the wedding-party, to which hosts of friends as well as family were invited. Our first wedding was held in Widjilan, where the daughter of the house was the bride. This involved the dismantling for ten days of the temporary lecture-rooms, somewhat dislocating my syllabus. But usually the preparations for a wedding took longer than that and all the female relations would be drafted to help with the decorations, invitations, cooking, dresses and so forth. Girl students might disappear for a whole month, excusing themselves on the grounds of some cousin's wedding. The Widjil wedding was a grand affair owing to the bride's royal connections, and it was carried out with all the traditional customs. Unfortunately owing to a muddle over transport we arrived half an hour late, missing the most interesting part of the ceremony, the meeting of the bride and groom and her washing of his foot. On later occasions we often saw the meeting, but never again till our very last night in Jogja did we have the opportunity of seeing the foot-washing, where the bride kneels at her husband's feet to wash off the egg he has trodden on; for this custom is out of favour with modern feminist ideas.

Still, we had plenty to study as we sat in the massed ranks of lecture-room chairs, sipping orangeade and nibbling rice rolls. The bride and groom sat facing us, side by side on the bridal seat in a bower of banked bouquets and symbolic decorations. Their costumes and make-up were rich, exotic and surprising. Both wore gold-braided jackets, his rather like an ambassador's, hers of knee-length velvet embroidered with gold flowers, above identical gold-painted *kains*. Jewels glittered on her broad belt and the triple moon of her necklace was like those worn in the court-dances. But their head ornaments fascinated me most. The groom wore a high black fez with gold bands, while his ears had strings of white buds hanging down and leaflike ornaments projecting above that made them look pointed like a devil's. The bride's whole head was made up so artificially that I could not tell if she were pretty or not. Her face was covered with a sickly yellow powder and her eyes were blackened with lines curving up at the corners like crow's feet; her hair was shaved back from the brow and black leaf shapes were painted on her forehead. To my unaccustomed eyes it seemed to make her look old and ill, and I preferred the back of her head with its glittering arrangement of jewelled stars and white flowers. After a time we rose to inspect the presents and the ancestral four-poster, the traditional bride-bed guarded by male and female clay images and illumined by tall many-branched oil-lamps; and so, amid much handshaking, away.

There were many styles of Javanese wedding, according to the district and status of the families involved. East Java differed from Mid-Java, Solo from Jogja, Pakualaman style from Kraton style, high class from middle and middle class from peasantry. We attended all sorts and gradually came to recognise the common factors, the essentials behind the variations. Like most Javanese religious ceremonies marriage was a variation upon Islamic law with survivals of Hindu or animistic custom. In Islam marriage is a legal contract rather than a sacrament, and so the signing of the agreement between bridegroom and father was really the central moment of the ceremony. But whereas in Egypt at a village wedding at the foot of the Pyramids we never saw the bride, in Java, where women always enjoyed a certain position and never underwent the veil, the bride played a leading role on her great day, though her legal position was that of her Moslem sisters elsewhere. In the old days she had no say in the selection of her future husband and might not even know him till her wedding-day, since she was confined within the walls of her father's home from puberty till marriage. She had to obey her parents' choice, a situation which provided a fruitful theme for the early Indonesian novelists, the conflict between duty and love. But in modern times, with girls meeting boys freely, their own choice was consulted and the couple would be agreed before the parents were approached. Nevertheless, for all the Western ideas of emancipation and romance triumphant, the consent of the parents was still essential and it was they who made the actual arrangements.

First the boy would tell his parents of his wish to marry the girl. After private enquiries about her character and that of her ancestors, they would pay a formal call on her parents to ask if she were free. If the proposal was accepted, the boy's parents then visited the girl herself with gifts of clothing, jewellery and nowadays a ring. The exchange of rings (worn on the left hand) constituted the bond of engagement, and if the girl broke it off, she was supposed to return twice the value of his presents. The next thing was to choose a lucky day for the wedding, a difficult business as not only the day but the month and the hour must suit the natal and nominal influences of bride and groom. In due time, after some wise elderly relation had consulted their horoscopes and ancestors, the day and hour were fixed and the preparations began. It was always easy to tell where a wedding was due, for the house of the bride's father would sprout a forest of bamboo scaffolding and soon an open pavilion would cover the front garden or court. Arches of yellowing coconut leaves curved between the poles and the doorposts were thick with bunches of bananas, sheaves of rice, sugar canes and a pair of young yellow coconuts, all symbols of fruitfulness, prosperity and happiness.

Meanwhile the bride had to make herself spiritually and physically ready. A week before the wedding a *selamatan* was held to seek the blessing of her forefathers. From then on she would stay indoors, treating her skin with a yellow paste of herbs and sweet flowers to make it clean, fair and fragrant. On the eve she was bathed by nine happy and prolific old women in water mixed with rose petals and her hair was dried with the smoke of incense; then came the make-up. The strange arrangement of the hair represented the seven leaves of a lotus, the yellow face-powder was the colour of the budding flower, and the spot in the centre of the forehead (suggestively reminiscent of an Indian caste-mark) stood for its heart and symbolised virginity. That evening was known as 'Angel Night' and the bride might not sleep before midnight, so her friends came to stay with her and keep her awake. The interpretation of the Angels was confused, perhaps forgotten; most told us that she had to await the visit of angels who would bless her with happiness and beauty, but a more interesting story connected the custom with the legend of the wedding of the angel daughter of the Goddess of the South Sea.

Next day, at the lucky hour, the marriage took place. Typical of a modern middle-class wedding was that of Maryati, daughter of a police superintendent and student of English. The little house and its front court were crammed with row upon row of hard chairs, the women inside and the men outside. Dress varied from full Javanese costume to lounge suits, and a similar ambivalence was apparent in all the surroundings—traditional decoration and flashlight photographers, symbolic *batiks* and jazz, the Koran and American comics. Soon the bridegroom arrived, his black Eton jacket sandwiched between *batik* headcloth and *batik* skirt, above an embroidered belt with a *kris* at the back. Chains of sweet-smelling *melati* flowers, white and fragrant as jasmine, hung round his neck and from the hilt of his *kris*. Accompanied by his friends but not his parents (who are not allowed at the wedding ceremony), he was led to a table in the porch where the bride's father, a white-turbanned mosque official and two clerks awaited him. For some twenty minutes the priest prayed, palms upwards, and instructed the groom in his duties, after which the token bride-price of five rupiahs was paid and the marriage contract was signed. The Moslem part of the ceremony was over.

Now came the big moment of the meeting. The bride was led forward by her eldest women relatives to the front door. In her lotus make-up and elaborate coiffure with white strings of *melati* draped over her left shoulder and a long jacket of yellow brocade I could hardly recognise the westernised girl I had taught. The pair faced one another across her father's threshold; each was given a handful of rolled *sirih* leaves, which they threw at the other. The one that hits the other, they say, will be the ruler of the household, and Maryati dutifully made a very feeble throw. But she did not wash his feet. They walked side by side to the bridal couch, where they sat surrounded by bouquets, pineapples, plaited palm-leaves and triple-horned coconuts. An elaborate symbolism regulated all these customs and ornaments, the design of the couple's *batiks* and every other detail; I never learnt them all, but the general meaning is the same the whole world over— love, happiness, fertility, wealth. Now all that remained to do was to queue up and shake hands with the couple and her parents, after which a wedding luncheon was served. The unmarried girls eagerly consumed the lucky yellow rice in the hope of following suit.

After a few days' stay with her parents the pair would remove to his parents' home, where another, but less elaborate, reception would be held to celebrate her acceptance as a new member of the family.

It cannot be said that these receptions were very exhilarating affairs, stuck as one was in cramped ranks and with the sexes segregated, generally unable to see or even hear anything amid five or six hundred other guests. We found a wedding *selamatan* in the *kampong* more picturesque. Late one afternoon we noticed a gay band of youths in green and white 'blazers' passing our house. They were on their way to fetch a bridegroom and cour- teously invited us to the party that evening. So we set out about 10 p.m. and after much wandering discovered the hut down a narrow pathway behind the facade of modern villas, only a few hundred yards away. We were welcomed with hospitable polite- ness and introduced to the central figures. The bride, a simple girl in her 'teens, no longer in wedding finery but with the tell- tale shaven forehead, was sitting with the old ladies, while the groom wandered round with his friends in a gaudy sarong and jacket of pink sharkskin. In the centre of the pavilion on the spread mats squatted a *gamelan* of some twenty musicians with a dancer sitting quietly in their midst. One side of the space was filled with chattering women and children, but the main part of the hall was occupied by circles of cross-legged men, absorbed as usual in their cards. Beyond them a half-curtained doorway gave a glimpse of the piled bolsters of the marriage bed. The men did not glance up even when the dancer bared her shoulders and rose to dance in the usual slow and decorous style. She was adorned with bridal chains of melati and frangipani flowers and was indeed far more striking than the shy village girl in the pink blouse who was the real bride. We left about midnight amid many votes of thanks and handclasps laid on the heart. But the celebration went on till dawn, for they made the most of their gaieties in the *kampongs*.

Though the woman is granted a fair share in her wedding, she still has much less than equal rights in her marriage. The law is that of Islam, which allows a man four wives and comparatively easy divorce. True, in these modern days it is mostly princes and peasants that take advantage of the law, while the intelligentsia and bourgeoisie practise monogamy. Moslem apologists assert that the law in fact, under modern conditions, enjoins monogamy since it states that all the wives must be given equal treatment—which is impossible, Q.E.D. This casuistry, however, did not prevent the Sultan from having three wives or our hotel boy from having four. Among the poor, paradoxically, it might even be profitable to have several wives, as their work in the fields or market contributed largely to the family economy. The daughters of Kartini, however, were determined to assert the Rights of Women to legal protection and monogamy, and the *Perwari* (Indonesian Women's Association) had prepared a new marriage charter or 'bargain' with ten conditions, including the husband's promise to allow the wife a divorce if he married again without her consent. The first girl to get married under the terms of this charter was the Mayor of Djakarta's daughter in July 1955. This was why the feminists were so furious with President

Sukarno for taking a second wife: he was the symbol of the new Indonesia and they felt he had betrayed them.

After marriage, birth—and a birth was expected to follow pretty soon. But there were ways to deal with the situation if the relations considered the delay excessive. One progressive and strong-minded Professor's wife told Coral that her son's wife went for over a year without pregnancy; the mother-in-law therefore stole a garment from a new-born baby and gave it to the young wife, for such things, if genuinely stolen, retain a magic influence. At any rate, the daughter-in-law was now pregnant. Even stranger was the case of another member of the Club, an aristocratic lady with two grown-up daughters. One of them had been married for a year and a half with no sign of a baby. The mother duly stole a tiny vest from the local *kampong* and hid it in her handbag; but unluckily she forgot to hand it over till too late—and the next time we met her, the mother was pregnant instead of the daughter!

For the first baby there were certain special ceremonies before birth. When our garden-boy of the moment, a youth of eighteen, was expecting his first child, he invited Coral to witness his wife's pre-natal bath, which takes place when the mother is seven months pregnant. They drove out through the ricefields to Tukiyo's home village and were welcomed with dignity by his father to their simple bamboo home. The women then set off across the fields in a little procession, leaving the men sitting on their mats in the courtyard, smoking, eating rice-rolls and sipping cool tea. The leader carried a flat basket of offerings, a clay water-pot and two baby coconuts. These smooth pale yellow nuts were the most important items, being decorated with symbolic *wayang* figures; one bore the image of Djanoko, another name for Ardjuna, and the other that of Sembodro, the most beautiful of his many wives. Other women followed carrying burning incense and a coconut scoop, then came Coral and the wife, and at the end Tukiyo, the only man among them.

So they went along, gaily teasing the young couple, till they reached the clear shallow rivulet hidden under sandy bush-covered banks. Here the husband and wife went forward into the stream, she clad only in a *kain* up to her armpits and he in short black pants, and squatted together in the water, facing upstream. Then seven old women, happy and fruitful, took turns to pour water with the scoop over their heads and shoulders, seven times each in alternate directions. When the pair came shivering out of the water, the old women wrapped the wife in a new *kain* and pushed the two decorated coconuts down between her breasts, catching them as they fell out below—a symbol of easy delivery and lovely children. Then back to father's for refreshments. Proudly he showed Coral round; one room with a little compartment for the beds and a carved and painted dividing screen. Children, chickens, goats and fruit-trees (banana, mango, breadfruit, soursop) completed the picture of a humble but contented home, of rustic peace and patriarchal unity.

In the towns, the same ceremony took place but the scene would be a modern bathroom instead of a country stream. After that there were no more preparations till the actual birth; it was not considered right to anticipate the will of the Almighty by making ready any baby clothes, and when it was born the child was wrapped in pieces of an old *kain* of its mother's. In the villages the birth would still be attended by the local *dukun*, an old woman who, though not officially qualified as a midwife, was accepted owing to her experience and superior powers—which often overflowed into witchcraft. As their knives of sharpened bamboo and traditional roots involved a very high death-rate from infection and bleeding, the government health service gave them scissors, pincers and a short course of hygiene as a temporary measure till it could train a sufficiency of proper midwives. The round of *selamatans* of course continued inexorably; first, for the women only, on the actual day of birth; then, after five or seven days for the naming of the child; then after thirty-five days for its first birthday by Javanese reckoning.

The question of the child's name and birthday was extremely important for its future, as both were believed to have a dynamic magical influence. The birthday naturally could not be changed and the child was saddled for life with the resulting number, based on a combined calculation of the Javanese five-day week and the international seven-day week. Each day had its mystic number (as indeed most things and ideas had) and by adding together the two relevant numbers you got your own. The Javanese 'market week' was said to derive from the grouping of villages at the four points of the compass around one centre, each with its market day; at any rate it had only five days, *Pon*, *Wagé*, *Kliwon*, *Legi* and *Pahing*, with the values 7, 4, 8, 5 and 9 respectively. The seven-day week, beginning with Sunday, was worth 5, 4, 3, 7, 8, 6, 9. Thus a child born on Friday-*Kliwon* (a particularly auspicious combination) would be worth 14, and this would affect his prospects and character and guide him in the choice of good days for important actions, such as marriage, starting work, building, even looking for lost articles. It would also limit his choice of a wife, for her personal number should fit his in accordance with some mysterious rules, and if they did not suit each other numerologically, it was better to break the engagement. Using this system the *dukuns* and wise men would divine the future, advise on all the problems of life and make magic as required. And though the modern generation might scoff at such superstition in theory, they did not flout it any more than the English flout theirs.

To the Javanese therefore the day of his birth was more important than the date, and as the same combination recurs every thirty-five days, they celebrated their birthdays ten or eleven times a year. Big families naturally could not hold an almost monthly party for each member, but at least on the birthday of the head of the family a small private offering was usual. A decorative basket of coconut leaves filled with rice, shrimps and sweet flowers and a banana-leaf plate of eggs, vegetables and more rice under a green dunce's cap—such was the specimen sent us by Paku Alam's sister on the day of her husband, a Law Professor. The anniversary of one's birth might also be celebrated, but even there a problem arose; President Sukarno's anniversary was celebrated every 365 days on 6th June, but the Sultan's came round every 354 days in accordance with the Moslem calendar. At the birthday party of a High Court official, where we were faced first with a European cake, complete with candles and the creamy words 'Happy Birthday to You', and then with a special rice dish served in bowls of young banana-leaf (symbolic of continuing vigour), we were far from clear as to the exact nature of the day.

Names were more convenient than birthdays, for in case of need they could always be changed. On the seventh day, when the naming feast was held, the neighbours' children were told the name of their playmate-to-be and ran to tell their parents. Only one name was given, usually with some significant content, for its inner power would affect the bearer. Normally this name was kept till marriage, and whenever I found a student with more than one name I asked the reason. Many had merely added their father's name as an unofficial surname; others were Christians or bore Arab names; but one at least had had to change his first name, though he retained it as an initial. As a child he had been seriously ill and his parents hastily altered his name to deceive the angry spirit who was causing the illness; demons think it is a different child when it bears a different name. Perhaps he ought to have discarded the initial too, for he was still sickly. Sometimes it was not the child that fell ill but one of the parents, and then more drastic measures were needed, as it meant the child was unlucky for them. They must get someone else, generally a relative, to adopt it. One of our closest friends had two sons, one his own and the other his brother's. In their love of children they made no distinction between true and adopted ones, and even couples with several of their own readily took others' offspring into their families. Perhaps it was easier where there was none of our obsession with carrying on the family name, since family names did not exist.

Five days after marriage the child-names of the pair were changed and they both received the same name, often made up of the elements of the names of their respective parents. Married names thus tended to be longer and more complex than unmarried; whereas the names of my students were reasonable, those of my colleagues were often tongue-twisters like Purbotjaroko or Tjokroatmodjo, most confusing until I learnt to sort them into their component parts. Even after marriage the process of nominal flux was not ended. Court or local officials in the Principalities were awarded official names by the prince according to the job and rank they held, and with every change their name was changed too. The Curator of Jogja's Museum, for instance, Raden Wedono Kusumobroto, had a different rank and name at the time of his marriage. The change misled his wife's Western friends, who embarrassed her with warm congratulations, not on her husband's promotion, but on a presumed new husband!

As the children grew, their progress towards maturity was duly marked with further *selamatans*. For the boys there was the ordeal of circumcision, which used to be a big feast—and still was so in the villages. In East and West Java this Islamic ceremony took place about the age of seven or eight, but in Central Java not till thirteen or fourteen. It was regarded as the initiation into manhood and they waited till the boy himself asked to become 'grown-up'. When the thirteen-year-old son of a friend was circumcised, the occasion was like a rather grisly birthday. On the evening after the operation we assembled for one of the usual parties, males and females separated in close ranks of chairs and festoons of flowers. The unfortunate hero of the day was lying in his decorated bed in a side room, surrounded by piles of modern presents and traditional offerings. In the villages there would be a *wayang* performance and the victims rode in procession through the streets on horseback before the operation. Owing to the expense, combined *selamatans* were often held for several children at once, brothers or friends—and sisters, too, since female circumcision was regularly practised, though at a much earlier age and involving a very minor incision. I heard of an aristocratic ceremony for three boys and two girls and of a mass operation for twenty sons and nine little daughters of the local poor at a princely *pendopo*.

For the girls maturity was marked by a *selamatan* held seven days after the end of their first period. As with other customs, it was among royalty and peasantry that the full ceremonies were best preserved, and when Coral attended a puberty party it was in one of the stately homes of Solo. The girl was a niece of Prince Paku Alam and the reception was held in the spacious halls of her grandfather, Prince Hadiwidjoyo. But the centre of interest was not the reception hall but the bathroom, outside which all the ladies congregated. Inside on a stool sat the fourteen-year-old princess, covered in yellow paste and wrapped in a white cotton cloth. Three old ladies anointed her with oils and perfumes, then bathed her in rosewater, after which she slipped on a new *kain* and *kebaya* with a dressing-gown on top. She was led into the bedroom and seated herself on a mattress before her royal grandmother to submit to her first full-grown make-up. While the grandmother painted and powdered her face and pencilled her eyebrows, the court hairdresser dried her long black locks with incense, oiled them and twisted them into a figure-8 bun, plumped in Solo fashion with green pandanus leaves. From a big silver bowl were added seven diamond and ruby pins and a diamond comb, and her perfumed body was wrapped in a rich lime-green breastcloth, handwoven with gold thread, pinned back with a diamond pin.

Now she was ready to be led out to take her place among the adults. All through the bathing and dressing, while the old ladies told her of their own time and teased her about the man she would marry, she sat silent with lowered eyes; and the same shy modesty surrounded her amid all the chatter of the reception. Throughout the whole ceremony, the day that celebrated her marriageable status, she never spoke a word.

Besides all these personal celebrations of the family there were the annual religious feasts of Islam. In Java these had become rather unorthodox owing to the people's tendency towards syncretism, which was as noticeable in the modern blend of Islam, Hinduism and animism as in the Hindu-Buddhist compromises of their ancient temples. In the Principalities, for instance, there were some very strange celebrations during *Sekaten*, the week preceding the Prophet's birthday on the 12th of the month that the Javanese call *Maulud*.

The month of the Fast was the one that affected the individual most personally. Not that the Fast was very strictly observed in Mid-Java. Cigarettes and tea were passed round during a Senate meeting, although a minority refused to partake; and in our Faculty office I noticed glasses of tea on all but one of the nine desks. Nevertheless the custom of taking meals after dark and shortly before dawn meant disturbed nights and drowsy days with all their increased inefficiency. During the nights when the Revelation of the Koran was expected, drums and rockets assisted wakefulness. At last the Fast ended and on the first of the new month came the biggest family day of the year, known as *Lebaran* or Ending. Early in the morning the people would go to pray in great gatherings in the square outside the mosque; alms of money or rice were distributed; and the rest of the day was devoted to visits and *selamatans* among the family. The younger members would visit their elders and ask forgiveness for all the offences of the past year, kneeling and kissing their right knee. Everyone wore new clothes. For us *Lebaran* meant little but the expense of a complete new outfit for all of our servants, but for them it was a happy time with something of the spirit of Christmas about it; family gatherings and feasts, presents and charity and goodwill towards mankind.

Nor were the ancestors forgotten. Graves and holy places were visited and the spirits' blessing sought. But this was done more in the month before the Fast, called *Ruwah* or All Souls. During the last two weeks of *Ruwah* we used to see little processions taking offerings to the cemetery; our friends vanished for two or three days to visit their home-towns; and one evening at dusk we saw an elderly couple, dressed up in their best, lay some offerings in the middle of the road junction by our front gate. For a while they squatted there, regardless of the traffic, fanning the burning incense, then quietly departed, leaving the incense and

H

the banana-leaf basket of rice and fruit in the roadway. We
learnt that when people were too far or too poor to return home,
they left the gifts for their ancestors at a cross-roads. If they
could reach the family tombs, they spent at least one night close
by, communing with the spirits who descended to revisit their
family in this month. My Dean went off to Semarang with his
wife and daughters, cleaned the graves, burnt incense, strewed
flowers, and spent the night praying for forgiveness and reading
extracts from the Koran—though the custom is not Moslem at all.
The tombs of past heroes like Senopati at Kota Gede or Sultan
Agung at Imogiri would be surrounded by sleepers, who hoped
to acquire power through contact with the influence that emanated
from them at this time.

The world of spirits was very much part and parcel of Javanese
life and coloured their whole outlook. The original animism of
the inhabitants survived beneath the successive layers of Hinduism, Buddhism, and Islam, and their easy gift of compromise
enabled them to combine many of their old beliefs with a sincere
profession of the Moslem religion. This made for their notable
lack of fanaticism—which was not the same throughout the
country. In Sumatra, Celebes and even West Java the practice of
Islam was much stricter and consequently more belligerent; the
Darul Islam rebellions in the Sundanese hills, Makassar and Atjeh
were symptomatic of their more uncompromising spirit. To the
Javanese there was a spirit in everything, and anything out of the
ordinary implied a special mysterious power, of which it was
possible with due concentration and self-discipline to partake.
Thus the spirits of your ancestors, in which you naturally shared,
had great influence; the power of great men was still effective;
your name and birthday had their special aura; and even seemingly inanimate but striking things, like ancient monuments,
great stones and tall trees (especially the banyan) were the abode
of important spirits. On Thursday evenings (really the eve or
beginning of Friday, since the new day started at sunset) we used
to find offerings at the foot of our tall fir-tree, left by our maid's
old mother; and others could be seen by the holy fig-trees in the

palace square and on the steps of the pillar at Tugu crossroads, just below the newly inserted traffic lights.

With all this background it was natural that the spirit of the dead should be carefully cherished, and the funeral was only the beginning of the ceremonies of death. When someone died in such a warm climate the funeral had to follow next day, and there was only one night for a hasty reception for the relatives and friends. The body was laid out towards the north on a low table; when the family had assembled, it was taken into the garden and bathed seven times with water and flowers. After the face had been powdered and perfumed cotton stuffed in the mouth, nose, eyes and ears, the corpse was wrapped in a white cotton winding-sheet, tied in seven places from the top of the head to below the feet. That night the body lay in state with incense and prayers for the soul's pardon, and the visitors stayed till late, keeping the bereaved company with tea and rice and cards. Next day the funeral took place, and as the coffin was lifted and paused outside the door, the children and grandchildren walked back and forth three times under it. When the procession bearing the coffin, under the shade of an umbrella, reached the burial place, the knots of the winding-sheet were loosened and the face exposed. Then the corpse was laid in the grave on its right side, facing Mecca. The priest prayed, earth and flowers were thrown into the grave, and it was covered over, often with a temporary wooden memorial at head and foot. So the mourners returned to the house, leaving the dead in the scented shade of the white-armed frangipani trees.

On the third night the first of the seven memorial *selamatans* would be held. These took place on the third, seventh, fortieth and hundredth day after burial, on the first and second anniversaries and finally on the thousandth day. The poor, who could not afford such a series of expenses, had to celebrate at least two, the most important being the last. These feasts, with their accompanying prayers, were supposed to celebrate changes in the status of the dead man's soul. Till the third day the soul was still in the house and the family must be careful not to sweep the floor or pour hot water on the ground, as the soul might get hurt and angry. Up to the seventh day it was still wandering about the yard, and until the fortieth in the neighbourhood. After that it occasionally visited the earth, but the *selamatans* for this period were not so important till the thousandth day. Then a big party was held, culminating in the release of two white pigeons, symbolic of the dead soul flying away. The soul had finished its haunting of its earthly habitation. The grave was strewn with a flower whose name, *telasih*, means 'No more love', and usually the permanent tombstone was then set up. And after that it was not considered shocking for the widow or widower to remarry.

The belief in the power and ubiquity of spirits led naturally to a superstitious fear of ghosts and the widespread practice of magic. Whereas satisfied spirits could help the descendants or others who invoked them, wronged or neglected ghosts could bring terror and disaster. Generally they confined their attention to those responsible and were visible only to the 'wanted' person; but sometimes they took more general revenge on humans. It was possible, however, if you knew the right formulas and practices, to counteract and even control the spirits, and the *dukun* (a generic name for medicine men, male or female) was often an expert at magic as well as a practitioner of rough medicine. Sickness was attributed to malign influences, and when it could not be cured by compounds of herbs, holy water and other more mysterious ingredients, spells and *selamatans* might do the trick. But magic could be offensive as well as defensive, and the *dukun* might be called upon to assist in the attainment of some less desirable object, such as revenge on an enemy or the charming of a reluctant woman.

We never had personal experience of Javanese ghosts or magic, but we heard stories of *guna-guna* from European friends and modern-minded students that showed the strong hold such ideas had on the minds of the people and the physical results of such psychological warfare. The garden-boy of a Scottish couple, a strong cheerful lad of twenty, suddenly fell sick and began to fade away. A European doctor was unable to diagnose the cause, but the people of his *kampong*, to which he retired to die, asserted he was bewitched and suggested a *selamatan*. His employers, unwilling to refuse any chance, paid for a *dukun* and a *selamatan*—and it worked. The boy soon returned to work, relieved of the burden of a curse laid on his father, who had died of a dispute over some banana-trees. A student told a similar tale of a village family she knew. The son, given up by the hospital doctors, was taken to a *dukun*. She was a medium, and lying beside the patient amid the fumes of incense, she fell into a trance. A dialogue followed between the spirit possessing the *dukun*, who now had a man's voice, and that possessing the patient, who complained that his house had been destroyed when some big rubber-trees were cut down; so, having no place to shelter, he occupied the boy who had done it. A *selamatan* was held on the fatal spot and the spirit, duly appeased, left him.

Ghosts were legion and might inhabit any place, though they were naturally more frequent in dark and lonely places. A European friend in Surabaya had trouble with a ghost in his brand-new steel and concrete chocolate factory. Soon after opening the building the workers, mostly women, went on strike and refused to return to work on the grounds that the place was haunted. Perhaps he had omitted to bury a buffalo's head under the foundation stone. At any rate a *selamatan* settled the ghost and the strike. Then there was the tale we heard, when we first arrived, of a pretty girl who used to wander in Malioboro and beg lifts on the back of young men's bicycles; soon after they set off with their fair passenger, they crashed and awoke to find themselves in a dark cemetery. This, I later found, was a modernised variant of the myth of the *Puntianak*, who entices youths at night to follow her, but, on arrival at a deserted place, reveals her true nature, floating in the air and scaring them into a faint. I was told of many other species of spectre, but only at second-hand. Like our English ghosts, many of them were unhappy souls that had died sudden or unfortunate deaths or had not enjoyed proper burial. The *Gendruwo*, who pelted roofs with graveyard gravel, was the spirit of someone killed without being prepared for death; the *Wéwé*, who stole children, was a childless woman; the *Peri* a disappointed virgin; the *Medi Potjong*, a carelessly buried corpse howling for his headstring to be untied; the *Tjumpelung*, the rolling skull of a severed head; or there was the arm-bones ghost who clicked and clacked in the night, and the bowels ghost that glided like a snake or flopped squashily on the ground. There were also the ghosts of natural phenomena, generally prophetic of plague, famine or disaster; the rushing roaring *Lampor*, the flaming *Kemamang*, or the *Ridjal*, which was a ghost of sound without form. Daylight ghosts were rare, but the fiery-haired *Banaspati* would leap out of the ground exactly at noon and run swiftly on his hands, chasing and devouring any child he saw. The *Buta* caused eclipses by swallowing the sun, but as he had no body the luminary soon reappeared from his neck, a process that could be hastened by the beating of alarm gongs to scare him.

Steps could be taken to guard against evil spirits by charms and amulets and Arabic formulas. Politeness also paid, such as addressing the ghost as 'Grandfather', just as one did a tiger, when passing through the jungle. Words have power to conjure up the objects or ideas mentioned and great care was therefore required in their use. An unscrupulous *dukun* might practise black as well as white magic. Thieves might be supplied with soporific sand from the cemetery to throw on intended victims' roofs; would-be lovers could be made temporarily irresistible with the Smile of Semar; and enemies could be struck down by the deadly *Tenung* or slowly destroyed by powdered bamboo, introduced with suitable incantations into their food. The sudden death of General Spoor, the Dutch Commander-in-Chief, was widely attributed to a patriotic *tenung*.

On the other hand supernatural or at least superior powers could be acquired by the practice of holiness. Javanese legend is full of tales of heroes and wise men who retired to a hermitage to recruit spiritual strength and through *tapa* obtained mastery over the spirits, immunity to magical attacks and ability to perform acts like flying. *Tapa* was a form of concentration, something like *Yoga*, mystical and ascetic; a purification process achieved through abstinence, withdrawal and meditation. Solitude and mortification of the flesh, as with the early Christian saints, assisted the mystic communion with a higher power. Sometimes it was required before undertaking some sacred work like making a *kris* or playing the Holy *Gamelan*; but it could also be used for short-term purposes such as success in love or business or revenge—or even, apparently, examinations! I do not know if my successful students ever practised *tapa*; but I found that some, who not only failed but actually fainted, had unwisely combined cramming with fasting.

It was difficult to get the modern Javanese to speak about their customs and still more about their superstitions, for they were afraid that the rationalistic Westerners would laugh and consider them primitive. When we told them something about the ghosts and haunted houses, the superstitious habits and irrational beliefs of Europe, they were amazed, for they cherished the impression that we were utterly scientific-minded materialists.

The younger generation, however, was becoming more rationalistic itself. From my students I heard such remarks as these:

"The old customs and traditions are getting out of date as people begin to think logically."

"*Selamatans* for the dead are uneconomical and worthless too, for the important thing is not the feast but the prayer."

"It is only in the villages, where the doctor's help is difficult to get, that they still believe strongly in the *dukun*."

"The ghosts probably originated as indirect suggestion to teach children to avoid sunstroke (the *Banaspati*) or prostitutes (the *Puntianak*), and so on; but the people have forgotten the teaching and kept the ghosts."

Yet the Javanese belief in the importance and ubiquity of the spiritual world and the superior power of the East in mystic matters is something so deep-rooted that even the most western-ised adherent of modern scientific theories is unlikely to fall into the agnostic vacuum in which so many of us drift. Modernism will be accepted and adapted into new forms of mysticism—in fact I heard of two new mystico-scientific movements in Jogja alone. One, the theory of an uncle of the Sultan, was so esoteric that he had forbidden its translation into English for fear of dangerous errors. The other, whose followers included at least one Professor, used to hold meetings (till the prophet moved to Djakarta) in a house that was subsequently taken over by an American friend.

The idea of the devotees lying entranced on that now-so-hygienic floor seemed somehow to illustrate the different approach of East and West to the problems of life.

6

THE PALACE

THE core of Jogja, historically and physically, was the palace. Without it the city might still be a mere village in a wood. It was born with the Sultanate, just over two hundred years ago, when a family quarrel split the dominions of the Susuhunan (Sunan) of Surakarta, the heir to the empire of New Mataram. Jogjakarta was the new Sultan's answer to Surakarta.

By the middle of the eighteenth century New Mataram, founded about 1600, had sadly declined from its greatness. The major factor in this process was the Netherlands East India Company, which established a permanent base at Batavia in 1619. In return for military aid to the Sunan the Company demanded ever-greater concessions, until they held most of the major ports of the north coast. Not content with mere trading as middlemen and carriers, they began to seek control of the sources of production, interfering more and more in the internal politics of Mataram and even enforcing the appointment of their own nominee as Sunan in 1704. But strangely enough, the events that led to the final downfall of the empire began with a series of troubles that did not concern the Javanese at all.

In 1740 the Dutch countered a rebellion of the Chinese in the Batavia area with a massacre of all those within the city walls. This roused the Chinese throughout Java to a general anti-Dutch insurrection, and Sunan Paku Buwono II, thinking it a chance to rid himself of his burdensome allies, unwisely joined in. He seized the Dutch fort in his capital, Kartasura, and murdered the officers of the garrison. But the Chinese failed to capture a key fort and the emperor began to have second thoughts. Learning of this contemplated re-doublecross his new allies turned against him, sacked Kartasura and set up a puppet Sunan of their own; and in the end it was the Dutch who restored the vacillating ruler to his throne in 1743. Naturally they exacted a stiff price: the whole north coast and the right to supervise the appointments to the major offices of state—in a word, complete economic and political domination.

These concessions caused violent discontent among the proud Javanese nobles. The Sunan's ambitious brother, Mangkubumi, rebelled, and when the Dutch intervened to cancel the peace-offering of a province a general war followed. In 1749 the miserable monarch expired and Mangkubumi proclaimed himself Susuhunan. But the Dutch had extracted the final and fatal concession from the emperor on his deathbed—abdication for himself and his heirs of the sovereignty of the country in favour of the Company—and they nominated his nine-year-old son as his successor. Mangkubumi, however, proved too formidable a fighter to be suppressed by force of arms, and after ten years of warfare a compromise settlement was reached, under which the Sunan ceded to his uncle an independent principality—a bigger grant than the original cause of all the trouble. But the Dutch had gained, too. The empire was fatally partitioned and they were rightful suzerains. In 1755 the Governor-General solemnly proclaimed Mangkubumi as Sultan with the title of *Hamengku Buwono*, 'He who has the World in his Lap'.

The new Sultan set up his capital in a village close to the Hindu ruins of Old Mataram and the holy tombs of his ancestors at Kota Gede and Imogiri. The name he chose for it was derived from the city of the heroes of the *Ramayana*, Ayudhya. The *Kraton* or walled town extended over a square kilometre and the palace was endowed with all the attributes of Javanese royalty on the model of Surakarta, which it was to rival. But the *Kraton* as it is today differs considerably from that built by Hamengku Buwono I. For one thing, large areas were then covered by a lake, in the midst of which the Sultan, in true eighteenth-century style, built himself a fantastic water-palace. For another, in 1812 the *Kraton* (like the White House) was stormed and sacked by the British.

The first Sultan reigned for thirty-seven years, dying peacefully in 1792 after firmly establishing his infant dynasty as the equal of the senior branch at Solo. His successor, Hamengku Buwono II, had an excessively stormy reign, being twice deposed by the colonial powers and twice restored. This recalcitrant prince first came into collision with Marshal Daendels, the ruthless 'strong man' sent out by Napoleon to govern Java after the French had occupied Holland. In 1810 the Sultan was removed and his young son set up in his place. But he was allowed to remain in the city, and a year later the overthrow of the Dutch by the British expedition under Lord Minto, the Governor-General of India, emboldened him to assert his independence by resuming power.

The Lieutenant-Governor, however, appointed by Minto as his deputy in Java, was not a man to be trifled with. Thomas Stamford Raffles was by no means prepared to accept unilateral repudiation of treaties made with the preceding colonial power. For the moment he had not enough spare troops to risk an open breach, but he boldly paid a state visit to the Principalities to gauge the spirit of the two rulers. Wisely he went first to Solo, where the Sunan was as complaisant as ever and readily signed a treaty. Then he proceeded to Jogja, where John Crawfurd, the able but tactless Resident, was already at daggers drawn with the court. The Lieutenant-Governor could only muster about nine hundred men, but he did not hesitate to assert the precedence of the paramount power over the Sultan. It was a gamble, and, but for the force of his personality, might have been a massacre. First he insisted on taking the leading carriage in the state entry into Jogja, then on having the seating arrangements changed in the audience hall, where the wily prince had deliberately placed Raffles' throne in a position inferior to his own. At one tense moment the Sultan and many of his chiefs actually drew their *krisses*. But Raffles' cool courage prevailed, and a treaty was finally agreed—though both sides were aware that a more decisive test lay ahead.

The second trial of strength, physical this time, came in the following year, 1812. While the main British army under its dashing leader, General Gillespie, was away in Sumatra on a punitive expedition, the Sultan of Jogja seized the opportunity to urge the other princes and regents to join him in a general rising. But the Javanese rulers took too long to make up their minds, while Gillespie wasted little time in negotiations at Palembang. By the end of May the victorious army was back in Batavia and Raffles decided that immediate action was required against the Sultan, who was busy training his troops and liquidating suspected opponents; he had even degraded the Crown Prince, his temporary successor and substitute.

On 17th June 1812 a small advance party, including Raffles and Gillespie, reached the Dutch fort in Jogja. The Sultan moved troops to cut the road behind them and hostilities began on the 18th with an attack on a British reconnaissance party. The *Kraton* was then bombarded from the fort; the Sultan's artillery replied; and as the British made no further move, he sent a demand for unconditional surrender. He had strong grounds for confidence in a formidable fortress and vastly superior numbers; Raffles estimated the troops in the *Kraton* alone at eleven thousand. Next day, however, the main body under Colonel McLeod pushed its way through to the fort, and Gillespie, with something over a thousand well-trained troops at his disposal, at once laid on an assault of the *Kraton*. Zero hour was dawn on the 20th and, to quote Raffles' despatch:

'Gillespie was himself. The assault was made by escalade; we soon got possession of the ramparts and turned their guns upon them . . . at nine o'clock the Craton was ours . . . the Sultan was taken in his strongest hold . . . the loss to our side very inconsiderable and comparatively nothing; on the part of the enemy dreadful.'

A last stand was made by the Javanese in the precincts of the mosque, but this too was cleared by noon. Here Gillespie, as usual in the forefront of the fighting, was wounded in the arm. But it was a small price to pay for what amounted to the pacification of the whole of Java, since all the other rulers were waiting to see the result of the struggle between the Sultan and the British.

Visiting today's *Kraton* I found it difficult to visualise the stirring scene of the storming of the walls by Gillespie and his men. Despite six years in the army my powers of military appreciation are not marked, and I could not imagine where they had the drawbridges, the bastions, the glacis and all the rest of the fortifications described by Raffles. True, considerable sections of the surrounding walls and some heavy ornamental gateways still existed, but though they might be eight feet thick, they were certainly not forty-five feet high, and the little projecting pepper-pots at the corners, hardly big enough for a couple of sentries, surely could not be called bastions. The wall on the north side, where the main entrance lay and where the main assault was made, no longer existed except for a curly conventional gateway to the palace square. The queer thing was that this great green, which Crawfurd described as a 'Javanese field of Mars', was on a lower level than the buildings to its north, where the main town now lay. The Dutch fort stood only a few hundred yards from the *Kraton*, yet at an advantageous height above it. The palace stretched out behind with its forecourt of *Pagelaran* at the far side of the square, but only the audience hall of *Sitinggil*, the 'High Ground', stood at a more commanding level. It was all very different from our normal idea of a fortress as something perched on an inaccessible hilltop.

The plan of the palace was a series of great open halls. This spaciousness gave a certain dignity, but none of the buildings were palatial in the European sense and Western visitors were often disappointed. Coolness was the grand desideratum in Java, and it was obtained by a succession of open tree-lined courts and wall-less pavilions with polished marble floors, carved wooden pillars and vast pyramidal roofs. Only the roof was available for ornamentation with climbing patterns of elaborately carved, painted and gilded beams; a rich display of furniture was precluded where the courtiers had to squat on the floor to be on a lower level than the seated prince, whose throne was a simple, backless, golden stool. Even the telephones were fixed close to the floor, lest anyone should address the Sultan, albeit invisibly, from a superior height.

It was not the architecture or the décor but the traditions of the *Kraton* that interested me most. Behind the High Ground lay a public courtyard called the *Keben*, open at each side to the streets. In the middle stood the Pavilion of Justice and on a marble dais the Sultan would sit when he paid some high offender the last honour of watching his execution. On the far side was a high wall with a great gate, locked and guarded by the royal bodyguard, whose dark blue jackets, long *kains* and tall lances accentuated the impression of length and thinness that marked the *Kraton* type. The private quarters of the Sultan within used to be seen only by privileged guests on great state occasions; but nowadays, though there were no more grand balls and banquets for the Europeans, permission to visit the palace could be obtained on request. What is more, for the first time the common people were allowed to see the sacred precincts. Every Thursday morning an awed throng of peasants, dressed in their best, could be seen waiting in *Pagelaran* and gaping at the wonders of the court.

In the first courtyard beyond the sentry-boxes stood two pavilions that housed the special *gamelans*: the two mighty sets of the Holy *Gamelan*, and two smaller ones for the Sultan's salute and for royal circumcisions. Two stout silver-washed giants, such as guarded the entrance to the Hindu temples, knelt in their sentry-boxes before the next gate, which led to the residential court. The comparative modernity of many of the buildings was illustrated by the date over the porch, 1928; while within the court the 'Yellow Pavilion', an airy house with carved lintels of filigree delicacy, was still unfinished, having been begun by the Sultan's father. The older buildings occupied the middle of the courtyard, jutting out from the right side, behind which lay the closed women's quarters. In the centre rose the *pendopo* known as the 'Golden Pavilion', where the Javanese dances were held, and stretching out from its side was the glassed-in 'Sweet Pavilion', where European balls and dinners took place—the last one in 1939. Behind the Golden Pavilion lay another wide but very dark hall, the *Prabajeksa* or Holy of Holies, where the sacred heirlooms of the Sultanate were kept. It was hard to distinguish anything by the red glow of the single ever-burning lamp, whose extinction would mean the extinction of the kingdom. But we could dimly discern racks of lances, ancient flags, *krisses* resting on cushioned stands, a lifesize photograph of Hamengku Buwono IX in full court dress, and the Great Bed, which we were told was purely symbolic and never used.

Separated from the main courtyard by the Golden and Sweet Pavilions was a garden with a ring of empty birdcages surrounding a low marble platform. Here once a year in the first month, *Sura*, the family *krisses* would be ceremonially cleaned. To sit polishing the hilt of a *kris*, listening to soft *gamelan* music and the song of birds, was the way, I was told, to achieve the true Javanese atmosphere. For the *kris* has a mystic significance for the Javanese, and every aristocratic house jealously preserved these heirlooms in a special central chamber. They had straight blades, not the wavy Malayan type, and the handles and scabbards might be richly chased and jewelled; but the scabbard's hilt was limited to certain shapes of polished wood. The invention of the *kris* is attributed to the legendary hero, Raden Pandji, and the old smiths were greatly revered. *Kris*-making was a sacred art and a period of abstinence and meditation was required before the chosen day for starting the work. This *tapa* period gave the smith supernatural powers which went into the weapon—magic *krisses* are a favourite element in the legends of Java—and these powers were transferable to whoever owned or wore the *kris*. Hence the vital importance of keeping them safe. They still formed an essential part of ceremonial dress, worn in the belt behind the back.

Prince Paku Alam told me that, when representing Indonesia

at Queen Elizabeth's coronation garden-party, he was approached
by a ferocious Arab sheik with a scimitar jutting from his cum-
merbund, who asked him curiously:

"Why do you wear your weapon behind your back?"

"In dangerous company," answered the Prince, "we carry it
at our elbow, thus. But we put it behind us when we do not
expect attack—as at Buckingham Palace."

The last time Coral and I visited the *Kraton,* our ways parted
here. The Sultan had given special permission for her to see the
women's quarters and his brother, Prince Murdoningrat, was
personally conducting us round. This prince was the only male
besides the Sultan himself who was allowed to visit the female
part of the palace—at least, so we gathered. So, while he led
Coral away, I made my way through a gateway on the left to
the *Kesatrian,* or young princes' quarters, so called from the
Hindu warrior caste of the *Ksatriya.*

In the forecourt an old stable had been converted into the
palace library, full of heavy Dutch tomes in brown paper covers
and bright modern magazines. I noticed *Picture Post* and *Life,*
Lilliput and *Esquire* and *Vogue*—whose tattered condition indicated much more use than the dusty books. In the *Kesatrian*
itself the *pendopo* was used as a storeroom with ten or so vast
chests full of *wayang* puppets, some ornate mobile frames for
screens, and the *gamelan* that broadcast 'Music from the Palace'
each Sunday. On the verandah I found half a dozen blue-uni-
formed officials sorting and labelling the costumes for a *Wayang
Orang* performance: though there were no more dance performances in the palace itself, the costumes were lent out to the
dance schools. Above the busy scene brooded three full-length
portraits, dark, severe, and neglected, of the seventh Sultan, his
mother and stepmother. These were the work of Raden Saleh,
the nineteenth-century pioneer of Indonesian painting, and they
did not strike me greatly till I realised how unique and unorthodox
his work was—for Java. It was not their quality, but their existence at all that made them extraordinary.

At the Sekaten celebrations

Female rice-mountain   Male rice-mountain

The sacrifice of the dolls
at the chalkpit

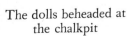

The dolls beheaded at
the chalkpit

Merapi Volcano from the Campus

Palm-leaf houses of the salt-winners at Winevendors Bay

Meanwhile Coral explored the mysteries of the harem and found them less romantic than they sound. The women's quarters were like a small village, with streets of detached bungalows, a disused mosque, a narrow foodstall that sold tea and fruit and ready-cooked dishes, some big family barracks and two large villas, for the Queen (*Ratu*) and the Queen-Mother. Her general impression was one of shabbiness and neglect; dusty windows and stained walls, empty rooms and verandahs thick with faded photographs. Yet it could not be called a Deserted Village; the Sultan's mother, three unmarried sisters, and three wives with their respective children lived there together with a troop of tough old harridans armed with *krisses*, who guarded the ladies from male intrusion. But there was no longer the bustle of youth and beauty that must have enlivened it when the Sultans had their dozens of concubines and troupes of *Serimpi* dancers. Coral met two of the sisters, girls in their early twenties, taking lessons in the *pendopo* of their mother's house. Though never allowed out socially unless escorted by Murdoningrat, they took part in public dance performances—one indeed was a star dancer. The Sultan's mother pleaded age and illness as an excuse for not appearing, but the illness was perhaps diplomatic, as we heard that she insisted on visitors wearing the old-fashioned court dress with bare shoulders like servants. Coral also saw the eldest of the wives, but she was not living in the *Ratu's* house, which stood across a lawn from the back of the Sultan's Yellow Pavilion. This well-kept and freshly painted villa with a terrace of roses and a romantic bench, was occupied by No. 2.

But what struck her most were two incidental sights: the royal washing being carried across a court under the shade of a golden umbrella, and a group of workmen repairing a pavilion. True they were under guard, but there they were, men in the theoretically forbidden zone—unless it could be that the lower classes did not count?

As we were leaving the central court, reunited, we were conducted to the southern gateway, not in order to pass through (as it only led to more courtyards, another High Ground and another

I

square of less importance and interest than their northern counter-
parts), but to admire the ornamentation. Along the wall-top
undulated two dragon-like serpents with their tails intertwined,
which dated from the original foundation—in fact they themselves gave the date. By the ingenious system called *Tjandra
Sengkala* (moon-dating) the figures are first reversed and then
each number is indicated by one of its many symbols, chosen to
make a sentence. The palace was completed in 1757, which
according to the Javanese *Saka* calendar is the year 1682. The
snakes' intertwined tails give the feeling of unity; and thus, as
snakes count 8 and feeling counts 6, two snakes feeling as one
gives us 2861, the reverse of 1682. Q.E.D.

The Water Palace was quite different, a far-from-traditional
whimsy of the first Sultan. But the lake in which it stood had
long since dried up and given way to streets and markets; the
high brick buildings of two or three storeys had largely collapsed;
and a wilderness of bamboo huts, ditches and banana trees
effectually blurred the ground plan. So shockingly tumbledown
were these damp and discoloured chambers and archways that the
official guidebook was ashamed to mention the place. But to the
Anglo-Saxon eye with its Gothic passion for ruins the Water
Palace was more suggestive and romantic than the official one.
The real name was *Taman Sari*, the Beautiful Garden, and in its
day it may have rivalled in fantasy the Villa d'Este or Hellbrunn.
The taste for playing about with water, so marked in the poten-
tates of baroque Europe, was perhaps more excusable on the
Equator.

There is a tale that might explain the irregular plan and in-
secure construction of the buildings, which so embarrassed the
compilers of the guidebook. When Mangkubumi was set up as an
independent prince, he agreed to provide the labour for the erec-
tion of a Dutch fort in his new capital. But first, of course, he
had to build his *Kraton*. The formal palace took only two years.
Then in 1758 he began work on his pleasure-palace of *Taman
Sari*—and a quarter of a century later his masons and carpenters

were still all engaged on this work. Nicolaas Hartingh, the local Dutch governor, commented sourly on the Sultan's experiments in 'fountains, grotto-work and conduits, which when completed, he orders immediately to be pulled down, not finding them to his taste, thus squandering some little money'. He was also squandering his workers' time, so that they were not available for the promised fort—a new version of Penelope's loom. Still, the work was finished eventually, for there is a description of the Water Palace dated 1791; and the fort was there for Raffles.

We visited the ruins several times, growing more and more confused as the different guides explained the details in words that, even half-understood, were clearly inconsistent. The main lines, however, remained reasonably clear. Entering by a wide avenue, we reached a thick ornamental archway, where snaky-banistered stairs led up to a platform on the top. Here the Sultan could sit and take the air to the sound of the *gamelan* playing in the court below. Thence we proceeded down a wide flight of steps to the royal ladies' bathing pools, surrounded by high but crumbling walls and stout stone flowerpots. There were two wide chickweed-covered tanks, separated by a causeway, and a third smaller one through a gateway on the left. The last was reserved for the Sultan and his Queen; and originally, we were told, there was only one big pool for the rest of his womenfolk. But the second Sultan, having forty wives, had to add another tank. On the far side another gate led to what was the garden court, now bare except for some heavy vases and a badminton court. But the stout ornamental archway beyond was blocked, and we had either to turn left to the sleeping-quarters (low dark rooms with niches like catacombs) or skirt the arch to the right, dodging among the trees and huts and streams of a *kampong*, till we reached a tall brick ruin like a blitzed warehouse. Being a two-storey building, it proved an easy victim of the earthquake that brought down the Water-Palace. On the ground floor were the music and dance halls; on the first floor the *Serimpi* girls' dormitories; and on the roof, reached by a slippery, hollowed stairway, a platform overlooking the clamorous market-place.

It was strange to reflect that in the days of its grandeur the whole area for half a mile around us was covered with an artificial lake, and that from this rooftop the Sultan would once a year hold a marine review of his troops, who paraded past him in boats. From the building's foot a maze of dark stone tunnels plunged down to ruined dining halls and towers. Only once did I manage to penetrate one of these underground passages, as they were usually flooded with water—an odd reversal of their original role, when they were subaqueous rather than subterranean and formed the only dry way from building to building. Through the tunnel we came to the bottom of the tower that was the Sultan's most original fantasy. It was a hollow cylinder made of two superimposed circular cloisters with the connecting stairs rising in the open centre around a fountain. The outer walls boasted windows and through the glass the occupants could watch the fish swimming by: an aquarium in reverse. When Major C. F. Reimer, Inspector of Canals, Dams, Dikes and Waterways, wrote his account of the *Kraton* in 1791, it impressed him as a remarkable feat of hydraulics. The upper floor was used by the Sultan and his brothers, the lower by the *Ratu* and her ladies; and each floor had a Moslem prayer niche as its only private corner. The Major's description of the place as a house of prayer (mosque, one of our guides called it) therefore seems the most probable explanation of its use, rather than the lascivious conjectures of later Western writers.

As we returned through the banana groves, I tried hard to picture the gorgeous state barge and the ladies in their skiffs and the shoals of fish; and I wondered at the rashness of Lieutenant Hector Maclean, who (doubtless for strictly military reasons) rushed down one of the tunnels towards the Sultan's harem, only to reel out again with a ghastly *kris* wound in his neck. Invariably as we passed through the last archway, a bitter wizened hag would attack us with loud demands for money, having whisked her broom perfunctorily over the passage-way. Each time she would reject with contumely the small but undeserved tip I offered and pursue us with volleys of curses; and the last time she became positively menacing. No doubt it was only a coincidence that the same evening at a party of ours my white dinner jacket was mysteriously befouled and all the lights failed. But at dusk amid the mouldering ruins of the Water-Palace it was not so difficult to believe in witches.

After the capture of the *Kraton* Raffles deposed and banished the Sultan and partitioned his territory with the grant of a semi-independent principality to his brother Notokusumo, who had led a force on the British side. The new prince took the title of *Paku Alam*, the Nail of the Earth, and Jogjakarta has boasted two royal houses ever since. But the stubborn spirit of Jogja's princes was not broken and thirteen years later it flared out again in a still more dangerous outbreak.

The old Sultan lived on in exile, while his son, grandson and even great-grandson succeeded rapidly to the throne. Meanwhile Britain had fulfilled her pledge to the Stadtholder's government-in-exile to restore Holland's colonies in the East Indies. This move was not popular in Java, but no major trouble broke out till the revolt of Prince Diponegoro in 1825. This proud and fanatical patriot was the son of the third Sultan and one of the Regents for his two-year-old nephew who became fifth Sultan in 1822. Chafing under the brash interference and disregard of his rights by the Dutch, he finally lost patience when the colonists began to build a road across his estates without his permission. On 19th June 1825 came the armed clash that set aflame the Java War, the greatest anti-colonial struggle till 1945.

At first the Dutch assumed that this was just another dynastic quarrel and Diponegoro wanted the baby Sultan's throne for himself. So they brought back the prince's grandfather from exile and he reigned a third time till his death in 1828. But it soon became obvious that Diponegoro's campaign was something much more serious for the colonial power. The common people regarded him as their champion and, because of his asceticism and Moslem fervour, as a saint, and the revolt became a holy war of liberation. He gained repeated victories and at one time held large areas of the countryside. But in 1827 General de Kock introduced a hedgehog system of forts throughout the war area, which upset the prince's communications and mobility and turned the tide against him. But despite his waning resources Dipone-goro still refused to give in, and it was only by the treacherous trick of arresting him at a truce meeting in Magelang that the Dutch finally suppressed the rebellion in 1830. The prince was exiled to Makassar, where he was imprisoned till his death in 1855. But his name remained a legend of patriotism and today he is remembered as the greatest of national heroes. The Jogja army command was called the Diponegoro Division; there were Diponegoro Streets everywhere; he was pictured on coins and banknotes; the anniversary of his death on 8th January was a national celebration; and every place connected with him was a shrine.

We visited two of these places of pilgrimage near Jogja. One was the cave of Selarong five miles south-east, which was his first field headquarters. There, after the Dutch had burnt his home, he took refuge with his family and was soon joined by a force of thirty thousand followers, flying red-and-white standards—now the national colours. It was not an easy place to get to even now, despite its proximity to the city. A narrow wooden bridge over a ravine compelled us to leave our jeep and walk the last mile or two. Loaded with picnic baskets, we panted along through the bamboo groves, past bicycle parks and eating shacks, into the cul-de-sac of hills that had formed the rebel prince's hideout. Melting, we arrived at the foot of a narrow graceless flight of concrete steps that led up to the cave, high on the cliff between two thin waterfalls. The misguided zeal of the public works department had also built a low concrete wall and platform in front of the cave, neatly spoiling the romance of its position and its past. The cave itself was not impressive, merely a shallow, carved-out chamber under an overhanging cliff, but the austerity of the stone couch of the mystic hero might have been moving, if the walls had not been scored with the squalid memorials of tourists.

It was Sunday and the place was swarming with trippers; the enclosed valley made the airless heat fiercer than ever; Coral cut her fingers on a sardine tin; and a sudden downpour, as we plodded home, marooned us in a shabby shack. We did not feel we had been in the presence of history.

There was more of the atmosphere of tragic dignity that should go with the memory of Diponegoro in the fatal room at Magelang, a town some thirty-five miles north of Jogja. The Residency was a long, colonnaded building on the edge of the town with a clear view across to Sumbing volcano, and its spacious marble-paved verandah, opening into a fountain court in the centre, made it one of the most attractive of the tropic-Doric palaces favoured by the Dutch. We signed our names at the police post and were conducted to a small room on the far side of the verandah. Before unlocking the door the policeman requested us to remove our shoes.

In the centre of a small square room stood a little marble-topped table with a stiff wooden armchair on either side. On the table and the worn straw seats lay handfuls of withered flowers, while two more chairs stood against the wall beside another table, bearing a brass coffee set, a charcoal brazier and four small cups of blue and white porcelain. These were the actual chairs and cups used by Diponegoro and three Dutch officers on the morning of 28th March 1830, when he met them for truce talks in this room. His troops were not allowed to enter the town, but the prince, trusting to the truce terms, came to the Residency and sat down alone in conference with General de Kock and two others. The chair used by Diponegoro could be distinguished by the deep scratches said to be made by his nails, as he tried to control his fury at their arrogant demands for his surrender. Finally, after two hours of useless parleying, the General ordered the arrest of his opponent. Significantly, he had already asked authority to do so. Meanwhile his reinforced garrison had disarmed the prince's troops outside the town. The negotiations seem to have been a deliberate trick to lure Diponegoro into a trap. It was successful; without his leadership Javanese resistance was broken, and the

Java War, which had cost the Dutch fifteen thousand lives and twenty million guilders, was over.

The victors were anxious that the prince should not become a legend or the room a place of pilgrimage. They locked the room and set two guards over it day and night, so that the furniture remained undisturbed for a hundred years. Yet when the Japanese opened it, the famous chairs had disappeared. After the liberation the Ministry of Culture made a search and in 1954 they were located in a local village, in the home of an eighty-five-year-old ex-official. He had been a district head under the Dutch administration, and his son a clerk in the Magelang Residency office. In the years of the depression one of the Resident's economies had been to cut the two watchmen and sell the old chairs at auction. The clerk bought them for four guilders and presented them to his father. The old man took good care of them. He covered the nail-marked chair with white cloth and those of the Dutch with black, and every Friday he burnt incense and prayed for the victory of the White and the downfall of the Black. Now his prayers had been answered and the task of caring for the holy chairs was fulfilled. He presented them to the Ministry to be returned to their original home, refusing all reward for what he regarded as a duty and an honour.

It is an instructive story. A hundred years of propaganda by Dutch teachers and history books, portraying Diponegoro as an ambitious and self-seeking rebel, could not destroy the living tradition of the people. Diligent government servants still nurtured the memory of national resistance and the hope of national liberation. Legend is one of the great forces of the world.

7

THE SULTAN

A T our first *Lebaran* party with the University Women's
Club Coral was introduced to a youngish, heavy-jawed
man in glasses and a lounge suit, whose name she did not
catch.

"Are you working at the University?" she asked convention-
ally.

"Not exactly," he replied.

"But you are connected with it?"

"In a way."

"Do you live in Jogja?"

"Part of the time."

"Have you managed to find a house?" (Houses were rather on
our mind at that time.)

"Yes, I have one."

"Do you have to share it?"

"Well, a number of people live there."

The going was distinctly heavy and Coral took the first excuse
to leave him. As she reported to me her encounter with this
weighty gentleman, a friend sitting beside us gave an exclamation.

"Do you mean the person you were talking to in the passage
just now?"

"Yes, who is he?"

"But that's the Sultan!"

Hastily Coral went back, taking me with her, to make her
apologies. The Sultan, far from being offended, had been
amused. He spoke excellent English and had, he told us, spent

two months at a tutoring establishment in Rottingdean, as well as visiting London with an Indonesian students' dance group, which performed at the Queen's Hall in 1936 on behalf of the Chinese Red Cross. He preferred Rottingdean, as it was quieter and he was himself an outdoor type of man.

In this informal manner we first met Kandjeng Sultan Hamengku Buwono Senapati Ing Ngalogo Ngabdulrachman Sajidin Panatagama Kalifah Allah Ingkang Djumeneng Nata Kading IX Ing Ngajogjakarta Hadiningrat, usually called simply Hamengku Buwono IX. It was not so surprising that after nine months in Jogja we had never before seen him, for he had spent most of his time till recently in Djakarta, serving as Minister of Defence. Even on his visits to his home he seldom made public appearances, being a shy man who avoided as far as possible all the pomp and ceremonial surrounding his position. Nor did he ever entertain in the *Kraton*, preferring to receive even the most eminent visitors at his office in his capacity as Head of the Special Area of Jogjakarta. The days of magnificent receptions and balls at the palace, attended by hundreds of Europeans, were over. The reason was partly economic, partly political; in the new democratic age he did not consider lavish displays of luxury tactful or tactical. In fact the only public reception of his reign was held at his coronation in 1940. The palace was no longer the centre of social activity nor the Sultan himself a social figure. Such occasions as he attended, like the present celebration, appeared to be matters of duty rather than pleasure.

His elusiveness was not, however, the result of a retiring nature. On the contrary, he was a man of formidable energy and ambition, who preferred to devote his time to public work rather than the social graces. In serious conversation his remarks were fluent and to the point, but for party chitchat he was apt to relapse into giggles or silence. His ideas were modern, progressive and far more democratic than those of his subjects. For most of the millions of Mid-Java he was still a mystic personage, surrounded by an aura of majesty and holiness as the representative of the ancestral feudal and religious power. Inside the

Kraton he was bound by tradition and his family and household insisted on his keeping up at least the shadow of the hallowed customs of royalty. But outside it he behaved with far more modesty than the new great men of the Republic.

We happened to travel with him once from Djakarta to Jogja by Garuda Airways. At Djakarta airport we were requested to wait till the Sultan and a gold-braided army officer—his A.D.C. we presumed—had boarded the plane first. At Bandung, where we made a stop, a crowd of glittering officers was waiting to greet them, as seemed right and proper for one who was an important man in his own right as an ex-Minister and territorial governor, apart from his hereditary status. But when we returned to the plane, we were surprised to see the Sultan walking with us unaccompanied and carrying his little red airways bag like any other passenger. The glittering brass and the fanfares had all been for the Colonel!

Coming to the throne in 1939, at the age of twenty-seven, he inherited a position of empty show, politically a mere puppet of the colonial government. As one of the select influential persons that the government needed, his education was placed in Dutch hands from the age of four, first living in the family of a Dutch schoolmaster, then studying at the Dutch schools in Jogja and elsewhere. At the age of eighteen he was sent to Holland, where he spent the next nine years at Haarlem High School and Leyden University, taking his first degree in 'Indology', i.e., colonial civil service law. He was about to take his final doctoral examination when he was hastily summoned home in September 1939. His father, who was in failing health, met him in Djakarta; but on the return journey the eighth Sultan fainted in the train and on arrival in Jogja was hurried to the Catholic hospital. Whether there was in fact a clap of thunder from a cloudless sky as the Sultan collapsed, whether his estranged wife had really prophesied that he would not die in his palace, the suddenness and drama of his death at the hospital next morning evidently stirred the people's imagination.

His heir did not accede at once, as he had first to negotiate a contract with the colonial government before they would sanction his succession. Only in the case of the Sultan and Sunan were negotiations allowed; all the other princes of the Indies were simply presented with readymade 'Short Contracts', and if they refused the terms they forfeited their inheritance. Hamengku Buwono IX proved unusually stubborn and difficult, and an interregnum of over six months passed before he finally agreed to the contract in April 1940; even then, he told me, he only signed because he got the feeling that the Dutch would soon be gone anyway. Yet the government assumed that his education in Holland must have made him pro-Dutch; actually, though he had used his time to study Dutch mentality, it was far from making him Dutch-minded.

A wartime history of the Indies proudly related how he received the conquering Japanese in the full dress of a Dutch Major-General; but the inference proved wrong. Defiance of the new occupying power, rather than devotion to the old, was the meaning of this gesture. His attitude towards the Japanese authorities was so unco-operative that they changed their local governor three times in three years. To be anti-Japanese, however, was not equivalent to being pro-Dutch; he was pro-Indonesian.

Among the many unpleasant shocks suffered by the Dutch in 1945 was the support of the Revolution by the princes of Jogja. A week or two after Sukarno's proclamation of independence in Djakarta, the Sultan and Prince Paku Alam VIII, of Jogja's secondary royal house, issued a joint message placing Jogjakarta under the central government of the Republic of Indonesia and declaring themselves responsible to the President in their administration of the region. Next day the President issued a charter confirming the princes in their positions and designating Jogjakarta province a Special Area. The moral effect of this unhesitating alignment of their historic leaders with those of the new Republic was vital in uniting the nationalist movement in Java. No one could then know how wise a move this would prove, changing a shadowy sovereignty into real political power. No one could guess that it would make Jogja the spiritual centre of a new, great country. No one could doubt that if the gamble failed and the Dutch regained control of their colony, deposition and exile would be the princes' fate, as it had been of so many of their ancestors. Though the Sultans had been quiescent for the last hundred years, they had always sought to assert their independence whenever the chance arose. The ninth Sultan was acting in accord with the spirit of his ancestors.

But he was not content merely to fight for the past. His placing of his province and influence under the orders of the President showed that he had wider views than personal aggrandisement and took an Indonesian rather than a purely Javanese outlook. His democratic ideas were put into practice in a series of experiments in local government that made Jogja into a kind of laboratory for pioneer tests of popular responsibility—a People's Representative Council, trial elections, economic and social reforms, a local People's Army, an embryonic national university. Everywhere he gave the lead in turning his realm from a feudal reservation into one of the most progressive, democratic and national-minded provinces of the still shaky Republic.

It is hardly surprising that, when on 4th January 1946 President Sukarno moved the Republican government's seat from Djakarta owing to its re-occupation by the Dutch, he chose Jogja as the Republic's new capital. It had both practical and psychological advantages. As a historic seat of Javanese sovereignty, as a traditional centre of resistance to the Dutch, as an area where the old order was in full accord with the new, as the scene of revolutionary progress, and not least as a refuge remote and difficult to attack from the Dutch-occupied ports of the north coast, it was an obvious choice. But there were disadvantages, too, about its remoteness and lack of facilities. It was out of touch with the world; and the world, with its attention fixed on the Premier's negotiations in Djakarta, failed to realise the uncompromising strength of the people's will for independence. Few journalists penetrated to the interior, and the 'Voice of Free

Indonesia', broadcast by the feeble local radio station, made little impression in a noisy war. Another disadvantage appeared later, when the Dutch decided to blockade the Republic and force its submission by virtual siege. The south coast had no ports to speak of, the north was held by the enemy; the only line of supply was a roundabout and hazardous air-lift via Sumatra, constantly in difficulties over lack of fuel, lack of recognition and armed interception. Only a few buccaneering adventurers would risk their planes on blockade-running flights, and by 1948 the capital was reduced to a desperate and primitive condition of living.

But the determined intransigency of the Republicans never wavered and the people patiently bore with rags and under-nourishment. The Sultan was appointed Minister of State in October 1946, and was charged with the co-ordination of defence in January 1948. On 19th December 1948 the Dutch finally lost all restraint and unleashed a sudden attack on Jogja with bombers, parachute troops and tanks. The whole government was captured and interned except for one Minister, who happened to be in Sumatra, and the Sultan, who was confined to his palace. Whether or not the Dutch authorities believed the story with which they indoctrinated their troops, who marched with the slogan 'On to Jogja to free the Sultan', they did not dare to remove him from among his people. They also hoped to induce him to play their game by offering him the headship of one of the federal states they were busy organising as counterweights to the Republic —a state that would be considerably larger than his inherited territory.

The Sultan, however, simply shut himself up in the *Kraton*, fasting and doing penance, and refused to see any of the Dutch authorities, civil or military. The people also steadfastly refused to collaborate with the occupying administration; of some ten thousand civil servants in the area no more than one hundred and fifty remained at work, and that only at the express order of the Sultan to keep up the essential sanitary and hospital services. They were encouraged by a message that their leader had seen a vision of his great ancestor, Sultan Agung, who told him not to worry as the invaders would be gone in three months. But he did not neglect active measures too. He was in hourly communication with the guerillas outside the *Kraton* and early in 1949 he planned a general attack with the double purpose of raising morale and impressing the United Nations, which were about to discuss the Indonesian problem once more. On 1st March two-thirds of the city were recaptured by the guerillas and it took tanks to dislodge them.

Next day the Dutch General and the local Governor demanded an interview and threatened to break through the *Kraton* gates in a tank, if need be. The Sultan granted them ten minutes and received them with his luggage ready packed behind his chair. He would discuss nothing but the evacuation of Jogja and announced his readiness to be taken away to exile. Hastily the Dutch disclaimed any such idea and their host thereupon passed on to reminiscences of student life in Holland. After exactly ten minutes he terminated the interview and left the room.

With such a record as the leader and symbol of resistance during the eclipse of the Republic he naturally emerged with enormous prestige. When the Dutch agreed to release the banished government, his orders for a cease-fire were at once obeyed. In the reconstituted cabinet he was Minister of Defence. When the Premier, Dr. Hatta, went to Holland for the Round Table Conference, he took the chair, and he represented the Republic at the triumphant moment of the transfer of sovereignty on 27th December 1949. In the federal cabinet of the new United States of Indonesia, he held the same post. But the federal system soon broke down and on 6th September 1950 the first government of the unitary Republic of Indonesia was formed, with the Sultan as Vice-Premier.

Instead of being a feudal relic in a tiny state, he was one of the biggest figures in the biggest Moslem country of the world.

When we arrived in Indonesia in September 1952, the Sultan was once again Minister of Defence, after a few months out of office during 1951. But a crisis was brewing over the question of the reorganisation of the army, which burst in the mysterious affair of 17th October. Newly arrived and remote from Djakarta, I could not clearly follow the cause and course of events; but it certainly looked like a half-hearted coup d'état by the army—and the army was under the direction of the Sultan. At all events, certain military units under senior officers seized the house of Parliament, broke up some of its furniture and forcibly prevented the members from entering. Others trained field-guns on the Presidential Palace; but after the President had come out and addressed them, they meekly withdrew and the whole affair petered out.

No official explanation of the events of 17th October was ever published, nor any court-martial held. For over two years an investigation was pending, but evidently too many important personages would have been involved. In the end the embarrassing matter was decently buried by the so-called 'Jogja Charter' of February 1955, when senior commanders of all areas met and signed an agreement that the army should heal its split and eschew politics in future. A sentimental ceremony at the grave of General Sudirman, the army's first leader, and a ritual signing in the presence of the Supreme Commander, President Sukarno, completed the reconciliation—till the next time.

The true background of the affair is thus impossible to trace with confidence. The Sultan himself later assured me that it was not a coup but a rather ill-thought-out demonstration by some progressive army leaders against political interference. The outside world interpreted the affair more dramatically as a struggle between the Sultan and the President for control of the army, and ultimately for supreme power. Foreign commentators, who saw in Hamengku Buwono a more reliable leader than Sukarno, wishfully hailed him as Indonesia's coming Strong Man. But if it was in any way a trial of strength, there was no doubt who came out on top. In the next few weeks three out of the seven territorial commanders appointed by the Sultan were forcibly relieved of their authority by their own seconds-in-command! The usurpers proclaimed their loyalty to the Presi-

Borobudur

Borobudur

A Buddhist monk

Stupas on the upper
terrace

dent but defied the orders of the Minister. When the latter visited East Java command, the new commander vanished on manoeuvres and, thanks to a signals truck dogging the ministerial car, could not be caught. In Makassar the mutinous colonel merely announced that he would not let the Minister land. The government would undertake no disciplinary action, leaving the impotent Sultan with no choice but resignation. His political career was ended, and he swore he would never resume it.

After that the Sultan devoted himself to his other interests, of which he had no lack. He was President of the Indonesian Olympic Committee, and the country's first Chief Scout, and Chairman of the Tourist Board. Immediately after his fall he tactfully departed on a foreign tour as leader of the national football team. He could perform as well as preside, as I found when I took part in a comic match between the University staff and the local journalists during Gadjah Mada's fourth birthday celebrations. For our eleven the Sultan, as Patron, and Paku Alam, as Chancellor, played as goalkeeper and centre-forward respectively. It must be admitted that the princes were more skilful and in better training than the rest of us and were largely responsible for our holding the newsmen to an honourable draw.

But his prime interest was his principality and his threefold job as local Governor, Chairman of the Provincial Government, and Sultan. He was tireless in all these roles, and his special enthusiasm was his plan for the industrialisation of Jogja. He was always exploring new ideas for bringing prosperity to his overcrowded and undernourished province—tobacco plantations, sugar factories, chemical works, mining; but whether the resources and business skill for his plans would be found, remained to be seen. At any rate it would not be for want of trying on his part. Jogja produced one of the heaviest Communist votes in the country at the first General Election in 1955; but the Head of the Special Area—royal, religious and feudal attributes notwithstanding—remained the undisputed leader of his people.

K

A Professor of Law told me that in his boyhood, before the present Sultan's birth, there was a prophecy current in Jogja:

'Poor widow's only son shall reign,
And Java shall be free again.'

Strangely enough Hamengku Buwono IX fulfilled the requirements, for the word *rangda* means a separated wife as well as a widow. His mother had been put away by his father and he was her only son. Her poverty was perhaps relative. When she married her cousin, the Crown Prince, he borrowed large sums from her, since she was rich. When he took other wives, she demanded her money back. Furious, he turned her and her son out of the palace; but he never promoted any other to First Wife and thus had no *Ratu*, or Queen, when later he acceded to the throne. Otherwise there might well have been a different ninth Sultan, as the rules of succession do not go by pure primogeniture. The heir must be a son of a reigning Sultan, but the sons of a *Ratu*, the crowned First Wife (first in rank but not necessarily in chronological order) take precedence over the others.

This conjugal ranking system explained a paradox that had mystified me at first. We were assured that the Sultan was unmarried, and at the same time that he had three wives and ten children. As a Moslem he was of course allowed four legal wives at a time; but the point was that none of his three was *Ratu*, and so they did not count! Nor was Paku Alam 'married' in the eyes of Jogja, despite his two wives and sixteen children. The secondary royal wives played no public part in social life, though they were no longer confined within the walls of the *Kraton*, as in the old days; so the leadership of society devolved upon the ladies of the University.

However, there was quite enough royalty about to be going on with, even on the strictest interpretation of the word, which should be applied only to the actual children of a Sultan. There were all the Sultan's uncles and aunts and brothers and sisters. The eighth Sultan had been comparatively modest with a mere twenty-nine children, but his father, who reigned in the grand old style from 1877 to 1921, had had no less than seventy-eight. One of the seventh Sultan's innumerable grandsons explained to us how such numbers were achieved legitimately with a ration of only four wives; whenever one of the 'unofficial wives' became pregnant, the prince would temporarily divorce one of his official team and marry the mother-to-be, reversing the process after the child had been duly born in wedlock. No wonder Jogja was full of titles! For though the term royalty might be comparatively limited, the blood carried with it a succession of diminishing honorific initials down to the sixth generation, after which came the almost indefinite continuation of *Raden*.

Fortunately, though these titles still figured in formal documents, the modern tendency was not to insist on them publicly and we were not troubled by such inextricable problems of protocol as sorting out GPH from BPH, gauging RMA against KRT, and so forth. Mrs. Hardjono, for instance, was the full sister of Prince Paku Alam, and when she took Coral to visit her mother at the palace of Pakualaman, all the distinctions of address, precedence, and language were duly observed. But outside the court she had dropped her honorifics and ranked as the wife of a Professor. Or there was the case of Professor Purbodiningrat, son of a Crown Prince and a leading light of the Communist party. Rumour had it that his egalitarian enthusiasm was really a matter of sour grapes, since his father had died before succeeding to the Sultanate and thus deprived his sons of any hope of the throne for themselves.

As with titles, so with ceremonies. I had read in books of Victorian travels the patronisingly romantic descriptions of the 'hollow pomps and make-believe royalty' of the Javanese principalities; and I once got hold of a privately printed booklet entitled *The Garebegs in the Sultanaat Jogjakarta*, apparently written about 1930. It was full of fascinating information about the four great feasts of Javanese Islam, the *Garebegs*, when the Sultan would appear in all his glory, riding in a gilded coach, escorted by his Guards in fanciful uniforms and followed by the royal treasures, the court dwarfs, and so on. The sight must have been impressive but at the same time rather pathetic. In the photographs the troops were so obviously toy soldiers in their quaint and obsolete accoutrements, while the reality loomed up in the stout, walrus-moustached figure of the Dutch Resident, the 'elder brother' on whose arm the Sultan leaned.

Now all that had changed. The Dutch had gone, but so had the great processions. The old customs were kept up, but privately and modestly; and the only occasion when we could get a hint of the ancient splendours was at the feast of Mohammed's birthday, the *Garebeg Maulud*, which was preceded by a week of celebrations peculiar to Solo and Jogja, known as *Sekaten*. The origin of these celebrations was attributed to Raden Patah, the first Moslem prince of Java, who overthrew the Hindu empire of Modjopahit. Wishing to extend the faith, he decided to attract the people to the mosque through their love of *gamelan* music, and at *Sekaten* time the Holy *Gamelan* played for seven days continuously in the courtyard of the royal mosque.

The Holy *Gamelan*, which was only played during this one week, was both older and larger than any other. In fact it consisted of two complete orchestras, known as *Kyai* and *Nyai Sekati*, or 'Mr. and Mrs.', one being regarded as male and the other as his female counterpart. The gentleman was alleged to be of great age, as old as Modjopahit; the lady's age was tactfully unspecified. But both were built on the same extra large scale with huge mosque drums, three-foot-wide disc gongs and racks of bowl gongs that needed three men to play them and eight to lift them. Their wooden frames were magnificent with red and gold carving, and their hammers were made of whole buffalo horns. A crowning touch of the extraordinary was given by their weird seven-tone scale; one year we were permitted to sit with them in their kiosk and were quite bewildered as well as deafened by the holy music. Seven days before the Prophet's birthday the *gamelan* was brought out of the palace into the *Keben* square, where it played from nightfall till just before midnight, surrounded by a busy market of flowers and fruit. Betel leaves figured prominently among the wares in the baskets, for it was believed that if a woman was chewing betel at the moment the *gamelan* struck up, she would remain young and beautiful all her life. Then the orchestras moved to the mosque in time for midnight and stayed there for a week, till the midnight preceding the Birthday festival.

We watched the procession one year, waiting in the mosque courtyard. The first sign of the *Gamelan's* approach was when pots of tea were put ready in the kiosks on either side of the court. Soon after 11.30 the procession appeared, looking in the shadowy dimness like a visitation from another world. First came two great oil lampstands, then pairs of candles fluttering in holders of Venetian glass; next followed the instruments in their red and gold frames, borne by teams of crimson-shirted coolies and guarded by a sombre escort of long thin spearmen with long thin spears; royal yellow umbrellas indicated the particular holiness of the two great drums and gongs; then there were the trays and baskets of food-offerings; and at the end the musicians, trailed by vast crowds. Only the band-leader's smart mackintosh struck a jarring modern note. As they moved across the palace green, the blaring loudspeakers from the fairground fell silent. They pushed their way into the mosque yard and settled down, one in each kiosk, for their week of non-stop music.

Actually it was non-stop only in theory. Officially Mr. and Mrs. Sekati should take it in turns to keep up the music continuously throughout the seven days. But when we asked the players themselves, they revealed that trade union ideas had penetrated even the Holy *Gamelan*, and they now worked limited hours, 8 a.m. to 2 p.m., 3 to 5, and 6 till midnight—a mere fourteen-hour day. Meanwhile in the square the *Sekaten* Fair, unlike the ordinary evening bazaars, went on day and night, and the merry racket outside the mosque walls competed with the solemn reverberations within, till the *gamelans* returned to the palace in the eve of the feast.

In 1955, being the lucky year *Dal* (the fifth of the *windu* or cycle of eight years), the final service of the week was honoured by the Sultan himself. According to custom he entered the court-yard about 8 p.m. and visited each bandstand, throwing a largesse of lucky but non-current coins from the steps, before entering the triple-roofed mosque to pray. So dense were the crowds that we missed this scene; but at last we forced our way up and over the gateway steps and, thanks to a would-be-English-speaking policeman, we gained places in the front row of the mob that lined the royal exit route. On and on droned the priests through the booming microphones, and the Sultan did not emerge for over two hours. As he hastened past to his car, we saw him for the first time in Javanese dress—dark, flat turban, flowery blue jacket and brown *kain*—modest and unassuming as ever except for the splendid golden umbrella above him and the train of white-jacketed princes behind him.

On the following morning, Mohammed's birthday, took place the queerest and least Islamic ceremony of the lot, the procession of the *Gunungan* or Rice-mountains. Like the *Gamelan*, the *Gunungan* were brought from the palace to the mosque in state; but such was the vagueness of the Javanese as to time that the hour varied each year and we only once contrived to be in the right place at the right time. Our one successful foray, however, was a lucky one, for we got an unusual opportunity to study the rice-mountains at leisure and close quarters. We reached the mosque gate just as the procession was passing—a series of red-painted litters with the oddest erections of bamboo and dried vegetable products arranged in many-coloured patterns. There was only one specimen of each kind of rice-mountain, the male leading, then the female, followed by two attendants of different shapes. Six or seven big trays, covered with white cloth, brought up the rear. This was all that remained, the token observance, of the glittering parade when the Sultan rode to the mosque in state, followed by hundreds of *gunungans*. Now their only escort was a section of khaki-clad police, clearing a passage for the coolies through the surging mob. They made for a high wooden door on the right of the courtyard, and we were swept along in the press behind them; but the police held us vigorously back till the doors could be slammed in our faces.

Infected perhaps by the oriental passivity around us, we hung about, vaguely hoping to see something more. Unexpectedly our patience was rewarded when a file of white-turbanned priests pushed their way up to the gate and, in response to our smiles and gestures, beckoned us to follow them inside. We found ourselves in another courtyard, where the rice-mountains had been laid on the ground to be dismantled. Fortunately we arrived in time to see them in full fig. The male mountain was a tall and suggestive cone of bamboo framework, lined with banana leaves and decorated with a hairy covering of red chilis and long green beans; its apex was gay with duck eggs, pear-shaped lumps of fried cassava and a multi-coloured tuft of sticks of rice. The female was bowl-shaped and her wide top bristled with discs of black and white rice, each one tufted in yellow, red, black and green, with a big tuft in the middle and bow-stringed sticks drooping over the sides. The first attendant resembled the lady, except that she had stars instead of discs; but the other was a smaller one, barrel-shaped and garlanded with green leaves, whose sex I could not determine. As the decorations were pulled off, they were distributed to the privileged few present, mostly court attendants and palace families, and we ourselves were courteously presented with a disc, a star and a cassava pear.

Then the stripped frames were taken back to the *Kraton*, and we made our way home with our trophies. Our maid's old mother received them with much joy and reverence; for these holy relics bring fortune and prosperity. The peasants eagerly seek them for their ricefields and will even buy them—and I dare say the old lady sold them.

The 'hollow pomps' that Western writers described so humorously had been swept away by the tide of social revolution. It was not fitting that displays of idle splendour should challenge the general poverty in a modern democracy like Indonesia. The ancestral customs were still piously observed, but with the minimum of expense and exhibition. It is the way of the modern world.

Yet, paradoxically, the 'make-believe-royalty' of which these pomps were the expression had changed into something much stronger. The Sultan now enjoyed real instead of nominal power. Though he was the servant of the government, equivalent to a provincial governor, his hereditary status and his personal prestige made him a figure that could not be ignored—or dismissed. Thanks to him the Special Area was a privileged and progressive place where the old way of life and the new could co-exist, as they did in his own person.

A few hours before his progress to the mosque beneath the great golden umbrella, he was seen in another procession, marching down Malioboro in his shirtsleeves among the other civilian officials in an Army Day parade.

Interlude in Bali

8

DEMI-PARADISE

BALI was Java as it might have been—Java before Islam and without the Dutch. The Balinese were Hindus, the cultural descendants of Modjopahit; and a period of less than forty years in the present century saw their subjection to and liberation from the colonial yoke of Holland. These facts explained the difference between the two islands so closely related geographically and culturally; the flourishing of all the arts in unbroken tradition, the natural gaiety undimmed by Moslem puritanism, and the welcoming self-confidence that contrasted with the reserve and inferiority complex of their long-colonised cousins. Their ancestral community life had not been invaded and their religion had gone on unchanged, so that the schizophrenic stresses of the outside world had not yet affected them. Bali was still the centre of the world for them and the Balinese way of life the most natural and best; as long as they conformed, they could lead well-adjusted and happy lives.

The atmosphere, so it seemed to me, was one of innocent enjoyment of living; everything was livelier, easier, more colourful and more open than elsewhere. They were happy and busy in their religion, their work, their arts, their communal life, and they carried them on undisturbed by the cloud of tourists buzzing round and the artists and writers who settled among them. With unselfconscious pride they accepted the interest of strangers as a compliment to their civilisation, unlike the touchy Javanese, who suspected they were being treated as anthropological specimens and equated with the Papuans or the tribes of darkest Africa.

In consequence this small island has attracted the attention and affection of Western writers to a much greater degree than its larger neighbours. A number of books have made the delights of Balinese living, its natural beauty and artistic vigour, its exotic customs and fascinating beliefs, familiar to the West. Somewhere I had read about it in my university days and I had always had a dream, though I never expected to realise it, of seeing the 'Last Paradise'. Now unexpectedly I found myself within reach of this legendary isle, and at the first opportunity, the Fast vacation of 1953, we made for it. From Jogja to Surabaya, the great port and naval base of north-east Java, was a train journey of some six hours, and from there to Bali a mere hour and a half by Garuda Airways.

My dream had come true, and Bali proved to be indeed a dream-island. By this I do not mean that it was the island of my dreams (for my ideas were extremely vague), but that our visit there had a curious dream-like quality, a sense of living at a slight remove from reality, a few feet off the ground. We soon came to accept the extraordinary as natural, the surprising as only to be expected. I had been fearful of disappointment, and the conflicting opinions of our American friends (for you either fall for Bali or you don't) had prepared me for squalor and misery as well as picturesque beauty. But it was better than I had hoped; there was a magic about it that I have found only in one other island, Corfu. No doubt, as the critics noted, there was lots of dirt and the women's lives were physically laborious, a far cry from the standards of hygiene and labour-saving gadgets of the U.S.A. But it didn't seem to matter to them and certainly not to us. Who worries about such things in a dream?

Our stay of three weeks was too short and my impressions were too impractical for me to attempt a rounded picture of life in Bali. This has already been done better by others. A straightforward account of what happened to us there (for we cannot claim to have planned our doings) may perhaps convey something of the strange whirl in which the days flew past.

Even before we reached the island, at Surabaya airport, the aura of improbability began to enfold us. We were accosted by an elderly American with an amazing resemblance to President Truman, who was on a lonely trip round the world. He asserted he had the longest ticket in the world; stretched out, the tickets for his whole journey, which were joined end-to-end instead of book-fashion, extended for several yards, even though some feet had already been clipped off. He too had been a Professor in his day, but had turned to tomato-canning as a more profitable line. He reckoned he must have been a millionaire at one time and now he was spending his millions. He had allotted two nights to Bali.

The island's airport was by the seashore and we had a truck journey of thirty kilometres or so to the capital, Denpasar. The countryside in this flat area was much the same as around Jogja, ricefields and coconut palms predominating. But we at once saw a difference in the human element. The long lines of women padding along the roadside were of sturdier build than the slim Javanese, with rounder faces and more slanting eyes; many were naked from the waist up, regardless of the government decree against such innocent nudity; and they carried their loads, piled baskets or tall pitchers, on their heads, which gave them a better carriage than the bent Jogjanese. The villages, too, looked neater and more compact than the shabby straggling conglomerations of Java, as the houses were walled round in family compounds, each with a group of tiny shrines to the family gods peeping over the thatched walls from the top of bamboo poles. Denpasar had its suburban bungalows and an up-to-date hotel, but a walk through the back streets brought us straight into the other world again. Fantastic gateways of brick and carved stone in flowery whorls of dragons, giants, birds and beasts, lined the dusty village streets, full of squatting men stroking their fighting cocks, graceful women whose black locks drooped sideways from a dingy turban of Turkish towelling, low-slung pigs with backs so hollow that they looked broken, and rickety carriages—but no *betjas*, as they were considered 'inhuman'.

That evening a Balinese student of mine called and we planned an expedition for the next morning to the beach at Sanur.

We did not, of course, go to Sanur next day. First the tomato-canning professor offered us a lift in his taxi for a tour round the island, which is not large though it supports a population of nearly two millions. Next came a message from an English friend, urging us to join him at a youth camp in the hills. Luckily we could combine the tour with a visit to the camp beside the mountain lake of Bedugul. After arranging to stay with Michael next morning, we sped off with the impatient American, who was in a hurry to get back to the airline office at Denpasar, to confirm his onward passage to some new tourist highspot next day. So we whirled through the knobbly hills and winding dales, past the jigsaw of rice-terraces and the berried coffee-groves, stopping just long enough to snap a procession of white umbrellas and streamer flags or to run up the steep stairs of a hillside temple. Even our lunch at the resthouse at Kintamani, high on the rim of a vast crater that contains a great lake as well as a still-active cone, was a hasty affair, for we had lost half an hour at Singaradja on the north coast. All the roads had been closed till the President of the Republic should pass, unmolested by other traffic. The police told us politely but firmly that we must wait an hour—or two—the President's movements were not quite certain; and we raged to ourselves at this example of democratic arrogance, which would be impossible for a mere King. Luckily the President flashed by quite soon, in a cloud of motor-cyclists à la MacArthur. We got back to Denpasar about 5.30 p.m., physically exhausted and mentally blank. For all the nine hours of bumping through that rich and exotic landscape, we felt we really had seen nothing. Our Professor, however, was satisfied that he had duly done Bali and was quite upset when he found he would have to wait another whole day for a seat on the plane.

Our day was not yet over. After dinner we attended the hotel's weekly dance performance in its own *pendopo*. It was given each week by a different company from the local villages; for in Bali every self-respecting village had its own dance troupe and *gamelan.* This was not the first time we had seen Balinese dancing; on our last night in London we had watched the first night of the tour by the Dancers of Bali at the Winter Garden Theatre. There we had been dazzled and deafened and bewildered by the glitter of their costumes in the glare of the footlights and the clash of the metallophones in the enclosed auditorium, while the whole conception of Oriental dancing had been strange to us. Now we saw it in its natural surroundings, an open pavilion with dimmer lights and the soft Balinese air all round us; and in Jogja we had learnt to appreciate the grace of arm movements, the harmony of the *gamelan* and the background of Indian legend.

Nevertheless the music and dancing was a shock to us at first. We had become inured to the gentle tempo and timbre of Java and forgotten Bali's vigour. The first dance was the classic favourite, the *Legong,* one of the oldest Balinese dances, which is a pantomime representation of a story recited by the *dalang.* It was rather hard to follow, since the traditional gestures were far from obvious and the characters were acted by three small girls, one of whom danced the introduction as a servant and reappeared at the end as a bird, while the others played a king and a princess. But it was sufficient just to watch and listen. The costumes were striking enough in themselves, the scarlets and greens and yellows and purples richly painted with gold leaf, yet all harmonising, as the Balinese have a brilliant sense of colour and a flair for decoration of any sort. Wide glittering collars, a long embroidered apron and a tremendous crown of white flowers trembling and fluttering on gold wires made the costumes of Jogja seem tame by comparison. The movements, too, were far more flaunting, and if the rapid, wide-kneed steps, the swooping turns, the fluttering fan and fingers, and the eyes flashing from side to side had belonged to a mature woman, they would have been distinctly provocative. But in Bali, as in Java, dancing was essentially a religious exercise, and whereas in Jogja decorum was preserved by the extreme slowness of the girls' motions, in Bali it was the dancers' age that protected their modesty. A *Legong* dancer begins her training at the age of about eight, reaches her peak at eleven or twelve, and retires before puberty. Ni Gusti Raka, the prima ballerina of the Pliatan troupe that had had such triumphs in Europe and the U.S.A., was only ten at the time.

After the *Legong* we watched a *Kebiyar*, or sitting-dance, a new creation only dating from the 1930s. The dancer, a man in a skirt with a wide train, hopped around with extraordinary agility in a kneeling or squatting position; but the fan, the eyes dark with mascara and the fixed simper gave a hermaphrodite impression. Finally there was an episode from the *Mahabharata*, featuring Ardjuna in one of his more edifying roles. Much of his time was spent in immobile meditation, as he was seeking through *tapa* to acquire the power to defeat the demon king; the dancing was mostly done by two tempting nymphs sent by the gods to test whether he was strong enough to be their champion. He triumphed, of course, over both Beauty and the Beast.

Next morning we bumped into the hills again to Bedugul. The youth camp was an experiment of the Resident, a purposeful holiday for students of English from all over Indonesia, where the different races could get together, meet foreigners in intimate companionship and practise their English all day long. Besides Michael there were some large idealistic Americans and a gaunt eccentric Dutchman. But we hardly had time to be introduced, for we found the whole camp in a whirl, expecting a visit from the President.

The great man, in fact, arrived two minutes later. We were introduced to him as friends of the camp and, in spite of our annoyance of the previous day, we could not resist the charm of his personality. There was no doubt about his magnetism, not only as an orator but as a person, which he cultivated and exploited with a natural instinct for public relations and the democratic gesture. Taller than the average Indonesian, with a handsome open face and a charming ready smile, he was always well dressed in immaculate but not showy uniform with a baton and a black velvet 'Merdeka-cap'. He greeted us all in English, and an international sing-song followed. There were songs from

Bali and Java, the Moluccas and the Batak country; there was an Indonesian version of 'One man went to mow'; then English ballads, negro spirituals, a soundless fish-song by the Dutchman, and a sentimental Greek duet by ourselves. Finally the President himself was called on and, firmly bringing forward one of the ladies of his train, he gave a spirited rendering of 'When You and I were Seventeen'. He insisted on remaining to share the students' lunch, sitting among us and eating glutinous rice with his fingers from a banana-leaf platter.

After his departure in a flurry of photographs and autographs, we made our way round the lake to Michael's borrowed bungalow. It was made of flimsy wooden boarding that allowed the evening breezes to play piercingly down our necks in bed. We had not reckoned with the chill of tropic mountains and spent the night hunched under our single blanket, wrapped in all the clothes we had, including socks and topped by pyjamas, warmed only by the glow of a memorable day. This had culminated in a dramatic reading at the camp of a Balinese tragedy, written by Jef, the Dutchman, in Shakespearean style and Shakespearean English. Sitting in the dark hut by the moonlit lake, lit only by the sharp pallor and shadow of a pressure-lamp, we watched him spouting theatrically in an astonishing accent, waving his arms and darting from side to side as he played all the parts, even sprawling on the floor in the numerous death scenes. Stratford-on-Bali was a weird place!

The following morning in the sunlight we visited a very different scene, still romantic but Wordsworthian rather than Byronic. Captain McConnel, a retired Scots sea-dog, had settled at Bedugul eighteen years before and devoted himself to botany. Unfortunately he was away, so we could not see round the gabled Victorian villa and the conservatory where he tended his orchids. But the gravelled drive and the neat flowerbeds, the view of the lake below and the pine-clad hills beyond, and especially the smooth-mown lawn shaded by a big fir tree, made me think of a Lakeland vicarage and filled me with nostalgia for the quiet pleasures of the English landscape and afternoon tea. From this

L

oasis of sanity we plunged straight back into the fantasy of Balinese life when we found a cockfight starting in the village below, in what seemed to be the parochial hall.

It was an open-sided pavilion like a *pendopo* except that the floor was sunk three or four steps down to make an arena. All round was a line of booths for food and gambling games, for the Balinese were inveterate gamblers and recklessly entangled themselves deep in debt over betting and cards. Much of the men's time was devoted to training the cocks, which were kept in big bell-shaped cages of wicker and shamelessly pampered. We watched the two owners rousing their champions into quarrelsome mood, lunging them at each other and dosing them with pepper. Then they bound a single spur, a three-inch blade, on the left leg. But the opening pair, as in a boxing programme, were not of the first class, and proved so faint-hearted that they had to be shut up in one small cage together before they would do battle—and then one gave in very quickly and feebly. This was enough to sicken us, though on later occasions we saw some spirited bouts, a flurry of feathers and cackling and blood as the cocks shot straight up in the air to slash at each other with the murderous spurs.

In Bedugul it seemed almost impossible to avoid cockfights. The next day we went down to a lonely temple on the lake's edge for a quiet morning of painting and writing. The lake-temple was ancient and very holy, though it did not boast the elaborate stone gateways and terraces of the larger shrines. Two or three slim pagodas of weatherbeaten wood and blackened thatch reached into the sedgy water, the tallest having no less than eleven tiers of roofs. The number of roofs was the gauge of sanctity and eleven was the maximum. Soon some villagers began to drift down to the compound where we were working, and formed rings to gape at me writing and Coral painting. The art critics for some reason seemed dissatisfied with her work, shaking their heads in distress and murmuring "Not good!" At last we discovered the cause of their criticism: with artistic licence she had only portrayed nine roofs. Amid relieved smiles she added two more. "Now it is good, very good." they assured her.

Actually they had come to see a cockfight which was due to start at midday in the temple precincts; and we soon had to retire from the scene as ever-growing crowds surrounded us. Two days later the same thing happened again at the same place. Life in Bali seemed to be one long holiday.

For us too it was a day of festival. England seemed very far away and we had no radio, but we could not let Coronation Day go uncelebrated. Dinner—of a sort—and a theatre—of a sort—made our programme. Perhaps the London ceremonies were still in progress at that very time, for Central Indonesian time is seven and a half hours ahead of Greenwich. Michael had brought a bottle of Chianti and loyal toasts were duly drunk. About 9 p.m. we went off to the village hall, where the blood and feathers had given place to hissing pressure-lamps and a drooping curtain. There was to be a performance of the *Ardja* or Balinese opera. The actors and actresses were still being made up on a nearby verandah and we went across to watch. The yellow face-powder, the eyebrow black, the elaborately decorated hair, were like the preparations for a wedding. But we had not realised how long they would take. By eleven o'clock, when the show at last began, we were in no state to appreciate it. Stiff from squatting on the hard damp steps, chilled through despite blankets, choked with the fumes of smoky kitchen-stalls, headachey from the dazzle of the lamps, our receptiveness was at a minimum. The singing did not help—shrill nasal wailing from the Princess, pompous booming from the comic Prime Minister, and twittering from his stooge. We left after about an hour, dead beat. To judge by the description of the *Ardja* in Covarrubias' *Island of Bali* we can only have seen the beginning of the introduction, which lasts some three hours—after which the play proper starts. The Balinese opera, it seems, is as relentless as the shadow-plays.

Worn out, we descended to the plains and the stolid normality of the Bali Hotel. We hoped for a day of rest on our holiday, a digestive pause, a prose passage in the romance of Bali. But even our neat tiled rooms were not proof against the all-pervading air of art. As we sipped our tea a handsome young aristocrat (at least he claimed the Brahmana title of *Ida Bagus*) would appear, hawking his works, charming flowery drawings in the traditional decorative style, full of amusing figures and stylised scenery. After dinner as we sat on the terrace, old women would unpack baskets full of tempting embroidered cloths or elegant wooden statuettes. Some of the wares, especially in the stalls in the hotel corridor, were meretricious mass-produced souvenirs for the hasty tourist. But we had time to explore and bargain in the shops of Denpasar and Klungkung, and the centres of silverwork and sculpture, woodcarving and painting, basketwork and weaving. Everywhere we went, we became more and more impressed by the universal artistic sense of the Balinese. Their instinct for bold colour harmonies was brilliant; their decorative sense, whether in stone or wood, silver or paint, straw or palm-leaves, was rich and gay; their music and dancing were excitingly alive. Only the bookshops were disappointing—nothing but a few flyblown text books. But in the museum there were some ancient strings of palm-leaf sheets beautifully inscribed with elegant Sanskrit-like characters; and I was told the arts of poetry and romance still flourished with the rest.

Bali was an artist's paradise, and it was no surprise to find that several European artists had settled there. The most accessible of the foreign painters was M. le Mayeur, who lived at Sanur beach, two or three miles from Denpasar. Not only was he near but he loved company. We were strolling along the white sands, fringed on one side with tall palms and on the other with reefs of red and white coral, when we saw a low spreading bungalow screened by scarlet hibiscus bushes and sweet-smelling frangipani trees. Suddenly we came upon the painter, clad only in a pair of khaki shorts and a vast floppy sun-hat, busy on a large canvas. He waved genially to us to wait and went on with his work, being one of those lucky artists who can concentrate even when surrounded by a mob of tourists. After a while he stopped and his model, who had been seated with a parasol under a hibiscus bush, rose to welcome us. For this was Pollok, le Mayeur's wife. He himself was Belgian and had settled in Bali some twenty-odd years before. Pollok was then the most famous *Legong* dancer in the island, and she was still notably beautiful, especially as she always wore the colourful Balinese *kain* and breastcloth, woven by herself on a hand-loom, with golden ear-rings the shape and size of big corks.

They invited us into the house, which reflected le Mayeur's own personality, richly and unashamedly romantic. The shady open rooms and balconies were filled with intricately carved and gilded furniture, designed by himself and executed by local craftsmen. The walls were covered with vast canvases of flowery and sentimental scenes, filled with figures of Pollok in a variety of graceful poses. But there was comfort too and such practical amenities as a modern bathroom. Life had been good to le Mayeur—because he knew what he wanted. Though he had had difficulties with over-nationalist youths in the revolution and was inclined to be *laudator temporis acti*, he was still a happy man. A glass of spiced palmwine, a bathe in the warm lagoon and lunch alfresco at the beach's edge, served by dark-eyed, bare-shouldered nieces, completed our sense of unworldly well-being.

Le Mayeur was only one of the Western artists who had built the home of their dreams in Bali. It was interesting to compare the various aspects of romanticism, as revealed not only in their pictures but their houses. We met another in the course of a grand expedition arranged by my patient and hospitable student, I Madé Warthe. As we drove along the dusty roads, halting every now and then in some village noted for its silver or basketwork, he explained the significance of his name. Warthe was his own name; *I* was a prefix indicating a male (the feminine was *Ni*); *Madé* indicated the second-born child. In Bali they still had the Hindu caste system, though more or less obsolete in practice; but they never had a caste of Untouchables. There were eight *Radjas* and numerous other nobles, though their power and their numbers were much reduced in the Dutch conquest at the start of the present century.

It was a surprising and terrible story. The Dutch did not

bother to assert their nominal suzerainty over the Balinese chiefs, ceded to the Company by the Susuhunan of Solo, until the middle of the nineteenth century, when trouble arose over the ancient Balinese practice of looting wrecks. In 1882 the Dutch established control over the northern states and the Radjas accepted a treaty that forbade piracy, slavery and shore rights. But in 1904 the Radja of Badung refused to compensate the owners of a Chinese steamer wrecked and looted at Sanur, and after two years of bickering the Dutch finally sent a military expedition to punish the recalcitrant chief. The punitive force landed at Sanur and, after repulsing a golden-speared army from Denpasar, advanced on the town. The common people fled, but the Radja and his retainers determined to die honourably rather than yield. The palace was set on fire, while the people of the court, worked up into a state of trance-like frenzy, marched out behind their ruler for a *puputan* or suicide attack. Men, women and children, dressed in their finest clothing, with ceremonial golden umbrellas and jewelled *krisses*, surged along the road till they met the Dutch forces. Orders and pleas to halt had no effect on the entranced Balinese. The soldiers were forced to fire and fire again, as wave after wave rushed madly at their enemy. The Radja's wives stabbed themselves over his body, the wounded were finished off with the *kris*, the chief's twelve-year-old brother led a final, fatal attack. At last the *puputan* ceased, when all the Radja's army lay in ghastly heaps of blood-stained silks and jewellery. That same afternoon of 20th September 1906 another Radja, borne in a golden sedan chair and surrounded by his wives and warriors, led another *puputan*. On the Dutch side the loss was physically negligible, but morally costly; their boasted paternalism was exposed as ruthless imperialism. Yet two years later the same dreadful story was repeated when a force was sent to punish the 'insolence' of the Radja of Klungkung, the last remaining independent chief and the highest of them all. Once again a *puputan* took place and the proud Radja with his whole family was inevitably massacred. It was difficult, as we wandered among the art-shops of Klungkung, to imagine such horrors in that pleasant sunny main street. There could be nightmares as well as dreams in Bali. We drove on.

Besakih lay in the foothills of the Gunung Agung, the Great Mountain, Bali's Olympus. We toiled up a tremendous flight of steps to a towering, florid gateway that led to a succession of wide courts and terraces, a forest of many-tiered pagodas. This was the Mother-Temple of all Bali, really a complex of temples, since there was one for each of the eight Radjas. The high-piled gateways were sometimes arched, sometimes divided, but always richly encrusted with soft stone reliefs of beasts and flowers, demons and dragons. Such gateways were to be seen in Java in the ancient temples of the Hindu-Javanese age and the ruins of medieval Modjopahit; but here they still led to something living. As we stood beside the three stone thrones of the Hindu Trinity, a party of schoolchildren came along, carrying baskets of offerings and flowers. A priest was fetched and they sat down at the foot of the thrones, clasping flowers between their palms. Warthe joined them unselfconsciously, unabashed by the presence of his Western teacher. For the Balinese their religion was a natural, living part of their daily lives; indeed a basic part, a well-spring of happy self-expression. The priest soon ended his prayers, and the children, tossing their flowers forward, resumed their chattering pilgrimage.

From Besakih to Iseh, to call on the Swiss painter, Theo Meier. From his flagged terrace we overlooked a valley that made a sweeping and brilliant pattern of glittering ricefields, typically tropical. Yet the home itself had something nostalgic, something reminiscent of his native Switzerland. The palm-wine was served by a graceful bare-breasted young beauty; but this traditional nakedness seemed so natural and innocent in those surroundings that there was nothing shocking or provocative about it. In the countryside we saw plenty of bare breasts, for the Government's ban was only effective where the authorities were likely to see them. Unfortunately it was mostly the withered old hags that clung to their ancient habits unashamed, while the younger women hastily draped a breastcloth around themselves at the rumour of a tourist. For it was not only Moslem puritanism that had ruined their innocence, but Western salacity. The Americans in particular displayed such a fixation about breasts, hunting them with ready cameras and bribes, that the women could not but feel the defiling touch of pitch.

We only had time for a glance at Meier's brilliant crayon sketches before pushing on, for the picnic arranged by Warthe at Karangasem, his home town, miles further on, was already an hour overdue. His family, after waiting for hours at the seaside Water Palace below the hill of Karangasem, had given up and returned home. But with undiminished goodwill they gathered the lunch baskets and brought them down again, and at about 3.30 p.m. we sat down to an elaborate meal, including sucking pig, at the edge of the ornamental lake. The Water Palace of the Radja of Karangasem was much smaller and better kept than that of Jogja, but it was Balinese only in its fancifulness—the style might be called Mauro-Chinese baroque. Dating from the mid-nineteenth century, it was a summer kiosk standing in the centre of the lake, connected to either shore by long, narrow, coroneted footbridges. We preferred the Radja's proper palace on the hilltop, a truly Balinese labyrinth of flamboyant gateways, sculptures, pavilions and pools. Thence we sped homeward along the coast through the gathering dusk and were just in time to visit the Cave of the Bats at Kusamba. Already from the dark cleft in the seashore cliffs a sinister cloud was starting to issue, circling and twittering thinly. It was, of course, a holy place and at the entrance stood three little shrines of wood and thatch. On top of one lay coiled a large and likewise holy python. We were not sorry to leave this ominous place, as the sun's last livid rays faded from the clouds above the still sea.

That evening there was another of the weekly dance performances at the hotel. This time it was a *Djanger*. The *Djanger* was a modern dance dating only from about 1920, something of a mixture between classical and folk dancing. The dancing took place within a square formed by two rows of seated girls and two of boys, who acted as a kind of Greek chorus. The singing and movements were directed by the *dag*, or conductor, and the story once again portrayed the inevitable Ardjuna's heroic *immobilisme*, followed by victory over the enemy in the shape, this time, of a monstrous bird. But the dancing had not quite the precision and expertise of the *Legong*, particularly in the swaying chorus movements. The *Djanger* arose from the natural desire of adolescents to take part in joint activities. They formed *Djanger* clubs where they could meet together and sing, joke and swing and maybe flirt. Their training was not the strict, intensive and single-minded discipline of the little girls of the *Legong*. But the *Djanger* craze was fading, ousted by the more audacious *Djoged*, where the dancer chose partners from the audience by tapping them with her fan. The arts in Bali were not static.

It would be rash to call any place the artistic centre of Bali, where everyone seemed to be an artist. But, as far as my own experience went, I would chose Ubud. Central geographically, it was not only noted for its group of painters but surrounded by other villages that boasted artistic specialities—Pliatan, famed for its *Legong*, Bedulu of the Monkey Dance, Mas of woodcarving repute. Its chieftain, the Tjokorda Agung, was a busy and practical patron of the arts, who had turned his palace into a guest-house and so brought custom to the local painters; and on its outskirts were the houses where Walter Spies, the musician and painter, used to live and Rudolf Bonnet, another distinguished painter, still lived.

One Sunday, therefore, we set out with Warthe to visit the Tjokorda. Pliatan was on our way, so we called in on the Anak Agung Gde Mandera, headman of the village and maestro of the Balinese dance-troupe that had recently returned from their triumphant tour of the West; whose opening performance at the Winter Garden on 26th August 1952 had been our first experience of Indonesian art. The story of their training and preparations, the adaptation of their programme for Western audiences, the last-minute snags and rush in London, have been told by John Coast in his book *Dancing out of Bali*. This young Englishman, who had taken part as a volunteer in Indonesia's struggle for freedom and flew to Jogja through the Dutch blockade, conceived and carried through the idea of bringing the first company of dancers from free Indonesia as a demonstration of the people's ancient civilisation and also of their new independence. It was not the very first time that Balinese dancers had been seen in Europe. The same Anak Agung had headed a group of musicians and dancers sent to Paris in 1931. But then they went as a part of the Dutch exhibit at the Colonial Exhibition, and they were carefully segregated against possibly subversive contacts. Now they came as the cultural ambassadors of an almost unknown state and created a sensation wherever they went. Headlines and photographs, film stars and ballyhoo, greeted and glamorised the little *Legongs* as exotic Oriental princesses. We feared that we would find some rather spoilt young persons with a veneer of Americanised sophistication.

As we halted outside the ornate gate of the Anak Agung's courtyard, we noticed a pretty little village girl sitting behind a market basket of peanuts and fruit. A few minutes later, as we sat with the maestro on his verandah, we saw her again, as she came shyly forward to greet us together with two slightly older girls. This was Ni Gusti Raka, the prima ballerina whose name had glittered in big letters outside the theatres of two continents, with her fellow stars, Oka and Anom. They had returned to their island and their old way of life, slipping quietly back into their allotted roles in Balinese society, unaffected by the pretentious egotism of the West. The Anak Agung himself was the same, a stout, simple, dignified nobleman at home. The fact that his home, and especially the projecting Garuda bird facing the gateway, had been pictured in so many travel books, was not important enough for him to call attention to it. This was the Balinese way. Any show of conceit or personal display would be fiercely resented by the rest of the community. The girls' Paris dresses remained in cupboards, the Anak Agung's station-wagon stayed curtained in its shed. Only Sampih, the brilliant *Kebiyar* dancer, got above himself and rushed noisily around on his motorcycle. In February 1954 he was summoned to dance for President Sukarno at Gianjar, but he never arrived. Three days later his body was found in the Ubud river, murdered.

We pressed the girls for their impressions of Europe and the U.S.A., and they showed us their albums of photographs and press-cuttings.

"This is the Winter Garden . . . here is the Embassy in Paris . . . that is Rome," they explained with halting modesty. "Here we are in New York . . . San Francisco . . . Los Angeles . . ."

The girls giggled self-consciously as we turned the page.

"This one shows us with Bing Crosby . . . and here is Bob Hope. They were very nice. . . ."

Other famous figures of the diplomatic and artistic world were to be seen in glittering groups with our host and the little girls. We noticed a famous ballerina.

"Did you see our Western ballet?" I asked.

"Yes, at Covent Garden."

"And did you like it?"

"Well," hesitated one of the girls, as she sought for words to express her feelings, "it seemed rather like . . . a sport!"

The gymnastic leaps and pirouettes of our style were evidently considered rather crude by Balinese standards.

From Pliatan it was only a short way to Ubud and the palace of the Tjokorda, a genial hearty man who showed us round the maze of small courts that formed his home. Unlike the bare spacious courtyards of the palace at Jogja, here every corner was as full of decoration as a Balinese picture. Through little doorways under fantastical gates we stepped into gardens thick with scented flowering trees, surrounded by thatched verandahs and picturesque balconies. In one court stood a tiny raised pavilion, formerly used for the tooth-filing ceremony. In this fairyland the guests had their rooms, simple as cells, except for the rich and strange paintings that hung on the walls. We wished we had known about the *Puri* of Ubud before. As the Tjokorda showed us round, wrinkled bare-breasted old retainers greeted him with a prayerlike Hindu clasping of the hands. Rows of bell-shaped wicker cages contained the princely cocks. The household gods were honoured in a forest of shrines. Nothing was wanting to complete the true Balinese atmosphere, nothing was there to clash with it, except the guests—and even they would be dressed up on occasion. He proudly showed us a photograph of a Balinese Malcolm MacDonald.

Ubud was the original centre of the breakaway from the rigid and monotonous themes of the old paintings, suggested and encouraged by Spies and Bonnet. What we usually regard as the traditional Balinese style is in fact only some thirty years old. Ida Bagus Madé was the leading spirit now, we were told; so we plunged down winding paths between the banana trees and through rough pig-infested enclosures, till we found the painter's hut. But he was busily occupied just then with another craft, dyeing and gilding a piece of cloth for the costume of a dancer. Though named to us as the best of the younger painters, he was typical in that he was no specialist and no individualist, but a craftsman taking his natural part in the artistic activities of his community. At another hut we found a group of painters and woodworkers, three engaged on the same painting, like the school of a Renaissance artist. Bonnet and Spies encouraged the Balinese artists to assert their individuality and make experiments, so as to escape from the strait-jacket of tradition; and the Western desire for a signature led some to scribble their names on the back of their canvas. But there was still no conception of exclusive and jealous egotism. Any new invention in style or technique, like the slim elongated figures in wood, was at once appropriated and copied by all the other craftsmen. The artists were distinguished by variations of skill rather than style. It would be a pity, I think, if the idea of personal distinction should prevail; for it was this artistic communism that made Bali a place where the arts formed so natural, so vital a factor in everyone's lives. Individualism implies exclusion.

As we drove away, after lunching amid the fantasy of the Tjokorda's palace, we saw Ida Bagus Madé sitting by the roadside with his friends, devotedly fondling his fighting cock.

The last three days of our stay were even more hectic than hitherto. The whole island burst into a single, universal and continuous festival, for this was the time of *Galungan*, when the spirits of the ancestors came down for a ten-day visit to their old homes. It was the New Year of the Balinese cycle, which was only 210 days. Everywhere enormously tall bamboo flagpoles bent over the roads with long strips of woven palm-leaf mosaic or tassels hanging down like fish on a rod. All the family shrines and images were decorated with gay cloths and piled with multi-coloured offerings of food. Everyone was dressed in new clothes, like the Javanese at *Lebaran*; only the colours here were brilliant reds and greens, orange and lemon, purple and gold, instead of solemn brown. We called on all our acquaintances, the Anak Agung at Pliatan, the woodcarvers at Mas, the Tjokorda at Ubud, admiring and felicitating.

We saw only one temple that day that was not decorated, the Monkey Temple at Sangeh. As soon as we arrived at the sacred forest, hordes of monkeys, small, grey and elderly-looking, poured down from the tall dark trees to demand tribute. They were bold and importunate, pulling at Coral's skirt and climbing all over the car, twisting the door handles and scrabbling at the windows. But they respected the peanut-sellers and seemed to have an arrangement with them, for they did not snatch at the little paper bags till they had been sold to the tourists. One of the hawkers led us up a dark and sinister avenue in the forest to the temple itself, which stood lonely and moss-grown in a neglected clearing. It looked as though it was left to the monkeys to look after it, for there were no offerings to be seen. They obviously took more interest in demanding offerings for themselves, and we only met one near the temple. He was a larger and more dignified specimen, whom our guide greeted as their King, the modern representative of Hanoman, who led the simian army in the *Ramayana*.

Back at Ubud, we lunched on the porch of an empty bungalow, above the gorge where two rivers met noisily below an ancient black-thatched temple. The view might have been composed by an artist—and in a way it was. For this had been the home of Walter Spies, the German artist known to the West as the 'discoverer' of Bali and in Bali itself as a friend of all their arts. Interned in Russia in the First World War, he used the time to study Tartar music; and the chaos of post-war Europe made him head further East. He spent some years at the Sultan's court at Jogja, having been called to organise a Western orchestra. Here he studied the *gamelan*; and when he visited Bali, he realised that he had found what he wanted and settled there for the rest of his life. His example and influence revivified Balinese painting; his choreography created the *Ketjak* or Monkey Dance; his volume on *Dance and Drama in Bali*, in collaboration with Beryl de Zoete, revealed these arts to the West. Unfortunately he died in the Second World War, when the ship evacuating him from his beloved island before the Japanese onslaught was torpedoed.

We drank coffee with Bonnet on his terrace a little higher up the bank of the gorge and were allowed into his locked studio, where his paintings and sketches impressed us by their strength and severity. But he seemed more anxious to interest us in the works of the Balinese painters than his own and took us down to another hut, where he was collecting a selection of pictures for an exhibition. Several displayed great originality of theme or treatment, though always within a recognisably Balinese pattern and style. The colours were more violent than the popular pastel shades and the subjects were bolder too, mysterious submarine scenes or symbolic cosmologies or fiery visions. Personally, I preferred the simpler, decorative scenes of Bali life or legend, which would remind me of the sunlit dream-world without the disturbing mysteries beneath the surface. But it was a healthy sign that the artists were not content to be bound to a new tradition, as they had been for so long to the old.

As we returned to Denpasar, we found the celebrations growing and all the temples busy. Everywhere the women were filing along the side of the road, balancing colourful and miraculously built-up offerings on their heads. At Kesiman, a mile or two out-side the capital, we met the full flood converging on the temple. Whole platoons of dark-eyed beauties came marching down the street, erect and graceful under their towering loads. The sym-phony of their bare brown shoulders, canary-yellow breast-cloths and orange waistbands, was striking and satisfying. But our eyes were riveted to the dishes on their heads. The narrow pyramids of fruits and sweets, green and yellow and pink, cemented with rice, were nearly as tall as the girls themselves—in fact one was actually taller, well over five feet. The temple gate was of the usual pattern, steps on either side leading to a low, narrow arch-way under a tremendous superstructure of stone, so that nego-tiating the entrance demanded the highest skill and equilibrium. Some of the Choephorae had to kneel and squirm forward in order to pass through.

We visited Kesiman again next day, twice. Once more, as evening approached, the ways to the temple were filled with chanting processions bringing their high-piled offerings; some-times a white or gilded purple umbrella accompanied some specially holy item; and then we saw the *Barong*. This was the mythical monster that protected the Balinese from the ghastly witch Rangda, the spirit of Evil (literally the Widow!), whose popping eyes and lolling tongue were paradoxically a favourite motif in their sculptures and silverwork and masks. The *Barong* could not be called a handsome beast, but it had the genial ferocity of a pantomime horse, which it resembled, being manipulated by two men inside; only it was much shaggier, wilder and more fan-tastic. During the period of *Galungan* all the *Barongs* would gambol about the streets of their villages, followed by music and umbrellas of state, merrily dancing around, chasing the children and generally enjoying themselves. Inside the precincts the offerings were still flowing in for the delectation of the visiting ancestors, received by the priests in front of a grotto where a stone dragon crouched darkly. But the scene took on an eerie and sinister atmosphere after dark, when we returned about 10 p.m. Now in the torchlit dimness of the temple courtyard we found a slow, monotonous dance taking place; a circle of elderly women swayed slowly round in the middle, making awkward and unco-ordinated movements, carrying smoking braziers and chanting drearily. We did not know what dance it was, but the hypnotic effect of the swaying and smoke and singing began to tell upon Coral and we soon left. Later we learnt that this was the *Mendet*, a true temple dance during which the priest or other mediums fall into a trance and become possessed of different spirits. On our way home we came upon some giant puppets, standing about ten feet high and entertaining a street-corner crowd with what appeared to be a riotous comedy.

The next day was our last in Bali. In the morning we went down to Sanur to say good-bye to le Mayeur and Pollok, bathe in the coral-ringed lagoon and enjoy their unfailing hospitality under the shade of the frangipanis. For the afternoon a special performance of the *Legong* had been arranged for us by an archaeologist, South African by nationality but Bohemian by nature, who evidently found the modern Bali as fascinating as the ancient. Command performances were not at all ruinous if the expenses were shared, and he declared that we should not leave without seeing the most brilliant dancer in Bali, a thirteen-year-old girl in the remote village of Saba. So much off the beaten track was this hamlet that we lost our way among the ricefields and arrived an hour late, about 5 p.m. Our friends, who had been waiting impatiently with their colour-films and cine-cameras, were not pleased; but for us the fading light and a flaring sunset behind the silhouetted palms added the last touch of magic to a scene straight out of fairyland. We sat in a little thatched pavilion in the village courtyard with the *gamelan* players seated on the ground on either side of the dusty dancing space. Every village had its *gamelan*, highly ornate, higher and narrower than the Javanese type; the players were peasants all day and musicians only in their spare time, unlike the professional orchestras of the courts of Java. Yet the standard was professional enough, and at Saba both music and dancing were a crowning delight. The dancer was everything that had been promised. Her solo as the

The Shiva temple at
Prambanan

Reliefs at Prambanan

Terrace wall at Prambanan

Two little princesses in
old-style court dress

Sorting tea, Central Java

attendant in the *Legong* was a masterpiece of beauty, grace and tirelessness in a series of sensationally rapid gyrations, arms, fingers, body, feet, head and eyes all moving in their different ways with perfectly co-ordinated precision. At last the brilliant, beautiful, glittering artiste ended her triumphant performance—and a few minutes later a simple village girl emerged from the changing-hut and ran shyly off to join her playmates. It was all part of the village's daily life.

Still marvelling, we were swept off by our archaeologist straight into goblinland. Not far away, in his home village of Bedulu, there was to be a Monkey Dance. In the growing darkness we were led onto the brow of a steep bank above what seemed to be temple precincts. We balanced on rough bamboo benches and gazed down into the dim courtyard, which was lit by a single branching torch of coconut lamps. The light flickered on the glistening arms and shoulders of a hundred and fifty shadowy brown figures, sitting in close-packed circles about the lamp, clad only in loin-cloths. There was no orchestra, no instruments, only the chanting of the men as they swayed rhythmically from side to side. Gradually the tempo increased, the excitement mounted, the singing changed to wild monkey-like chattering, then a sudden shout and three hundred arms shot up with fingers outstretched, etching an unforgettable pattern against the primitive light. From their chattering *tjak-tjak-tjak* comes the name of the dance, *Ketjak*. Now and then a sinister, shadowy figure would leap into the middle of the circle and do a grotesque apelike dance or duel with another intruder. At last the chattering sank to a mutter, the swaying ceased, and in eerie silence and darkness the dance ended.

For us the dream was over; but it had lasted to the end. The enchantment never failed; we were never brought down to earth. Luck was with us all the time, enabling us to see so much in those few days without strain or indeed initiative. True, there were plenty of other strange and fascinating things we had not seen, the famous funerals or the mysterious *kris*-dance, for instance.

M

But we were satisfied, overwhelmed with the impression of an idyllic land of primeval poetry and happiness—not, as some have called it, a 'living museum', but rather, in the words of Pandit Nehru, 'a people and country as it was in the morning of the world'.

Part Two

OUT AND ABOUT

9

LANDSCAPE AND LEGEND

Our landscape was dominated by Gunung Merapi, the Mountain of Fire, one of the world's most dangerous volcanoes. From our garden we could see its plumed cone and from the open campus there was an uninterrupted view of both Merapi and its humpbacked fellow, Merbabu—if the day was clear. Except at dawn and dusk, though, the mountain was normally veiled in clouds and haze and one could not tell that it was more than a low ridge, unless, astonishingly, the peak appeared above the mists, floating in the sky, far higher than expected. It stood some seventeen miles north of the city, its steep triangle almost banally picturesque, the subject of endless obvious paintings and photographs. Its height was variable, as rocks and lava piled up in or were ejected from the crater; 9,700 feet in 1925, down to 9,500 in 1950, up again to 9,800 in 1953. The plug was well above the crater's rim when suddenly on 18th January 1954 Merapi breathed forth death and destruction. But there was no sensational display of fire or darkness, and in Jogja we knew nothing about it till we read the papers next day. For a week or two the weather was more than usually oppressive and overcast, but no flames or glowing lava streams were seen by anyone but a rather excitable German professor. It was almost disappointing to have to answer anxious friends at home that we had not even noticed the eruption.

But the other side of the mountain was more seriously affected. Actually it was not a true eruption but an avalanche of red-hot lava rocks, giving off clouds of suffocating gases, which descended on a mountain village and claimed forty-four victims. A lava flow followed, devastating a large area of fields and houses; but by then the people had been evacuated and the problem was one of relief rather than of rescue for the fifty thousand refugees. Merapi quietened down, but it still remained dangerous, as the vast cap had not blown off and the explosive pressure was unrelieved. Eighteen months later a Canadian geologist climbed up to the rim and reported that avalanches were still continuing, forty or fifty small falls a day; indeed, he and his party only just passed the screes in time before some glowing rocks rushed down past them. And then, on 3rd January 1956, the volcano burst into activity once more, just two years after its last effort. At 5.30 a.m., the rumbling and shuddering woke those staying at Kaliurang, the hill resort at Merapi's foot. The trouble was again on the far side of the crest and George, the Canadian, set out to investigate. He could not reach the higher observation posts; the streams were boiling and a rain of ash fell all day in Magelang, so that his jeep came back with a pall of grey dust. But once again we knew nothing in Jogja till we met the Sultan at a reception that evening. He had already visited the scene and arranged the evacuation of five thousand peasants from the danger zones. This time there were no fatalities and the refugee problem was less acute, since most of those evacuated in 1954 had never gone back. After a few days Merapi subsided again. But the frequency of its cycle, which had been five to seven years since the last major eruption of 1930 (which cost over 3,500 lives) was ominously increasing.

Merapi was only one of the hundreds of volcanoes in Indonesia, and although it was distinguished for its constant activity, it was by no means the most violent. Altogether there were some four hundred in the whole country, nearly a quarter still active; and Java had more than its share of these. The whole backbone of the island was a chain of volcanoes, rising abruptly from the plains, with mountain masses at the east and west ends. The tallest was Smeru in East Java, 12,000 feet high; but height was no criterion of violence and one of the most dangerous was its neighbour, Kelud, less than half its height. The most notorious was Krakatau, a mere 2,667 feet. This island in the Sunda Straits between Java and Sumatra exploded entire in 1883. A tidal wave swept away forty thousand people on the neighbouring shores, and all over the world the atmosphere was so filled with ashes as to cause weeks of amazing sunsets.

But danger is nature's price for her favours. The rich volcanic soil, and the changeless equatorial warmth made these islands immensely fertile, bearing crops all the year round and twice or even thrice a year in places. Rice was the staple and sometimes in adjoining fields we would see the crops in quite different stages of growth, seedlings and growing stalks, dry fields and waving golden grain that looked like our own cornfields. In a country that straddled the Equator, where the days were all of the same length and there was no winter nor spring nor autumn, times and seasons did not seem to matter much. Even the grand distinction between the dry and rainy seasons was not absolute. It varied according to the area; but rain might fall at any time and a sunless day was a phenomenon. In the rainy season the early hours were generally bright and fresh, but the atmosphere grew more and more oppressive till the storm burst about tea-time. In the dry the southern coast was made more temperate by winter breezes from Australia, so that from May to October we enjoyed a kind of paradoxical summer despite the hemisphere. But whatever the weather, the waters never failed and the greenness never faded.

The cycle of the rice started with the ploughing of the rice-terraces. Meanwhile the seeds had been planted in special seed-beds, where they grew for about four months, making patches of brilliant green. When all was ready for the transplanting, it was time for the offering to Dewi Sri, goddess of the rice. The rice-shoots were taken out of the seedbeds and tied in bundles, and the planting took place next morning after the offering. For this the peasant needed many workers; but he found no difficulty in obtaining help, however poor he might be, for the Javanese were proud of their tradition of *gotong-royong*, communal co-operation, mutual and unpaid. The workers got their food and sometimes a little money, but it was a gift, not payment. The heavy work with plough and mattock was done by the men, but the planting was women's work; and the long lines of bending backs and pointed coolie hats were one of the most familiar sights of the countryside. After a month or two came the harvest, again carried out by the women, who cut each stalk separately with a primitive cross-set knife. The stout golden bundles of rice-ears were carried home on yokes by the men and laid on the roadside to dry. Next the women had to husk the grain, pounding it rhythmically in a stout wooden mortar with a thick bouncing pole, then sift away the chaff by tossing it in a wide shallow tray.

All these processes were carried on in the ancestral way that has prevailed for hundreds, perhaps thousands, of years, and with much the same instruments—we often saw ploughs with wooden blades. The wet system of rice cultivation is certainly very ancient, for all the hydraulic ingenuity shown by the terraces with their ever-flowing streamlets trickling through the mud banks. Whether it was introduced, like so much of Indonesia's civilisation, by the Hindus, or dates from earlier times, is not proven; but patriots claimed that none of the words for the several stages of the rice (*padi* in the fields, *beras* when husked, *nasi* when cooked, and so on) were of Sanskrit origin. The Japanese during their occupation introduced improved methods of planting and stocked the flooded fields with fish; but after they left, the peasants soon reverted to their age-old ways. It will need much persuasion and education by the experts of the government and the agricultural faculties to induce modernisation.

Flying over Java one saw an endless pattern of flooded fields of all shapes and sizes, like the fragments of a gigantic broken mirror; in between stood clumps of palms like little islands; every hillside, every wood showed the hand of man. For those who wish to see wild nature, jungle untouched and beasts untamed, Java is not the place. It is far too thickly populated and assiduously cultivated to leave room for real jungle and most of the wild animals have been crowded out. Yet except where there were towns, it was difficult to discern any human habitation. The peasants' huts nestled beneath the tall palms and bamboos and each clump was a hamlet. Forty-eight or fifty millions (nobody knew the true figure, which was believed to be rising by perhaps a million a year) were packed into this one island: nearly 70 per cent of Indonesia's total population in 7 per cent of its total land-area.

It was rare, as we drove dustily through the countryside, to find the landscape empty of human beings, even at night. Here and there a dark hillside wood survived as a refuge for the monkeys or a salty marsh made a hunting-ground for the wild pig. But the mighty virgin forests of our imagination, with their tigers and elephants, rhinoceros and orang-utans, belonged to Sumatra or Borneo. The typical animal of Java was the water-buffalo. These stout grey cattle with moon-shaped horns and big flapping ears could be seen everywhere, patiently plodding through the muddy water pulling the ploughs, their dingy hides caked with brown flakes that protected them from the sun and insects. When not at work, they would wallow in the canals with only their foolish faces above the surface; and in the evenings we met them lumbering home to the village, ridden by two or three ridiculously inadequate little boys.

Near the hamlets we often noticed smaller islands amid the lake of rice-fields, with groups of twisted trees and mossy stones. These were holy places. The sculptural white limbs of frangipani trees indicated a burial place, the haunt of the spirits of the rude forefathers; a many-cabled banyan or a rough cairn might be the dwelling of the village's guardian spirit. Javanese animism, strongest among the peasantry, filled earth and air and water, trees and rocks, with spiritual forces, and these immaterial inhabitants demanded just as much attention as the living. Some were represented by living creatures; notably the *ular sawah* or snake of the ricefields, which was connected with the most important of all the rural spirits, Dewi Sri. In a country where rice was the universal and almost invariable diet, the legend of Dewi Sri was known to all.

She was the daughter of the King of Mendang Kamulan, a

semi-mythical kingdom that may correspond to Old Mataram. The old King wished to retire and called on his son, Sadono, to take over the succession. Unfortunately the prince also preferred retirement to worldly power and begged to be excused, as he wished to become a hermit. The autocratic father finally lost his temper and cursed his disobedient son.

"Very well, then, if you want to lead a free unworldly life, go! Not as a man, though, but as a little bird!"

Dewi Sri ran in just in time to see a *glatik* bird fly hurriedly out of the room. Her pleas for her brother only incensed the old King more and when she said she would follow him, he burst out:

"Follow your wretched brother then, if you want. But you shall crawl as a snake!"

Next morning a local peasant found a strange serpent in his ricefield. As he took up his sickle to kill it, the snake spoke, telling him who she was and promising him a rich harvest if he did her no harm. Hastily he brought her offerings of flowers and incense; and he was rewarded with a greater harvest than ever before, as the snake protected the crops against rats and other marauders.

According to some it was the prince who was turned into the serpent, while his sister was changed into the rice itself. But whatever the story might be, the peasants venerated the *ular sawah* as the protector of the rice crop and would not disturb it; nor would they trap the little blue-grey *glatiks*. And before the planting they never failed to make offerings to Dewi Sri.

Dewi Sri was a gentle and generous goddess. But outside her damp and fertile realm, in the ancient limestone quarries and the barren Thousand Hills and the raging waves of the South Sea we found fiercer spirits ruling and wilder customs.

The village of Gunung Gamping, or Chalk Hill, was only a mile or two west of Jogja, but we had never noticed a hill there— for the good reason that it no longer existed. A chance remark by our maid's mother about some odd ceremony called *Saparan*, which was held there, set us on its track. The old lady was our best source for local lore, but just what was due to happen and when (her calculations involved the permutations and combinations of Javanese and Western months, five-day and seven-day weeks, and all her fingers) was far from clear. A reconnaissance revealed that the so-called mountain was nothing but a tall limestone rock, undercut on one side, that reminded me of the Bowder Stone in Borrowdale. Nearby were some shallow chalkpits, filled with yellow water, in which a few workers were levering at the walls with crowbars or stooping chin-deep to heave out the loosened lumps. But there really had been a mountain once. George's geological enquiries unearthed an old drawing that showed Gunung Gamping as a ridge hundreds of feet high and a mile or more long, while in place of the shallow overhang that we saw there had been an enormous cave. This whole hill had simply been mined away and, but for the barbed-wire fence that now ringed the last rock, not a trace would remain today.

We found out that the ceremony of *Saparan* would take place four days later, on the 15th of the month *Sapar*, at an hour that seemed far from definite. Arriving at 9 a.m. we found ourselves with an hour to spare before the procession was to start out. At the quarry manager's house there were all the usual signs of a big *selamatan*, the temporary pavilion, the serried chairs, the matting stage and a full *gamelan*, already strumming quietly. What was unusual was the row of three miniature litters standing on tables at one side. They were like small cages with horned green roofs and wire-netted sides, decorated at the corners with sugar cane shoots and palm leaves. The first only held offerings, but the second and third each contained two dolls, moulded out of starchy rice flour and seated in wooden stools. Their heads were painted to represent a man's turban and a woman's hair; their yellow faces and necklaces of *melati* marked them for bride and groom; their necks were noticeably long and exposed.

At 10 o'clock the procession started out for the 'Mountain'. First went the bridal litters borne on long bamboo poles; a straggling group of *Djatilan* maskers and six black hobby-horses accompanied their progress with the monotonous beat of gongs and drums. These were not professional trance-dancers but some of the quarry-workers, putting on a special show for the lucky year *Dal*. Their amateurish costume and mild, shy bearing made them comic and pathetic rather than wild or mysterious. At the rock we were privileged to enter the enclosure under the wing of the Sultan's representative and first cousin, KRT Yudoku-sumo, director of the area tax office. He spoke excellent English and varied his explanations of the rites of *Saparan* with reminiscences of his student days in Sutton, Surrey. A pair of the dolls was placed under the overhanging rock, side by side, flanked by symbolic wedding coconuts. An old worker mumbled a short speech, then drew a large knife and ceremoniously cut off the dolls' heads. As he tipped them onto their backs, a symbolic libation of syrup trickled horribly from the bamboo stem in their neck. The decapitated dolls were replaced in their litter and the procession moved on through the fields to a deep chalkpit about a mile away. There the same sacrificial rites were performed on the other couple of dolls. Then the litters with their grimly suggestive loads and their gay escort of maskers made their way back to the factory courtyard, full of limestone blocks and holiday stalls.

As we sat under the thatched awning, watching the *Bondan* dance, Mr. Yudokusumo explained the significance of these sinister rites. In the old days the quarry-workers actually made human sacrifices to propitiate the spirit of the mountain and save themselves from accidents. The chosen victims, man and girl, were ceremoniously married first, then borne in procession to the cave, where their throats were cut and their blood poured on the ground. The modern symbolic version lasts three days with all the paraphernalia of a wedding; on the first, in place of the bathing, they make the dolls; on the second, instead of shaving, they paint the heads; on the third comes a mock wedding service before the sacrificial procession. Some years ago, he said, the workers used to make eight pairs of dolls, one for each of the pits being worked. Did they do the same, I wondered with a shudder, when the victims were real men and women?

There was no misnomer about the Thousand Hills, which formed part of the rough plateau known as the Gunung Kidul, or Southern Mountains. This range lay along the coast of the two principalities and its inhabitants lived a poor, isolated and primitive life. But the hillmen were proud, for all their poverty, and they claimed to be descended from the refugees of Modjopahit, who retreated after the empire's fall into what was then impenetrable forest. Now, however, the trees had gone and erosion of the soil was rampant, so that it was one of the poorest districts of Java with starvation as an ever-present menace. Under-nourishment was common enough throughout the country, but that was partly a question of diet; actual starvation, where nature was normally so profuse, was a rare phenomenon.

We saw this for ourselves when we visited a German doctor at Wonosari, the capital of the Gunung Kidul. He was the only doctor in the whole area with a population that was rapidly approaching half a million. Most of the town's public buildings had been burnt down in the clashes and remained as gaunt and blackened ruins. The government had given priority to the public health programme and built a new hospital. There was nothing very splendid about the bare bungaloid wards and tiny operation room, but at least it was clean and hygienic—and there. Even so the doctor had to use the wicker huts of the former 'hospital' for isolation wards, where skeleton-like figures with limbs lividly swollen from hunger oedema or wasted with syphilis lay apathetically on bare bamboo couches. There were some yaws cases with distorted knees, but this former scourge had been much diminished by a special campaign of the World Health Organisation. The doctor's chief worry was an aged woman on the brink of death. It was not her dying that troubled him, but her dying there, in his hospital. The people did not fear death but they liked to die in their homes, and the relatives removed them when the end was near. If he kept her and she then died, the relatives would be angry. He gave her an intravenous injection and risked it.

After his round the doctor threw off his cares and took us in his truck to the coast. It had to be a truck, the going was so rough. The region known as the Thousand Hills, endless conical hillocks of blackened pitted coral with a thin topsoil terraced for cassava and maize, was like a landscape of the moon. Indeed it was said to be really the sea-bed, heaved up in some cataclysmic eruption of pre-history. The rains of January had given the hills a sparse greenness; but, now the forests had been cut down, there was hardly any water and all would be brown and parched in the dry weather. A few trees marked the grotto where the only unfailing spring rose, but the stream soon sank underground. Miles further on, in the cove of Baron, the subterranean river emerged from a cave to form a romantic tree-shaded pool amid the sands. Outside the waves roared with a note like the thunder of distant cannon, but here between two headlands there was peace and beauty. Or there would have been, if the sands had not been thick with the droppings of cattle, brought from near and far to this, the only watering place for miles. Even so, in the dry season the peasants had to sell their cattle for sheer lack of water.

As we returned through the moonscape towards dusk, we noticed on each hilltop a silhouetted figure, lonely but proud, like a King of the Castle.

"They are watchers," the doctor told us, "to guard their precious crops against wild pig. They spend all night in those little palm-thatched shelters among the maize, banging bamboo sticks to scare the raiders away. I once shot a large boar, and the poor devils were so hungry that, Islam notwithstanding, they'd stripped it clean before I could even get there across a ravine."

"Do you have tigers here?" I asked.

"Plenty in the remaining wooded parts, but they're panthers really. They aren't man-eaters, so there's a truce between them and the peasants. Only once recently a panther carried off a child that was watching by night in a lonely shelter; so the villagers tracked down and killed that particular beast but no others."

"What about these stories of head-hunters?"

"Well, they do hunt heads in a way—but not those of the

living. If someone dies on a specially auspicious day, when, say, Friday-*Kliwon* falls on the first of a Javanese month, their skulls are considered lucky and wealth-bringing. So the family has to guard the grave against robbers, day and night for ten weeks or so. There was a case two or three years ago, and though the blame was officially put on a tiger, the family are still searching for the skull."

In that barren and savage countryside such tales seemed well suited to the spirit of the place. We were relieved, when we got back to Wonosari, to find that the old woman in the hospital had revived and escaped death away from home.

Below the plateau's western corner, where the cliffs turned inland, lay the beach of Parang Tritis, our only seaside resort. Despite the long coastline of southern Java there was practically no access to the sea. The roads ran parallel with the shore at some distance inland, for there were no fishing villages. The tremendous waves, crashing in endless succession on the steep sands, made it impracticable for fishing boats to venture out in most parts; indeed there was only one small port, far away to the west, in the whole length of the south coast. We once drove for miles, making vain sallies along tracks that petered out amid the marshes, before we finally got within striking distance of the sea. We still had to plod through hundreds of yards of blistering dunes and even then we could not plunge joyfully in to cool ourselves. The pounding waves roared up the sandbank and sucked back so greedily that we could only lie at the edge and cling to the sands for dear life. Battered, scarlet with sunburn, and plastered with gritty black shingle, we hopped back to the distant shade and vowed never to go exploring again.

There was a great contrast between the muddy, sluggish Java Sea on the north coast and the wild, clean and lonely depths of the South Sea. The shallow isle-enclosed northern waters are part of a sunken continent, but on the south side the continental shelf drops sharply into the vast stretch of the Indian Ocean, with nothing between Java and the South Pole. No wonder this stormy, awe-inspiring scene was the source of mythological inspiration, of the legend of the Queen of the South Sea.

There were many legends about this goddess. All agreed that she was the daughter of a King of Padjadjaran in West Java. Dewi Kadito was so beautiful that she was called the Princess of the Sun. The stories diverged over the cause of her leaving her father's court. Some said she refused to marry because her only desire was to rule as a Queen; others, because no suitor was the man of her dreams. But most attributed her exile to a wicked stepmother, who, jealous of her beauty or of the king's love for her, contrived to give the princess a horrible disease. In one tale she poisoned her step-daughter's bathwater so that all her skin erupted into dreadful incurable sores. In another version the king's second wife called in a revengeful witch to act as maid to the Queen and her daughter. The witch handed them enchanted garments that infected them with leprosy, which meant their banishment to the forests. At any rate Dewi Kadito fled from the palace, for she could not bear to show her ravaged face to her fellow-men. The legends joined again in relating how she wandered through the wilds till she came one day to the shores of the South Sea. As she sat there, exhausted and despairing, she fell into a trance and seemed to hear a voice calling to her from amid the roar of the moonlit waves:

"Come to me, come to the depths of the sea. Here you shall find your beauty again, here you shall find the man of your dreams, here you shall be a mighty Queen, ruling for ever in the spray clouds and rainbows and the deep green palaces of the ocean."

She rose and followed the mystic voice into the wild seas and was soon swallowed by the waves. Her body was never found, and from that day the Javanese believed that she lived on as Nyai Loro Kidul, the Lady of the South Sea.

She seemed to be a temperamental and thoroughly feminine goddess. We were warned, for instance, that we must never wear green when bathing at Parang Tritis, as the Queen disliked the colour and would certainly drown us. She also had to be appeased

Javanese dancer

Street market in Bali

at each visit with the offering of a coconut, and the small boys of the village did a thriving trade in supplying these to be cast into the waves. But there were worse difficulties than these about a bathe in the sea. The beach lay beyond a broad river with a temporary bridge that was washed away every wet season. Only in the dry weather, when the river was low, could one reach Parang Tritis by car. The villagers built up a wide sandbank as a barrier to divert the stream to either side, leaving a broad dry stretch in the middle, which was then connected to the banks by two short plank bridges. Though no further from us than Kaliurang, the sea was much less accessible than the hills.

We used to go early in the morning when there was still some shadow from the cliffs of the Southern Mountains and the sands were not yet burning. But even here, after all due precautions, it was unwise to venture too far into the Queen's embrace, as the great walls of water easily swept one off one's feet and the tug of the backwash was dangerously strong. By midday the shallow caves scarcely kept out the sun and we would head for home, exhilarated but exhausted. The best time of all, we were told, was a moonlight night; but the only time we tried it was a disappointment.

Our objective was not romance *per se*, but a Chinese water festival. All over the world on the fifth day of the fifth month of their lunar calendar the Chinese flock down to the water to commemorate the death of Chü Yuan, the patriot and poet who drowned himself in the river Mi-Lo in 278 B.C. in despair at the corruption that had ruined his country. Originally the *Peh Tjun* festival was held on a river and the race of dragon-boats symbolised the rescue party that searched for the poet's body. But any water will do now, sea, lake, or even swimming-pool, and in Java Parang Tritis was a favourite resort for the holidaymakers. There could be no boat-races among those waves, but the Chinese would spend the night on the beach, feasting and bathing, letting off rockets and making torchlight processions. As the festival fell on Midsummer Night one year, we hoped for something magical.

N

We drove down to the river crossing in the late afternoon, to find the ford flooded two feet deep by unseasonable rains. Nothing daunted, we left the car and waded across, trusting to find transport on the far side. Bicycles were at a premium, but luckily we found a niche in the back of a truckful of Chinese—luckily, because as we set out, black clouds rolled up and the road soon became a morass. We reached the line of shacks that made the village at dusk in a downpour. When at last it sank to a drizzle, we ventured to the corner facing the sea. There amid all the merrymaking three old women still remembered Chü Yuan; behind a little table loaded with offerings and censers, flaming candles and sweet-scented joss-sticks, one knelt with a book while the others intoned prayers. All round them their compatriots surged loudly and gaily, clad in shorts, pyjamas or bikinis; an ancient radiogram blared or murmured according to the fluctuations of an ancient generator; huge family groups sat in the huts gorging on pork and strange confections of black and pink jelly. Some boys and girls braved the drizzle and dark to bathe and a few rockets sizzled feebly into the pitchy sky. Then the rain quickened again.

We thought of our dry, quiet beds and sought out the truck. For a price the driver agreed to take us back early and we plunged and skidded through the mudpatches, scraping bogged motorcycles and tangling with another car's bumper. At last we reached the river and paddled thankfully back to our own car. *Peh Tjun* had proved too much of a water festival for us.

Perhaps the Queen of the South Sea was offended by this Chinese invasion of her realm. For Parang Tritis was particularly connected with her cult in its most exalted and intimate form; here she received gifts from her royal husbands. As the bride of both the Sunan and the Sultan she had the right to be proud.

The connection began with the greatest and most venerated of the princes' ancestors, Sultan Agung, the Great Emperor of the early seventeenth century. One day he met an enchantingly beautiful woman who invited him to follow her to her palace.

Being only human, he did so, and she asked him to share her kingdom and her love. She danced for him in a wonderful wedding dress. But after two days he remembered his own kingdom and people and resolved that he must return to them. Hushing her to sleep with a love-song, he stole out of her palace, and in a moment he found himself back in his own. Ever since then the Sunans of Surakarta had considered Nyai Loro Kidul as their bride, who would visit each new monarch for two days at his coronation and receive regular presents from him. When the Sunan's empire was split in 1755, the newly created Sultan of Jogja claimed and set up all the same sacred rights and customs for himself, including marriage with the South Sea. Though the Queen did not visit him in his *Kraton*, reserving this honour for her first line of husbands, she was quite ready to accept the Sultan's attentions and presents—which were regularly provided for her to this day.

We had heard tales about offerings of clothes to the South Sea, but we were in serious doubt about the custom's continuance till we actually saw the ceremony ourselves. As with the *Saparan*, so with the *Labuhan*; only in our fourth year did we learn of this fascinating annual occasion, and again we were the only Westerners—indeed the only outsiders—present. The *Labuhan* procession took place on the morning after the Sultan's birthday. The starting point was the village of Kretek at the crossing of the river, three miles from the beach. At the headman's office we found some palace officials in blue-black jackets, embroidered belts and glittering *krisses*, checking and packing the packages of gifts. The Queen's list contained thirty-one items; but there were other addresses too. A car was setting out for the holy mountains Merapi and Lawu, loaded with three officials, several boxes and a royal yellow umbrella. I could hardly believe that the elderly gentleman in charge would really climb to the top of the volcano, but I was assured this was so. Maybe it was too— shortly afterwards I heard that he had died.

Meanwhile the Queen's trousseau was loaded into a triangular wicker litter, borne by four coolies and shaded by a golden umbrella of state. We set out in procession for the beach, but first we had to cross the river in rafts, since this was December and the rains had swept away the bridge. By the time our raft reached the far bank, the procession was well ahead, padding with amazing, tireless swiftness along the dusty track. Our party, three male and two female, did not relish the prospect of a three-mile run in that heat, so we hired three bicycles. The tiny Mrs. Kusumobroto perched with aristocratic ease and elegance on one carrier, but poor Coral found balancing on the bare bars in such bumpy going no joke. However, this means of transport enabled us to keep up, and about 10 a.m. we reached Parang Tritis and sank gratefully onto the strewn mats of an open hut, where the litter had been laid down.

After a tea-break, the unpacking began. Two wooden boxes were filled with a set of brand-new woman's clothing of special and unusual design, a *kain batik* and numerous breastcloths of dark blue, red and white, red and yellow, a check pattern, and others we had never seen in ordinary life. These were passed, one by one, to an official who smeared them with a patch of nutmeg ointment, the Queen's favourite scent. He handed them on to the villagers to be packed again on rough, flat latticework frames of bamboo, lined with banana leaves. More leaves were spread on top, then several heavy stones, and the whole was tied down with another frame. Two were filled with the trousseau of Nyai Loro Kidul and another with packages of the Sultan's old clothes and linen, which, being holy, could not be thrown away or disposed of in the ordinary way. Other packages, wrapped in straw sacking, and two black and gold fezzes, covered with white cloth, were left as they were. All were politely labelled with the Sultan's monogrammed card. Finally there were two mysterious red and gold boxes, filled with little bags. These, we learnt, contained the royal nail-parings and hair-trimmings of the past year, religiously preserved.

At last all was ready. The villagers lifted the weighted frames and packages and marched down to the beach. Alas, I could not stay to see the final consignment of the gifts to the sea, for I was already due back in Jogja for an examination board. The procession was heading for a spot called Parang Kusumo, nearly a mile along the sands, where a service would be held, the frames thrown into the sea, and the hair and nails buried. Of one thing, however, we were assured; though the Queen sometimes returned her husband's old clothes, she never, never gave back her own trousseau.

10

HINDU HERITAGE

BOROBUDUR and Prambanan, the two mightiest monuments of Java's ancient civilisation, stood on either side of Jogja. With Bali they formed Indonesia's prime tourist attractions, so that everyone was expected to pay them a visit, however short his stay might be. Vice-President Nixon flew up for the day from Djakarta; so did Mr. Adlai Stevenson; King Norodom of Cambodia beat the Americans at their own game by actually flying round the Borobudur. We ourselves first saw this monstrous pile on the third day after our arrival, and again with nearly every visitor who came to us. Yet such was the concentration on these two monuments that one never heard of the innumerable lesser archaeological remains that crowd the Jogja district—the vast Buddhist complex known, with pardonable exaggeration, as the Thousand Temples, only half a mile from the Prambanan group, was quite unknown to us for two years, till I learnt of its existence from a Victorian guide-book. After that we tracked down many other groups of temples off the tourist route and began to gain some appreciation of the extent of the civilisation of Old Mataram.

The Hindu-Javanese monuments of Central Java belong to a period of some two hundred years between A.D. 730 and 930. The first recorded date is 732, found on a stone inscription at Gunung Wukir, off the road from Jogja to Borobudur. Two hundred years later, in 928, the seat of the kingdom of Mataram seems to have been suddenly shifted to East Java, where a splendid new civilisation arose, culminating in the empire of Modjopahit.

Central Java sank back into obscurity till its glories were revived six hundred years later in Senopati's empire of New Mataram. The reason for the desertion of the older centre—whether it was some natural disaster like plague or eruption or some powerful political upheaval—remains a mystery. At any rate it seems to have been urgent, for the work at Prambanan is unfinished; on many buildings the ornamentation is partially or even completely wanting and elsewhere it is only rudimentary.

It is with these monumental remains that the history of Java really begins. The high development and sophistication of the architecture implies a much older civilisation, but the documentary or archaeological evidence is pitifully meagre. A few references, starting in A.D. 132, to mysterious and doubtfully identified kingdoms in Chinese diplomatic records or travellers' tales; a possible mention in the atlas of Ptolemy about 150; an early Buddha image in East Java; a Sanskrit inscription about a fifth-century Buddhist King Purnavarman in West Java; and the rest is all legend. Shrividjaya, the first great empire in Indonesian history, was based upon Palembang in southern Sumatra and extended across the straits of Malacca and Sunda, thus commanding the sea-routes between India and China. But how far its rule extended into Java is uncertain before the time of the Central Java temples. There is not even any clear evidence of Shrividjaya's existence before 670, when it sent the first of a series of embassies to China. A stone inscription found on Bangka Island, off Palembang, records an invasion of Java sixteen years later. And with that we come to the first definite date, the inscription of King Sandjaya in 732.

It is odd that Java, and indeed Indonesia in general, should lag, historically, so far behind its great neighbours of India and China; for prehistorically it can beat the world. The nearest approach to the 'Missing Link', the earliest known individual in human history, was found near the village of Trinil on the Solo river in 1891. The cranium and jaw indicated 'a large hominid at an intermediate stage of evolution between anthropoid ape and man',

who was named *Pithecanthropus erectus* or Java Man. Later
finds in the same area confirmed the type, which is supposed to
have appeared about the beginning of the Pleistocene period,
some four to five hundred thousand years ago. More discoveries
were reported in 1955 from Sangiran, about ten miles from Solo;
but the large jawbone may indicate an earlier type, an ancestor of
the *Pithecanthropus*. Their nearest rival from outside Java, the
Sinanthropus or Peking Man, is rather more advanced. After
this the evidence of further evolution is again provided by Java
with another ape-man, again found on the banks of the Solo
river; whence the name *Homo soloensis*. Finally we reach *Homo
sapiens*, genuine man, with some skulls dug up at Wadjak near
the south coast of Java, believed to belong to the end of the
Pleistocene period, a mere 12,000 or so years ago. Java, in fact,
by itself provides the most complete summary of the history of
human evolution that we have.

There follows a hiatus of ten thousand years. Even the legends
of Java do not go further back than the first century A.D. The
first year of the Javan era was the year 78 of the Christian era; but
as the Javanese year is slightly shorter, the difference is now less.
Thus on our arrival in 1952 we found it was the Javan year 1884
(not to mention the Moslem year 1372 and the Chinese year
4589). The Javanese system was known as the Saka calendar
from the legendary introducer of this and other sciences into Java.
Adji Saka was variously described as a prince or minister or
teacher from India, and to him were attributed the first systems of
law, religion and letters. He was a symbol or personification of
the cultural colonisation of the Indonesian islands by the Hindus,
that *mission civilisatrice* which resulted in the Indianised kingdoms of Shrividjaya and Mataram and the rest whose names we
do not know.

The story of Adji Saka's invention of the Javanese alphabet
was a charming combination of myth and mnemonic. This
learned and virtuous Brahmin came from India to save the people
of Java from the barbarous king of Mendang Kamulan, whose
habit it was to devour one of his subjects every day. Adji Saka

nobly offered himself as a sacrifice to die for the people, but he was so young and handsome that the anthropophagous monarch suggested that he should become his Crown Prince instead of his dinner. The Indian insisted, only stipulating that he should be given a patch of ground as big as his turban. But the turban was magic and never-ending, so that it covered the whole town, then the countryside right down to the South Sea, till the king, driven back to the shore, was thrown into the sea and turned into a crocodile. The grateful people duly made Adji Saka their new king and insisted he should stay among them. He therefore sent one of his two faithful servants back to India to fetch his holy sword, which he had left behind in the keeping of the other one. Unfortunately he had given the second servant strict orders not to hand over the sword to anyone but himself personally. A deadlock thus arose between the retainers, since one would not hand it over and the other would not go back without it. This led to a quarrel, in which both were killed. Their master sadly commemorated their exemplary loyalty with a rhyme that will be remembered as long as the Javanese language, since it is made up of the twenty letters of the Javanese alphabet:

ha-na tja-ra-ka	They were servants
da-ta sa-wa-la	They fought each other
pa-da dja-ja-nja	They were equal in valour
ma-ga ba-ta-nga	Both became corpses

Between the time of Wadjak man and Adji Saka various waves of humans had passed over the islands, but the last great group was of the type called Indonesian, who may have spread out from a dispersal centre in south-west China. Essentially they were of the same variety as the southern Chinese, without the latter's Mongoloid admixture, though Mongoloid characteristics did appear in the earliest Indonesian settlers in the islands of the archipelago, known as Proto-Malays, whose descendants include the Bataks of Sumatra, the Dayaks of Borneo and the Toradjas of the Celebes. But the last and most characteristically Indonesian wave was that of the Deutero-Malays, about two thousand or less years B.C., a more mixed type that formed the ancestors of the Javanese, Sundanese, Balinese and most of the other islanders, as well as the Malayans. The basic population of Indonesia is in fact Malay, though their earliest historic civilisation is Hindu. The struggle of Adji Saka with the king of Mendang Kamulan no doubt represents native resistance to Indian penetration; but, as in the story, the people seem to have welcomed the bringers of the higher civilisation. Today's Indonesians are proud of their Hindu heritage and feel a historic spiritual bond with India that has modern political significance.

The monuments of Central Java made a bewildering kaleidoscope of Hindu and Buddhist shrines, both in place and date. The Sandjaya inscription was Shivaite, and so were the contemporary temples of the Dieng plateau. Half a century later a temple was raised to Tara, a Buddhist goddess, at Kalasan, near Prambanan. The Thousand Temples and Borobudur, the largest Buddhist *stupa* in the world, followed about A.D. 800, and must have taken a considerable time to erect. Yet soon after, in 863, we find the Shivaites back in the Prambanan district, and in 898 the name of the Hindu kingdom of Mataram first appears. About this time the great complex of Shiva temples, known to tourists as Prambanan, was built. And then, before these new temples had even been finished, the whole area was deserted in 928, leaving hundreds of shrines, both Buddhist and Hindu, to moulder into ruin and oblivion.

The picture that emerges is of an earlier Hindu kingdom, taken over in mid-eighth century by Mahayana Buddhists for about a hundred years and then returning to the power of the Shivaites until it was abandoned for unknown reasons some eighty years later. The Buddhist dynasty that displaced the Hindus was called the Shailendras, or 'Kings of the Mountain', and they were evidently a family of great ability and energy. Not only did they set about the tremendous building programme of which we now admire the remains, but they spread their power into the Malay peninsula and Cambodia. More important, they gained control of the other great Indonesian empire, Shrividjaya—probably by peaceful means such as marriage, since we hear of no great war and both states were attached to Mahayana Buddhism. It is conjectured that the Shailendras transferred their seat to the older capital in Sumatra, and that the exiled Shivaites thereupon returned from East Java to set up the Hindu kingdom of Mataram and build their own temples amid the Buddhist shrines of the Prambanan plain, on a scale to rival all except the Borobudur. But it is not necessary to postulate a deadly and exclusive rivalry between the Buddhists and the Hindus. The Javanese tendency towards compromise and absorption, or 'syncretism' as the scholars call it, was evidently operative even then. The two religions were not fanatically opposed to one another; they mixed more and more readily, even in the same buildings and the same persons. At Plaosan, just beyond Prambanan village, there are remains where the inscriptions indicate a joint foundation by a Shivaite king and a Shailendra queen. Javanese Buddhism was inclined to multiply its pantheon and develop the Bengali ideas known as Tantrism, which included magic and female deities too. It was thus easy to harmonise the two pantheons. In the later shrines of East Java syncretism actually went so far as to show both Buddhist and Hindu symbols in the same building, while the kings ensured universal loyalty by presenting themselves as personifications of a united Shiva-Buddha! In modern Bali their religion is still in some ways a mixture of the two faiths.

Syncretism is part of Java's tradition. The unfanatical nature that could accept the superimposed religions of Hindu-Buddhism, and then Islam, on top of their original animism and keep something of them all, should surely be able to produce a satisfactory or at least workable synthesis between the claims of modern Eastern and Western civilisation.

In spite of the confusing intermixture of Hindu and Buddhist remains on the ground, it was still possible to obtain a fairly clear picture of the general historical development by considering the temples by areas, starting with those furthest from Jogja at

Dieng, moving eastward to the great Buddhist shrines of Boro-budur and Mendut, and finishing with the innumerable relics of the Prambanan area, taking first the Buddhist monuments of Kalasan, Plaosan and the Thousand Temples and finally the great Shiva shrine known as the Loro Djonggrang complex. This was not, of course, the order in which I viewed them—hence, perhaps, my confusion. For the sake of clarity I shall ignore personal chronology in favour of historical.

For beauty of setting, as opposed to archaeological interest, the Dieng group was my favourite. The plateau, north-west of Jogja, in the waist of Java, was almost inaccessible and could only be approached by car over a steep, winding, single-track road from the little town of Wonosobo on its south side. Beyond Wonosobo the countryside grew steeper and wilder, and we climbed through deep gorges, gay with the scarlet of poinsettia, and under bamboo aqueducts till we reached a rough wooded valley, ringed by tall mountains and lined with pale eucalyptus and strange Corot-blue trees. Only the villages, drab with black corrugated iron roofs, marred the scene. But this was not yet the plateau. In the hamlet of Kedjadjar a bar across the road and a death's-head warning about brakes marked the starting point of the one-way track. The times of entry and exit were strictly regulated, since vehicles could not pass on that narrow, precipi-tous road; barrels of water were disposed at strategic intervals for boiling engines; and the climb took about an hour. But the exhilaration of the air and scenery, with clouds drifting far below us, made me forget my archaeological eagerness in the sheer joy of feeling really alive. At last the road dropped over the rim into the plateau and we were in the village of Dieng. Some shabby corrugated houses and shops full of flies, a primitive and dirty resthouse with nowhere to sleep but the floor, some cabbage patches and an ancient wall—such were the village's amenities; and the people looked as primitive. The men and women were unkempt and ragged, the children unwashed and adorned with scraggy topknots; one of the red-cheeked girls was sorting manure with her hands. There was a strong smell of sulphur.

The surroundings were sinister but fascinating. This wide basin of land, nearly seven thousand feet high, was really the crater of a semi-extinct volcano with smaller craters still smoking inside it. The ancient temples belonged to a once flourishing religious community, which was not dankly isolated as it is now, for there were mighty stone staircases for the pilgrims north and south and a gigantic drain to draw off the plain's marshy waters. Then for nearly a thousand years the plateau was utterly deserted, till the first half of the last century. Raffles, as usual, was the first to take an interest in the historical remains, sending engineers to explore and survey the plateau. They reported some forty groups of buildings; a quarter of a century later Junghuhn mentioned twenty odd; today only eight are left in recognisable shape. The reoccupation of Dieng by the peasants and the discovery of its archaeological riches by amateurs of the antique caused more rapid and fatal destruction than all the volcanic upheavals and neglect of centuries.

We made our way to the group of tiny shrines we could see in the middle of the plain. Down a muddy lane we plunged, hedged by masses of crimson fuchsias, wild roses and coral-red lilac, through a marshy field, full of ponies and stone foundations, till we reached the line of temples. The central shrine was sacred to Ardjuna, who gave his name to the whole group. But they were all rather plain and tumbledown and empty. The House of Semar, a stone hut standing opposite the door of his master Ardjuna, was only interesting for its name. Our guide could only tell us the names and hazard a guess that they were perhaps two hundred years old—anyway from the time of Buddha, as the villagers call the Hindu-Javanese period.

We went on round the plain, re-discovering the pleasures of walking in that cool and invigorating air. First we peeped down into one of the wide vents of the ancient sewer, which later generations explained more romantically with the tale that a Kurawa hero burrowed along underground, popping his head up every so often to reconnoitre, in a subterranean attack on the Pendawas. Then we skirted the marsh, past the little shrine of

Gatotkatja and on into the cool pinewoods, where we found another temple, sacred to his father, Bima. This was slightly larger but equally void; its distinctive feature was the array of busts in the niches of the roof, which looked like curious tenement-dwellers, peeping at us from the windows. Beyond the woods we came to an area of bubbling sulphur springs, some hissing and steaming evilly amid the yellow-streaked clay, some popping to the reedy surface of stagnant ponds. The Lake of Many Colours was a disappointing monochrome that day, grey-green amid the misty pines. Here too in a sulphurous white bank at its edge we watched thick bubbles rising inside the holes and bursting like the wink of a huge frog; a vulgar burping and a brimstone smell accompanied the wink. It was like a prim Scottish tarn disturbed by a disrespectful and unseemly devil.

As we left the plateau, the clouds closed around us. We glanced at the source of the river Serayu, then wound our way cautiously down the precipitous track with the feeling that, romantic as it was, we would rather not spend the night at Dieng —and certainly not bathe at midnight in that bitter spring, even for the joys of rejuvenation.

Borobudur lay in the same direction as Dieng, but much nearer to Jogja. A side road between Muntilan and Magelang led down to the confluence of two rivers below a range of knobbly mountains, whose knobs were reflected in the humpy outline of the monument itself, lying at their feet. But owing to its position and grey colour it did not show up against the dark background until one was quite near. Only when we came right up to it did we realise its enormous size, covering the whole of a hilltop; for it was spread wide rather than high. The downward approach robbed it of the imposing grandeur that such a colossal conception should invoke, and for me the design itself was disappointing too. My feeling, influenced no doubt by the Gothic perpendicularity of our English cathedrals, is that a religious building should aspire to the vertical, should soar heavenwards. The broad base and comparatively low apex of Borobudur inspired me with less exalted images—a giant's wedding cake or a vast baroque dish-cover. Only when I saw it from above, as our circling plane revealed the harmony of the six square galleries crowned with the three rings of round terraces, did I appreciate the brilliance and originality of the architect's plan. From the ground Borobudur seemed to me heavy and oppressive, overcrowded with ornament, without clean lines or clear design, a squat and bristling mass.

The attraction of Borobudur was not in the immediate general impression but in the detail, not in the architecture but in the sculpture. Its interest was intellectual rather than aesthetic, leading one deeper and deeper into the study of Buddhist cosmology instead of striking one with emotional beauty. It was a sermon in stone, the heaviest in the world; and if one was to appreciate it, one had to know something of the language. To go there unprepared, ready only for open-mouthed wonder, was to invite disappointment. It *was* a wonder, of course; the vastness of the conception, the skill of the architect, the legions of builders and craftsmen needed to carry out the plan, the miles of reliefs, all made it a triumphant achievement. Yet it could not compare in its impact with the unadorned and soaring vastness of the Pyramids. The visitor must be prepared to study and not merely to gaze.

The road, emerging at last from the masking trees, still failed to make the right approach. It climbed close under one flank of the monument, never allowing a general view, then turned into a wide level area where you suddenly found yourself face to face with the stupendous mass. A mass it was, solid, impenetrable, built round the core of a hilltop; not a temple but a *stupa*, a monument like a funeral mound, raised to contain the relics of some Buddhist saint. In India the *stupa* developed from a hemispherical body into a variety of shapes—bells, bowls, bubbles— while the circular base often became a square or step pyramid. In Borobudur the different types were ingeniously combined so that the several essential characteristics, bell top, circular body and square pyramidal base, blended into a single huge hemisphere.

The plan also corresponded to the Buddhist cosmology, through which humans rise from the lowest physical world of men and animals (*Kamadhatu*) through the sphere of higher but still intelligible forms (*Rupadhatu*) to the highest sphere of the abstract and formless (*Arupadhatu*). Each stage has a corresponding aspect of the Buddha, and men may aspire to rise from their inferior human state to the highest abstract Reality through the stages of human Buddhas (like Gautama, the historical Buddha), then adepts (Bodhisattvas) of a higher order, then deities, and finally nothingness. Thus the reliefs of the base and the square galleries were accompanied by statues of the appropriate Buddha in niches above; thereafter three open circular terraces, devoid of decoration, represented the formless sphere and the Buddhas here were enclosed in bells of stone lattice work, so that they were half invisible in a transitional stage of being; at the top rose a huge crowning bell, completely enclosed, presumably representing the Highest Reality, utter abstraction. But just how it conveyed that idea is a matter of endless scholarly speculation and controversy.

Such was the theory of Borobudur. In practice it was slightly different, for the human sphere, the base, rapidly proved its inferior nature and evidently had to be changed by the original builders. The vast weight above must have caused sagging (the lower gallery walls leant outward alarmingly) and in order to prevent the collapse of the whole, the reliefs of the base were sacrificed and encased in a solid buttress all round, which took 12,000 cubic metres of stone. So the lowest part was lost to view till the secret of the hidden base was discovered in 1885. It was then uncovered section by section, photographed and re-covered; but the Japanese had the south-east corner exposed again, leaving visible two and a half of the hundred and sixty cautionary panels of the Law of Rewards and Punishments. These scenes showed extremely ugly human figures, teaching that wicked deeds result in 'deformity'—in fact, to drive the lesson home, the word (*virupa*) was actually written in the background in a script that indicates a date round about A.D. 800. It was a pity that the rest were buried; they looked the most amusing of the reliefs. As one rose higher, they became more and more inhumanly edifying and only the most devoted student of Buddhism would follow the complete course of the upper galleries. The first gallery, however, with its immense strip cartoon of the life of the Buddha on earth, had plenty of human interest.

It was best to take the Borobudur systematically, since it represented a system. We learned to start from the east side, where the story started. At the foot of the eastern stairway stood a sacred fig-tree, descended from the original Bodhi-tree under which the Buddha finally attained Enlightenment. This particular tree, however, was quite young, only brought to Borobudur in 1928; it was a shoot of the holy tree in Ceylon, which was itself a shoot of the original tree brought from India in the third century B.C. After a look at the horrors of the *Kamadhatu* we would mount to the first gallery and take the correct clockwise circumambulation. The upper series of reliefs on the inner wall told the story of the Buddha from his miraculous birth to his final enlightenment. The carvings, lively and lifelike in high relief, were filled with decorative and charming details of everyday life with a distinctly Javanese flavour about them. The lower series, which told shorter stories of previous incarnations, contained two famous panels, the graceful 'Ship of Borobudur' and a feasting scene that looked remarkably like a modern *Rijsttafel*, that endless procession of side dishes for rice that is supposed to be a Dutch invention of the last century. The walls of the upper galleries were occupied with an immense serial of four hundred and sixty panels, telling how the Bodhisattva Sudhana tried no less than forty-seven teachers before he achieved Absolute Reality. We were generally satisfied, and exhausted, by the Buddha story and took a short cut up one of the four staircases to the Abstract Sphere above.

On the Abstract Plane some of the *stupas* had vanished with their Buddhas, some statues sat in the open, but most were still enclosed in their latticed stone bells. One complete one at the top of the east stairs had become the object of superstitious veneration

o

to later non-Buddhist generations and faded flowers and offerings could always be seen in his lap. But why this particular image out of all the four hundred and twenty-three? There is a story of the first Crown Prince of Jogjakarta, who in 1758, among other misdeeds, insisted on visiting the Thousand Statues in spite of an ancient prediction of woe to the prince that should look on them, since one represented a *Ksatria* or Knight in a cage. The curse was evidently effective, for on his return the Crown Prince fell ill, spat blood and died. The 'Knight in a Cage' certainly sounds like a latticed Buddha, presumably the one still worshipped. But then, what of all the other statues, many equally caged? Were the Thousand at that time merely a tradition and a name, still buried under the piled volcanic detritus except for one, or what? The 'mountain of Borobudur' was known in Javanese verse of the early eighteenth century; but it was not examined till the indefatigable Raffles sent Cornelius to excavate the fabled hill. Unfortunately he does not tell us the state of the monument before excavation, and so leaves us with one more mystery.

But the crowning mystery lies in the topmost *stupa*. What did it contain? Did it indeed contain anything? What was the secret enclosed in the darkness of that hollow dome? Was it some relic of the Buddha of such surpassing holiness as to justify such a colossal structure? Was it yet another image? Or was it sheer emptiness and darkness and silence—the mystic Nothingness of the Highest Reality? What makes the problem worse is that a statue was actually found in the *stupa*, an insignificant unfinished little statue that can now be seen sitting meekly on a pile of stones in the temple court. It certainly did not strike me as having any of the qualities of a supreme religious finality. It looked like any of the other Buddhas, only less skilful, and I incline to the view that it was a bungled piece of work—a stone which the builders rejected. How then did it become the head of the *stupa*? Was it introduced at a later date by some busybody who felt that there ought to be some sort of statue in the centre? Before the restoration in 1907, there was a large hole in the topmost bell; but who would bother to drag a statue up all those steps from a mere sense of fitness? The figure, some argue, must have been left unfinished on purpose to indicate the impossibility of portraying the Adi-Buddha, the Highest Being, unthinkable, unapproachable, unrepresentable. The scholarly battle rages, but there is no answer from the *stupa*. Restored and closed again, it keeps its mystic secret in the darkness, silence and vacancy of an empty hidden room.

The other *tjandis* (as all ancient monuments, irrespective of their particular purpose or religion, were called) were dwarfed in size and importance by the stupendous *stupa* of Borobudur. But to me, as a layman, some of them gave greater aesthetic pleasure. The finest of the Buddhist remains was Tjandi Mendut, on the road leading to Borobudur. The great *stupa* was not isolated but the centre of a religious community; about fifty more temples were known in the Kedu district. As usual no serious investigation was made till Raffles set his experts to work; and if we may believe the fulminations of Scheltema in his *Monumental Java*, his discoveries only made things worse. The Dutch on their return attempted no serious archaeological preservation or restoration till the end of the century. Meanwhile the newly revealed ruins were used as stone quarries by villagers and by government engineers for the foundations of bridges, dams and other practical public works. Portable statues or loose reliefs were stolen or sold to decorate the residences of officials or amateurs. Mendut suffered pillage like the rest, but its fame was saved by the sheer weight of the three stone colossi that constituted its peculiar glory.

The whole building, originally about ninety feet high, was hidden by a huge mound of ash, earth and shrubs until 1836, when the ground was cleared for a coffee plantation. Restoration, however, did not begin for sixty years and was still incomplete; the flat top ought really to be crowned by a conglomeration of *stupas*. Round the base of the platform and on the wings of the stairway some decorative panels in low relief portrayed common folk-stories and fables, moral tales reshaped and connected with previous incarnations of the Buddha. It was interesting to compare our own favourites with those of the Oriental Aesops; the tortoise, for instance, beat a Garuda-bird instead of a hare. Up the steps and through a finely carved porch we entered the sanctum. Here in the semi-darkness sat three vast figures that were really worthy of their position, and their grandeur made it even more difficult to believe that the shabby little 'Unfinished Buddha' really belonged to the crowning point of Borobudur. In the middle brooded a superbly dignified Buddha, carved from a monolith ten feet high; his hands were in the wheel-turning attitude which indicates the teaching of the law; his feet were stretched downwards in the unusual 'European' sitting position. On either side sat two super-Bodhisattvas with only one foot down. These too were masterpieces of sculpture, only slightly smaller than the central Buddha, yet completely overshadowed by his personality.

One Friday morning we noticed fresh offerings of flowers in the laps of all three and incense still smoking at the great Buddha's feet. These statues were buried and unknown for hundreds of years, so they could not be the objects of long-established superstition like the Caged Knight of Borobudur or the Princess Loro Djonggrang of Prambanan. But what was once holy to the ancestors of the Javanese is still holy. And the statues of Mendut were indeed worthy of veneration.

In the other great area of archaeological remains at Prambanan ten miles east of Jogja most of the buildings were Buddhist, with a Shivaite core in the mighty Loro Djonggrang complex—or rather, since the Buddhist temples were there first, the latter must have been planted in their midst to rival or perhaps complement the neighbouring complex of the Thousand Temples. The lesser Buddhist shrines were more interesting for their number than for themselves, though each could boast some point of significance or attraction for the expert. Thus Tjandi Kalasan, the first to be met on the way from the city, was a mere battered hulk, foetid with the droppings of the bats that swarmed through its holed roof; but besides the first Buddhist date, it showed traces of stucco ornament on the south wall that suggested that this (and maybe all of them) was originally covered with white or multi-coloured plaster. It is an alarming thought that all these solemn grey monuments may once have glittered over the landscape in gay and glaring hues—almost as disillusioning as the loud and polychromatic reconstructions of Athens and Rome by ruthless Teutonic scholars. A little further along stood Tjandi Sari, which was distinguished by having two floors of three rooms each, with windows, so that some held it was a monastery rather than a shrine. The same plan, on the other hand, was also found in the central building of the northern Plaosan complex, on the far side of the Prambanan village, and this was clearly a shrine as it still contained several statues.

In the middle of these groups lay the biggest group of all, Tjandi Sewu, the Thousand Temples. The word 'thousand' was not used in an exact sense and merely meant a very large number; in actual fact the total of the shrines inside the walls came to 249. There were also several small temples in the vicinity, outposts as it were of the main group. It was strange that such a place should be so ignored, especially when it was situated only a thousand yards behind the tourist haunt of Loro Djonggrang. Maybe it did not compare with its neighbour in magnificence, but little reconstruction work had been carried out as yet. One could not blame the archaeologists for shying away from the deadly task of rebuilding 248 almost identical shrines, set in four lines around the central temple. There were slight differences; the second row faced inward, the others outward; the pediments differed in design; the empty niches inside varied between one and forty-one. But this was hardly exciting, even for an archaeologist, and so far they had only restored one specimen shrine. The rest were mostly piles of stones with a few stone Buddhas scattered here and there. At the gates on each side stood pairs of monstrous guardians, who formed one of the chief attractions. Kneeling on one knee, these giants still stood over eight feet high and they were stout in proportion. They were ferociously armed with club, sword and snakes. And yet for all their formidable bulk and attributes, their popping eyes and sergeant-major moustaches, there was something invincibly genial, irresistibly Falstaffian about them, so that they inspired amusement rather than awe. You felt no hesitation about entering the precincts under the eyes of these petrified boobs.

In the centre stood the main temple and this, I always felt, would repay the effort of restoration, for it had several unusual features of plan and decoration. The square columns of the niches rose to an almost Moorish arch and the lotus capitals had something that reminded me of Luxor. There was a faintly exotic air about it—exotic, that is to say, from the viewpoint of the normal Hindu-Javanese style. Unfortunately the main statues here were made of bronze, easy to break up and melt down after the abandonment of the temples. To judge by the size of the throne the central figure was so big that the temple must have been built around it, and it certainly could not have been moved if, as at Mendut, it had been made of stone. A mile or two away six bronze fragments were found of a Buddha's snailshell curls, of such a diameter as would make a seated figure of proportionate dimensions ten to fifteen feet tall.

Just over half a mile away, separated only by some ricefields and a belt of trees, rose the pinnacle of the Shiva temple, more than 150 feet high, the tallest building on the island of Java. With its companion buildings this proud affirmation of Hinduism stood in the midst of Buddhist temples, Sewu to the north, Kalasan and Sari to the west, Plaosan and Sodjiwan to the east and south-east. It was the last gesture of the great Hindu-Javanese civilisation of Central Java, and before it could be perfectly completed, the kingdom was removed to the east. These temples, however, were never utterly buried or forgotten and they lived in the memory and legends of the people. The first European visitors early in the eighteenth century found a tumbled ruin overgrown with vegetation, but one of the statues, that of Shiva's consort Durga, was still to be seen in the northern chamber of the central temple.

It was this slim feminine figure that gave the Hindu temples of Prambanan the name by which they are still known, the Loro Djonggrang group: for *Loro Djonggrang* means the Slender Maiden.

According to the legend, Loro Djonggrang was the daughter of a giant king of Prambanan, named Ratu Boko. The preliminaries are somewhat confused in the several versions, but the dénouement is clear. The lady's hand was sought by a powerful but rugged character called Bandung Bondowoso, but she was unwilling to marry him, either because of her love for another or because of his ugliness or because he had conquered and killed her father. Not daring to refuse outright, she set him what she considered an impossible task, to build a palace with a thousand statues in a single night. However, she had not reckoned with his supernatural powers, for he summoned thousands of spirits to assist him in his task. To her dismay the princess found at half-past three in the morning that her suitor had almost fulfilled his labour. Hastily she called on all her maidservants to start pounding rice in the wooden mortars, which woke all the cocks in the neighbourhood. When he heard the crowing of the cocks, Bandung Bondowoso gave up his stakhanovite effort, having achieved nine hundred and ninety-nine statues—only to find that it was not yet sunrise. In his rage he cursed the lovely but deceitful princess to be turned into stone and complete the required number in her own person. And there she has stood ever since.

Whether the lady's influence was benign or not seemed doubtful. The older books describe streams of women—villagers, aristocrats, Chinese, and even Europeans—visiting her to smear the image with *boreh* juice and beg the fulfilment of various feminine desires—a husband, a child, or escape from the consequences of some lapse; for the Slender Maiden was understanding, her own reputation being tarnished. On the other hand she was supposed to be jealous and vindictive towards happy couples, having missed marital bliss herself, and so even now no engaged or newly-wed pairs were allowed to visit Prambanan.

The cult image of Shiva himself in the central chamber was not discovered till 1885, when masses of fallen masonry were removed and piled haphazard in the courtyard. In 1918 the Archaeological Service began to sort out all the stones and fit them in experimental reconstructions of roofs, façades, cornices, and so on, on the ground. It was found that it would be possible to rebuild the entire Shiva temple and at last in 1937 the final reconstruction was embarked on. But war, occupation and revolution intervened, and when we first arrived, the silhouette of the temple was still blurred by a forest of bamboo scaffolding. It stood between two smaller ones, sacred to Brahma and Vishnu, the other aspects of the Hindu Trinity, and they were faced by three lesser shrines with two little court temples at either end of the intervening courtyard. The spaciousness and perpendicularity of the plan satisfied me much more than the claustrophobic density of the terraces of Borobudur. This was truly impressive, the other oppressive.

The statue of Shiva was the centre of the complex, but it was not the geometrical centre of the 370-foot square court. According to magical reckoning, the exact centre was a vulnerable point and therefore the statue might not stand there. The architects, however, carefully marked the true centre inside a miniature chamber on the left of the eastern staircase. Like Kalasan the main temple was a cruciform building with stairs at each point of the compass, leading up steep steps to a cell containing a statue of some manifestation of Shiva; the eastern cell acted as ante-room to the main chamber of Shiva himself. Doing the clockwise round, one came first to the image of Agastya, usually called *Mahaguru*, the Professor, a stout bearded figure appropriately equipped with what appeared to be a birch and a bottle. On the west side sat Ganesha, Shiva's elephantine son, and on the north side the supreme god's female complement, Durga, whose wifely qualities had become lost in her transformation into Loro Djonggrang, the Slender Maiden. Slender she certainly was, for one hand could almost span her waist, and she stood in a graceful and willowy attitude on the back of a bull. But her slightness did not imply weakness. She had just fought and conquered the bull-demon, and the lowest pair of her eight hands gripped its tail on one side and on the other the curly hair of a poodle-like demon emerging from its head. Shiva himself stood on a pedestal under which lay a pit or shaft containing the sacred temple deposit. In most places the deposits were looted long ago, but here the excavators found a stone box, filled with earth and ashes, scraps of gold and copper leaf, silver coins, pieces of crystal and some calcined animal bones. Such scraps represented the elements, material and spiritual, that form the cosmos, and were therefore the nucleus of the temple, which stood for the cosmos or, in its outward shape, the 'Mountain of Heaven'. At the same time they represented the elements as found in man, the microcosm, and so indicated a specific person as well as the whole universe; the cremated remains of a body might be added to the scraps. So the main statue might be the spiritual portrait of some dead and deified king of Mataram, perhaps King Balitung, who was supposed to have built the temple. The Slender Maiden might even portray his chief wife—many modern Javanese girls looked almost as slim. There are many layers of meaning in every detail of Oriental foundations.

The reliefs here rivalled Borobudur and were carved even deeper. On the base there were all sorts of charming animals, rising to celestial dancers and musicians on the balustrade. The instruments, such as the tubular drum, were familiar in the *gamelan*, but the dancers of that age clearly preserved the more vigorous Indian style, not yet watered down into Javanese solemnity. But the deepest and most striking reliefs were inside the balustrade of the terrace and told in strip form the story of the *Ramayana*. The carvings were full of character, action and humour, vividly and decoratively portrayed. The serial was continued in our next, i.e. on the balustrade of the Brahma temple. On the Vishnu shrine a different story was set out, telling of the youth of Krishna (yet another incarnation of Vishnu), a favourite subject in India but rare in the sculpture and literature of Java. The lesser sanctuaries still stood open to the sky, while their roofs

were being experimentally assembled on the ground. Meanwhile
such images as remained—the four-faced Brahma, the crowned
Vishnu, Shiva's humped riding bull lying patiently in the shrine
opposite its master—were more easily appreciable than the others
in the dimness of their cells. The two little court temples had
been completely restored; and at last, after thirty-five years, the
reconstruction of the main temple was finished.

On 20th December 1953 a grand opening ceremony was held.
For the first time we were able to admire properly the piled and
pinnacled domes and bells, climbing steeply on the five tiers of
the roof 157 feet into the sky. Under a temporary bamboo
pavilion hundreds of guests were ranged to listen to President
Sukarno, Muhammad Yamin, the Minister of Education, and
others. The Premier, Dr. Ali Sastroamidjoyo, was there too and
the Sultan and many other notables. It was a salute to the great
achievements of Java's past by the architects of her future.

That was the point made by the President in his address: that
Prambanan should be a symbol and an inspiration for the new
Indonesians, proving the greatness inherent in the race and the
potentialities of their future. I had never before heard the President make one of his famed orations, and I was deeply impressed.
Yamin, who spoke before him, was a man of no mean personality
and skill in words, but I remember nothing of what he said.
Sukarno struck much deeper, partly by his expert technique—the
repetitions, the pauses, the gestures, the slow spelling out,
syllable by syllable, of the major points—but more by the sheer
emotional force he managed to generate. It was not that the
ideas he put forward were specially profound or original; they
were simple and simply expressed—so much so that even I could
follow them. But he could infect his audience with his own
fervour. It was this oratorical power, this dominating personality, that had made him the unchallenged leader of the nationalist
movement, filling thousands and eventually millions with a single
will. He was a spell-binder. Even on such a mild occasion as an
archaeological celebration, in a half-understood tongue, one could
feel it.

To the south of Prambanan on a spur of the Southern Mountains there were yet more remains, traditionally known as the '*Kraton* of Ratu Boko'. Though the *Kraton* was dubious and the king mythical, the link between the defeated giant of Prambanan and the mountains was suggestive. One of the many legends of Loro Djonggrang related that she was her father's mistress; another told of her marriage to a dog. The princess, whose many faults included laziness, was weaving one day when she dropped her shuttle. She could not be bothered to get up and fetch it and promised to marry whoever should bring it back to her. The obliging individual happened to be a dog, so she duly married him and became the ancestress of a race called the Kalangs.

These people differed from the Javanese in physique and customs and were believed to be descendants of the old indigenous population. In the Hindu-Javanese era they were only partly Hinduised, and the tradition of the superior race credited them with brutish characteristics such as the habit of incest and rudimentary tails, doubtless the legacy of their canine ancestor. They kept to the forests, living as woodcutters and woodworkers; and even in recent times they were the carpenters of the courts of Central Java, living in isolated communities in the woods or special quarters of the towns. Did this *Kraton* mark the point of contact between the conquering Hindus of Prambanan and the primitive Kalangs, who had retreated into the then thickly-wooded mountains?

It was years before we ever heard of these ruins, which stood on the edge of a small plateau with a magnificent view over the plain and the other Hindu remains. A steep path led us from the wooded foot of the cliff up to the plateau, where we suddenly found ourselves facing a square-shaped triple gateway of a pattern unknown elsewhere in the temples and palaces of ancient Java. Behind was a paved and parapeted court, from which a flight of steps led to the foundations of a five-fold gateway. The rest of the area was a maze of terraces, walls, parapets, cut-away rock faces and a mysterious mound that might have been a cremation place. Beyond a straggling hamlet to the west was another area where, amid a chaos of worked and unworked stones of all shapes (bowler hats, tramway lines and what not), we climbed onto a wide terrace about sixty feet square, paved with heavy stone blocks, in which rows of small square hollows indicated the original position of wooden pillars. It must surely have been a roofed, open-sided pavilion like the *pendopos* of the stately homes of today.

The layout and architecture was all so different from the temples that the tradition of a royal residence seemed vindicated, though the discovery of Buddhist and Shivaite inscriptions pointed to the existence of religious foundations as well, royal chapels perhaps, where a politic syncretism would seem to have been practised. Some objected that the situation was inconvenient, difficult of access, barren and short of water. Perhaps it was only a hill-station, a summer palace. But then, secular buildings, even palaces, in ancient Java were not normally made of stone, which was reserved for the *tjandis*. The towns were mostly built of wood and bamboo, like modern villages, with brick for the foundations of the *pendopos*, for gates and for bathing pools. The sites of the famous capitals of the Javanese empires were almost lost. A few worn brick masses were all that remained of the glory of Modjopahit; the East Javanese capital of King Erlangga was unknown; West Java's Padjadjaran had vanished. In a few years the rains and the jungle wiped out all traces of the deserted cities, and often the only signs of their existence were heaps of broken potsherds and tiles, an earthen wall or some fruit trees growing in the midst of the wilds.

This opens up a wider question as to the meaning of the crowded monuments of the Prambanan plain. The natural first assumption is that these colossal structures must have adorned the capital of a Central Javanese empire. Raffles supposed this was the site of the fabled city of Mendang Kamulan; Professor Krom thought Prambanan the capital of Old Mataram. But then Dr. Stutterheim, the head of the Archaeological Service, noted the lack of potsherds and other evidence of human habitation in this district and argued that the *tjandis* were really mausolea of dead kings; that the word was derived from a name of the goddess of death and related to the persistent ancestor worship of the Javanese. Prambanan, he suggested, was a vast cemetery and not a city, for people could not live in a place of death. This gloomy theory, however, does not fit in with the apparently residential remains of Ratu Boko's *Kraton*, while at Penataran in East Java there is plenty of evidence of habitation as well as many *tjandis*. Stutterheim's successor, Professor Bernet Kempers (to whom I owe these learned reflections) considered that the *tjandis*, regarded not as funeral monuments but as contact points between the kings and their divine predecessors, might well have stood near the capital, though there was no factual indication of where the city, if any, was situated. These vast ruins, in fact, could only be described as 'more or less isolated features in an otherwise entirely mysterious situation'!

Mysterious or not, the fact remains that these impressive monuments exist and were the work of the ancestors of today's Javanese. The President was right. With the Revolution their significance has changed; they belong now to the Indonesians, not to the foreign archaeologists and tourists. No longer a reproach, they stand as a challenge to the generation that is reconstructing the country's greatness. The towering temple of Loro Djonggrang is still, after a thousand years, the tallest building in Java —but for how long?

I I

THE OTHER PLACE

ETWEEN Jogja and Solo, the capital of the next province,
there was a sort of Oxford-and-Cambridge feeling—except
that Solo had no university. Their rivalry was historic,
artistic, moral: the issue was which should be regarded as the true
representative of the best in Javanese culture. They were branches
of the same tree, and to the mere outsider their manifestations
were almost indistinguishable. The differences were in detail and
the ready contempt which the one expressed for the other applied
not to the ideas but to the style. While the Solonese regarded the
Jogja style as stiff, imitative and dull, Jogja considered Solo as
decadent, loose and corrupt.

There was no denying that Solo had seniority, though Jogja,
thanks to its part in the Revolution, was now in the lead. The
Susuhunan (or Sunan for short) of Surakarta (or Solo for short)
was the direct successor of the dynasty of Mataram, whereas the
Sultan was descended from a younger brother whose princedom
dated only from 1755. The principality of Solo was nearly twice
as large as that of Jogja and the country richer. The palace, the
arts, the ceremonies of Solo were the model for Mangkubumi,
when he set up his own capital; there was the *Kraton* with its
Pagelaran and *Sitinggil*, the *Serimpi* dancers and the Holy
Gamelan, the *Sekaten* fair and the great feasts of the *Garebegs*.
The Queen of the South Sea obligingly took the Sultan as her
second husband. One side of the royal cemetery at Imogiri was
allocated to the Jogja branch of the family. Jogja, in fact, according to my Solonese students, was merely a pale imitation of the

original grand source of Java's arts and civilisation. My students from Jogja snorted: Solo perhaps had priority, but it had long lost the essential Javanese spirit which was preserved pure and undefiled in Jogja.

Perhaps my judgment was affected by these arguments; for whenever we visited Solo, I found everything a little grander, superficially more impressive and attractive, and yet somehow unsatisfying. There was no doubt that life in Solo was livelier and gayer. How we wished there was a place like the Sriwedari amusement park in our town! Yet there was a pervasive air of demoralisation, not only in the shady gaieties of the park by night, but in the deserted and shabby palace area. No busy crowds of youth thronged these courts or gave new life to the old buildings. They belonged to the past, a past whose links with the present were steadily weakening. So that the question arose in the mind unasked, "What is going to come of it?"

We did not get the chance to view the palace on our first visit, as it had not been opened for sightseers like the Sultan's. But there was still plenty to see and enjoy. Solo was only an hour and a half's drive from its rival, and a tall formal gateway, marking the city limits, led us into a straight tree-lined avenue that seemed almost endless. In the middle of this boulevard were assembled the Park, the town museum, and the Dana Hotel, newly converted from a princely residence. The décor nicely combined tradition with modernity. The *pendopo* had become an airy lounge with its pillars freshly carved and painted in a colour scheme of cream, green and natural brown; the walls were hung with paintings of local scenes by local artists; and there was even—shocking evidence of moral laxity—a real bar with gay red stools and a striped awning.

A friendly old gentleman told us that all the carving and decoration was the work of Solonese craftsmen; and, with a lack of reserve that would never be shown in Jogja, he went on to suggest tea at his house, followed by a drive to the sugar mill that he once had managed. The tall green walls of sugar-cane along the road gave a new aspect to the countryside and it was new too to see a mill in working order. Most of them were burnt to gaunt ruins during the scorched earth campaign of the guerillas. I am not mechanically minded and almost any factory appears a marvel to me. At one end the canes, looking as inedible as bamboo, were fed into giant presses, where they were crushed four times successively. The extract then passed through various mysterious pipes and chemical processes till it emerged in the form first of thick brown treacle and finally, refined and crystallised, as white sugar shaking its way along a belt into the waiting sacks.

Such sugar-factories provided much of the wealth of the Sunan and Prince Mangkunegoro, and this one belonged to the latter, who had contrived to preserve much of his property intact and was consequently the richest of the Princes now. According to his brother the Mangkunegoro family was more modern-minded than the other royalties, and all the relations had been sent to work instead of living parasitically and looking down on business as too sordid for their attention. The Dana Hotel, for instance, was one of their enterprises. But the Sunan's once vast fortune was sadly dissipated—which is hardly surprising if the stories I was told of the tenth Sunan, who reigned for some forty years in princely, if impotent, splendour, were not too exaggerated. So lordly was his contempt for money that, when warned that some of his agents were cheating him, he replied simply:

"Well, why not?"

That evening we walked across the road to the Sriwedari Park, which contains two theatres, a cinema, a restaurant, a zoo and a bandstand. The night was hot and we decided against the *Wayang Orang* or the *Ketoprak*, as the halls were too crowded and stuffy. We wandered towards the music and found the band on a steep little island in the lake, reached by a hump-backed Chinese bridge. In the dimness of the winding walks we could see what made the puritanical moralists of Jogja frown upon Solo. The girls of Solo were noted for their charms, but not for their morals; a drive to rehabilitate the plethora of prostitutes did not seem to have had much effect. It was not a scene, though, that would have caused any raised eyebrows in, say, Hyde Park or the

Champs Elysees; even vice was modest in Java. It was the music rather than the company that drove us away, for they appeared to be holding an Amateur Night.

Next morning we wisited the Museum, where the exhibit that most struck me was the *Wayang Bébér*, a long scroll covered with a series of heroic scenes that was unwound like a primitive cinema. The zoo was our next call, where we duly admired tigers and little black bears, warthogs and crocodiles, monkeys and brilliant cages of tropical birds, the tiny, fabled mouse-deer and the aged and legendary elephant. Finally we entered the *Wayang Orang* theatre, where a professional troupe played each Saturday night and Sunday morning. The house was as crowded as ever with the common people in large and unsophisticated family groups, brought up from childhood to love the tales of Ardjuna and the antics of Semar. There was no suggestion of an arty fad or a fashionable occasion about these dance-performances; they were a commercial proposition, popular in every sense of the word. The show opened with a chorus of painted beauties who twirled and dipped and flicked the long bright scarves draped over their bare shoulders. After that, however, action and dialogue played a larger part than dancing, which was a little perfunctory, and the longest and most popular scenes were those of the clowns. It might not be the highest form of art, but it was certainly a lively one.

The *Kraton* of Surakarta was actually only a few years older than its counterpart at Jogjakarta, having been founded in 1743. This was due to the rulers' habit of changing their capital whenever they wished to change their luck. The capital of Mataram was exceptionally peripatetic. From Kota Gede, the seat of Senopati (the founder of the dynasty), it was shifted to Karta, near Imogiri, by his grandson, Sultan Agung: the Sultan's son, Mangkurat I, set up his court at Pleret in the same neighbourhood; when disaster overtook Pleret, Mangkurat II moved to Kartasura on the Solo river—all this within a single century. Finally after the Chinese desecration of Kartasura in 1742 the wretched Paku Buwono II tried to reverse his luck by building a new *Kraton* at

P

Solo, six miles away, with the reversed name of Surakarta. With such vicissitudes it was hardly to be expected that the palaces should vie in splendour with the more permanent foundations of other lands.

But while life moves, death remains. The palaces rose and fell, but the royal burial-grounds of Mataram endured and, thanks to Javanese reverence for their ancestors, they were as well or better kept. From Kota Gede, where Senopati lay buried, the dynasty's Valhalla was moved by his ambitious grandson to a prouder site on the hill of Imogiri, which has been used ever since. But the older cemetery was never neglected or forgotten and the village of the silversmiths was still a place of pilgrimage. Every Thursday and Friday the ancient wooden doors in the high wall west of the mosque were opened for the pious to visit the tomb of Senopati, where he lay surrounded by his parents and relations, including his unfortunate father-in-law. His father, according to legend, was only a peasant, but thanks to drinking the milk of a magic coconut he was fated to become the ancestor of a line of kings. The father himself rose to be governor of the desolate region of Mataram, under the powerful Sultan of Padjang, and his son Sutowidjoyo was appointed *Senopati* or General of the Sultan's forces and given a royal daughter in marriage. The ambitious Senopati then rebelled and after a long campaign defeated and perhaps poisoned the Sultan, thus winning the holy regalia of Modjopahit and with it the right to rule Java.

Yet though it was so near to Jogja, we never saw the tomb of the conqueror, who died in 1599. We often visited the precincts but were allowed no more than a keyhole glimpse of the grave-studded enclosure, since all visitors had to put on Javanese court dress. Nevertheless a visit was well worth while. First there was the sheer atmosphere of those ancient courts, shaded by enormous banyans and pervaded by the rhythmical clinking of hammers on silver. One of the banyans, it was alleged, was planted by Senopati and announced the death of members of the royal family by dropping a branch. Through wide courtyards and narrow brick gateways we would descend past the cemetery by a series of terraces to two roofed stone water-tanks, the home of the sacred White Turtles. How long these extraordinary creatures had lived in the pools and where they came from I never discovered. Scheltema's *Monumental Java*, which treats of the last quarter of the nineteenth century, mentions only one; but when we visited Kota Gede there were two, one in each tank, and one looked distinctly younger than the other. The colour was not really white but yellow, pale and splotchy in the elder but bright and clean in the small one. Usually they lay half-hidden under a mossy ledge in the shadowy greenish water, but twice the young one swam right out and poked its pointed snout up to the surface to peer at us. The farther out they swam, the better luck it augured; so I had high hopes of the turtle's favour.

A short way past the entrance to the precincts was another relic of Senopati, his throne. Javanese thrones were simple affairs and did not need to be high, as all the court sat on the ground. This one was like the Stone of Scone, just a flat grey rock about a foot high and three square. Four great royal trees guarded it, but the Stone had lately been enclosed in a concrete hut, reminiscent of a public convenience, which robbed the scene of any aura of majesty and tragedy that might have been conjured up by the memory of the ruthless usurper and of the rebellious prince who was stabbed here as he bent to kiss his master's knee in submission. We saw just a broad cracked stone decorated with inscriptions in Latin, French, Italian and Dutch! This unexpected display of Western learning was ascribed to a European prisoner who was chained to the stone for many years, until freed by the trick of a love-stricken village girl. The resigned tone of the inscriptions, which all said 'Such is life', was at least consistent with the tale.

In an even smaller and stuffier ante-room there were three round pitted yellow stones, alleged to be cannon-balls. The biggest had the magic power of granting untold wealth to anyone strong enough to carry it three times round the throne. I was hopeful that the holy turtle's attentions might augur success, but alas! I found that I could not even lift it.

Senopati's son took the title of Sultan, but the grandson was the most illustrious of the line, honoured with the title of *Sultan Agung*, the Great Sultan.[1] He reigned from 1613 to 1645 and asserted the suzerainty of Mataram over Central and East Java; and he even led an expedition against the new Dutch settlement of Batavia, thus showing more foresight than his successors. He took for himself a new superior title, Susuhunan, which is still held by the prince of Surakarta, and a new superior bride, the goddess of the South Sea. When he died in 1645, he was buried on the hilltop at Imogiri, from which through blue gaps in the hills he could see the Indian Ocean, the realm of his bride.

The same rules applied to the pilgrims at Imogiri as at Kota Gede; but the loneliness of the situation made dressing up a less embarrassing ordeal. So, when a party of University wives made an excursion to the tombs, two Western husbands were emboldened to accompany them and face the hazards of Javanese court dress. From the village at the foot of the holy hill we mounted a stupendous stone staircase, stretching straight and relentless for three hundred and forty-five steps up the woody grave-dotted hillside. At the top fresh flights branched out, straight ahead to the tomb of the Great Sultan himself, left to those of his Solonese descendants, right to those of Jogja. Led by Paku Alam's sister, who as granddaughter of a Susuhunan counted as Solonese, we took the left stair. By that time I was beyond counting any more, but we must have completed a step for each day of the year.

At the top stood a small *pendopo*, used for *wayang* plays featuring Semar, who despite his clownish antics represented the ancestral spirit. We walked along a paved terrace past a row of elaborate gateways, into one of which we turned and found ourselves in an enclosed forecourt. Here were our changing rooms. Tom, an atomic scientist from California, and I closeted ourselves with our Solonese mentor and wrestled with the *batik* skirts and high-necked blazers that had been kindly lent us. Wrapping the

[1] Not to be confused with the Sultan Agung of Bantam, who ruled in West Java in the second half of the same century.

kain tightly round my waist, pleats in front, I strapped it up with a broad girdle of purple satin, held by a green embroidered belt with a large enamelled buckle. Then came the jackets; but fortunately (for we were already glistening with sweat) they proved impossible to do up at the chest and neck, as the Javanese are of much slighter build. The alternative was to roll the jackets and tie them round our waists, which was not only cooler but excused us from wearing the turban and *kris*. We rejoined the ladies, who were by now transformed in a costume of *kain batik* and breast-cloth with bare shoulders and hair looped in a special way. The ensemble of brown, dark in the *kains* and light of the skin, was most attractive, and the pale Western women, freckled or tomato-patched by the sun, showed up poorly by comparison. Of the Western males, the less said, the better. It was a mistake to have photographs taken.

Now suitably clad, we retraced our steps and mounted the scorching bricks and paved paths of the central stairway. Through ever-higher terraces, crowded with tombs and pavilions, we came to the topmost courtyard. On a wide stone platform stood a plain wooden shed with a pyramidal roof. Here was no splendour of marble or carving, no display of pride except in the site. We squatted on the ledge of the platform under the wide eaves, watching the old priests chanting and burning incense before the narrow door to the tomb. A stream of villagers, bare-shouldered or torsoed, gradually filled the court. At last the service ended and the pilgrims were allowed to enter the tomb in twos and threes, there being no room for more. Squatting unsteadily we made obeisance, palms pressed together and thumbs to nose, before stooping into a dark passage, like the inside of Cheops's pyramid. A single oil lamp lit the small chamber, in which lay a plain humble Moslem tomb with no ornate decoration that I could see. My attention, though, was more concentrated on avoiding tripping over the folds of my skirt, as we shuffled on our haunches to strew rose petals and *melati* along the top of the grave. After every move we had to make a *sembah*, or salute, and by the time we got outside we were pouring with sweat despite the hilltop breeze. Ruthlessly the old officials waved us into his wife's tomb opposite and then another next door, where his grandson, Mangkurat II, lay in similar humility.

The missing generation was due to the unfortunate character and end of the Great Sultan's successor, Mangkurat I (1645-77), whose monstrous tyranny earned him the name of Java's Nero. Such 'Roman holidays' as stripping a hundred girls and throwing them to the tigers were revolting but perhaps not enough to cause revolt. What led to his downfall was his Stalinesque suspicion of his leading chiefs. Raffles tells of thousands of priests massacred with their families; of the execution of his father-in-law and family for an unlucky gift; of unsuccessful generals put to death; of the Crown Prince himself forced to stab his bride and sent into exile. The only surprise is that the rebellion did not start sooner. In 1674 a chieftain of Madura led a rising and drove the Sunan from his capital. Soon the Sunan fell ill and with his last breath he begged his son to bury his body where the earth was sweet. His corpse was piously carried across country till a suitable spot was found near Tegal on the north coast; and there the tomb of this monster lay, still venerated under the inappropriate name of the Prince of the Fragrant Earth.

Mangkurat II restored the family fortunes with the help of the Dutch and prodigies of double-crossing in every direction; and by his unscrupulous cleverness he managed, like Charles II, to avoid going on his travels again. In 1703 he was buried at Imogiri beside his glorious grandfather, where we paid him our reluctant respects. Then with trembling knees and frying soles we skipped hastily down to the main terrace and hurried along the Jogja side. Fortunately we were not expected to go right through the whole list of Sunans and Sultans—not even the first holders of the present titles, Paku Buwono and Hamengku Buwono. Not that I would have minded paying my respects to that tough fighter, the first Sultan; but I felt little admiration for Paku Buwono I, set up in 1704 as a Dutch puppet. Our objectives, however, were the grandfathers of the present princes, both of whom had long, peaceful, prosperous and powerless reigns.

More stairs, courts and gateways led us to a marble-floored pavilion, where a lace canopy overhung the plain marble tomb of the seventh Sultan. Here we repeated the exhausting process of creeping, thumbing our noses respectfully, strewing roses, and even kissing the foot of the tomb. Next came his Queen's tomb, then two more on his other side. These were the graves of the eighth Sultan and his elder brother, who died before his father. Strangely, Sultan VIII's tomb had never yet been completed; it was nothing but two carved wooden ends set in holes in the marble floor, with a golden parasol above them.

Our ordeal was still not over. We dripped and skipped along the terrace to the Solo side, using every scrap of cover under the scanty trees. This time we visited Paku Buwono X, grandfather of the present Susuhunan and also of our leading lady. The Solo pavilion was definitely showier, as befitted the older and richer branch of the family; more spacious, more glittering, with richly carved lintels and canopies, and tall golden crowns on the tombs. There was no humility here. Four more times we crawled and kissed, bowed and strewed, for the old Sultan, his Queen, his second wife and his successor. But by this time my body was so worn and melted that my mind refused to register any more impressions. At last we stumbled to our changing place and revived ourselves with tea, before descending by a rough field-track to the village. The older ladies were carried down in smart green sedan chairs; but for me straight legs and open breezes made the walk a welcome relief.

Two months later a prince of Solo was buried in state there in Imogiri. Funerals are urgent and sudden in Java and the news did not reach me till too late. But somehow I was not really disappointed.

One day the woman doctor who attended the ladies of the palace at Surakarta came to see me about a medical course in England, and through her I obtained permission to visit the *Kraton*. As we drove over to Solo with a Yugoslav friend, we argued about the rival records of the two principalities. I put the case for the spiritual superiority of the Sultan's realm with its tradition of patriotic resistance to foreign domination.

"Jogja was founded on victory," I declared, "or at any rate on non-defeat, and it has always been the centre of Javanese nationalism, the danger-spot for the colonial rulers. The British had to storm the *Kraton* to repress the Sultan's independence; Diponegoro held large parts of the state for five years; and Jogja was the capital of the final successful liberation struggle. In all these struggles the court of Surakarta remained on the fence."

Ernest scoffed at my idealistic talk of patriotism.

"Look, I am an East European and I have seen enough of nationalistic wars. The end is always suffering for the common people. The Sunans served their people better by keeping the peace, however ignoble. Just look round at the prosperous countryside of Solo and compare it with the devastated factories and buildings of Jogja province. What use is spiritual superiority to an empty stomach?"

I was not convinced and he proceeded with his theme.

"Take the facts and figures. During the hundred years of peace between the Java War and the Second World War the living conditions of the peasantry improved so materially, even with the notorious Culture System exploiting their labour and draining off such huge profits to Holland, that the population of Java rose from four millions in 1800 to twenty-eight in 1900."

"And yet," I retorted, "the whole country rose behind Sukarno in 1945 and preferred struggle and starvation to acceptance of the old humiliating tranquillity. I believe the full spirit is more important than the full stomach—as other colonial powers have learnt. If you ask an Indonesian whether he regrets the old order and the new muddle, he answers, 'But now it is our own responsibility; now we feel free'."

Not that the people of Solo were behind the rest in their enthusiasm for the revolution. Solo was a vital part of Republican territory, the headquarters of the Communists and the armed 'Wild Bulls'. In the *Kraton*, however, the old spirit of vacillation unfortunately reappeared and the young Sunan, Paku Buwono XII, was too reliant on the advice of his nervous elders, who feared that revolution would mean the end of the kingdom. At first, it is said, the nineteen-year-old prince went round telling his people:

"I am one of you. Just call me *Bung*. There is no more royalty; we are all just the same now."

But, whatever his motives, a Susuhunan cannot escape his heritage, and these democratic protestations impressed neither friends nor foes. The left-wing leaders found that an election on the question of the Sunan's powers, as demanded by the government, might go against them; so in May 1946 they seized control of the area by an armed *coup d'état*, leaving the prince with nothing to rule but his *Kraton*. The *fait accompli* was never reversed. By failing to range himself behind the Republic at once, like the Sultan and Paku Alam, the Sunan only provoked the storm he feared and lost the powers he sought to save. But even worse, when the Dutch occupied Solo in the Second Clash, the Sunan held a reception for them in the *Kraton*. He would appear to have learnt nothing from the history of his ancestors and the decline of their empire through indecision. Their only achievement had been an unheroic survival by sitting on the fence. But times had changed, and the fence had been removed; the consequent crash might well prove fatal.

The people no longer waited for his lead but decided for themselves. While he entertained the Dutch, the other young men of Solo went to the hills as guerillas. One of them, a student of mine, was still in the Junior Secondary school when he joined the Student Army, and he described his experiences to me. Ill-armed and inexperienced, they were strong only in spirit, believing they were guided by their ancestors and could not lose unless they did wrong. His own company, for instance, surprised in a dawn attack on their mountain headquarters on Lawu, escaped without casualties and, despite a short-sighted gunner and a rickety Jap machine-gun, they killed three of the raiders. They were scared, they ran, but they did not give up the struggle for liberty. They looked beyond Solo for a lead; the *Kraton* had forfeited its place as a sanctuary of the Javanese spirit.

It was a strange contrast to enter the palace of the Sunan after that of the Sultan. For the first time we saw the *Pagelaran* as it really was, a vast empty audience hall, unimpeded by wooden partitions and serried desks, files and blackboards, clerks and students. It was more impressive and dignified, certainly, but it was the dignity of death. As we climbed the steps to the High Ground, a row of ancient cannons faced us; but the biggest and most famous stood on the green outside. This was Nyai Satomi, wife of the sacred cannon of Djakarta that used to stand by the Penang Gate; both of them naturally had magic powers and received regular offerings and petitions. Beyond the second hall, we visited the music-store, full of *gamelans* ancient and modern; one particularly battered set of gongs was said to come from Modjopahit, six hundred years old, whereas another with peculiar bottle-shaped gongs and round drums was tuned to the Western scale. Nearby were the carriage-houses and stables. The state coaches were in the most elaborate Victorian taste—red and green upholstery, golden tassels, Venetian glass lamps, gold-frogged livery, and everywhere the monogram of the magnificent Paku Buwono X; but now there were only four horses. A couple of luxurious American limousines had replaced them in the stables.

The entrance to the palace itself, shaded by a corrugated iron porch with a peeling lintel of painted wood like stage scenery, was far from impressive. Under a bellicose emblem of the Sunan's role as Defender of the Moslem Faith we passed into a small court dominated by a four-storey Holy Tower used for highly un-Islamic offerings to the Queen of the South Sea. The top room was where the Sunans met their goddess-bride, when she visited them at coronation time; but the Tower was burnt down soon after our visit, and who knows if it will ever be required for another coronation? We were surprised and honoured to find a delegation of royal ladies waiting for us here to conduct us into the presence—three stout aunts and a beautiful cousin, Muryati, who had been engaged to the prince since the age of nine. Through another winding corridor we reached the main residential court, lined with shady trees; on the right lay the reception halls and dance pavilions, but we turned left to the row of stores and offices where two rooms had been converted into a small museum for obsolete regalia and unwanted presents. It was a hotch-potch of gilded umbrellas, Venetian glasses, bridal litters, spears and flint-locks, *wayang* figures, Sèvres china (one vase the gift of Napoleon I), iron horns for tiger-fighting goats, and a pair of English lorgnettes. It did not seem very well arranged or cared for.

Now a group of gentlemen in European dress came forward, led by one of the Sunan's elder brothers—by a secondary wife, of course. The party awaited the signal, then crossed to the reception hall, where a handsome youth with a straight narrow nose and almond eyes came forward to greet us. Paku Buwono XII was dressed in Javanese style with a high-necked white jacket, dark brown and blue *kain*, and an elegant *kris* studded with diamonds and rubies. In appearance and manner at least he was worthy of his high position, but the strength of his character was in doubt, that fatal defect of his predecessors. His friends admitted, and his actions showed, that he was weak-willed and content to relapse into the role of a gilded playboy, guided by old-fashioned, Dutch-minded counsellors and a dominating mother. He had been only eighteen when he succeeded to his troubled inheritance during the Japanese occupation, and the following year the Revolution broke out; but he had never enjoyed real power or initiative, for the coup of 1946 left him with only nominal powers before he was twenty.

The times demanded a man of decision and deep interest in the people and affairs of his principality; but the boy-prince was more interested in sport than business, in enjoyment than study. He told us he liked tennis and swimming, riding and driving; fast cars and films appealed to him, Comets and cameras, anything modern. His education, he himself admitted, was unfinished, interrupted by war and revolution. A year or two at a private secondary school in the town, and then at fourteen he made his only trip to Europe; but it was 1939 and he was hastily recalled with an evening at the Folies Bergères as his most vivid experience. Since then he had had private lessons in the *Kraton*, hardly the best place for developing a sense of modern political realities. The Republican government was pressing him to go abroad for higher studies, but he would not go further than Djakarta, as he feared that in his absence they might abolish his principality. The Sunan might be out of touch with the people, but he was no fool.

We sat down in a semi-circle of Louis Seize chairs and marble tables on a vast red carpet at one end of the long pillared hall, which was decorated in a colour scheme of pale blue and white. Behind the royal chair a stained glass screen graphically represented his title—*Paku Buwono*, the Nail of the World—with the globe dependent from a large nail. At the far end squatted a full *gamelan* orchestra with eight singers, and on the threshold behind us a dozen elderly women attendants with bare shoulders and red-and-gold neckbands sat patiently waiting. The scene was an odd mixture of tradition and modernism. The *gamelan* players wore 'Merdeka-caps'; the male servants had khaki uniforms and did not crawl; the palace guards wore dull-white army suits; our princely companions were in lounge suits. The atmosphere was friendly and informal. After an apéritif of beer, served in engraved goblets of crystal and gold ("Cheerio!" said the Sunan), we all rose and helped ourselves to an excellent buffet lunch, ending with a rich but perilous cream cake. The conversation was all in English, and while Coral at the Sunan's right was readily told of his life and views, I found his brother and his fiancée equally forthcoming. Information was far easier to come by than among my colleagues at Jogja, and Ernest was allowed to take photographs of the party within the sacred hall itself.

As we talked, the orchestra played softly in the distance and we learnt that a special programme of tunes connected with England had been arranged in our honour.

"This tune," we were told, "was composed in honour of the

signing of the treaty between Raffles and the fourth Sunan; the stormy ending reflects Raffles' disappointment at the subsequent hostilities with Jogja."

"Now they are playing a tune called 'Westminster', composed in 1935 by the Sunan's uncle, who was inspired by the chimes of the Abbey."

"Do you hear those notes like a clock striking? The name of this piece is 'Big Ben', inspired by hearing the broadcasts of the B.B.C."

The *gamelan* was itself broadcast every Monday, and the sacred *Serimpi* dance was still practised twice a week in the *pendopo* next door. But the holiest dance of all was the *Ketawang*, a *Bedoyo* dance performed only once a year on the anniversary of the Sunan's coronation by nine maidens dressed as brides; for this was the dance created by Sultan Agung in remembrance of his meeting with his bride of the South Sea and the words were those with which he had soothed her to sleep after her bridal dance. Muryati had often taken part and sometimes, she said, people thought they saw a tenth girl dancing—Nyai Loro Kidul had joined them herself.

Ten days later an unexpected echo of our visit was reported in the newspapers. The Sunan had suddenly ordered all the gates of the *Kraton* to be shut to prevent his mother leaving the palace; she had threatened to do so after discovering that at a recent reception for some foreign guests a certain unmarried girl had been among the ladies who received them. This could only mean ourselves and Muryati! Apparently we had got involved in a struggle between the mothers; hers wanted the match, his did not. The couple themselves, engaged since childhood, were perhaps not too much concerned; and in any case the Sunan already had several secondary wives. We had innocently precipitated the crisis, for it was not strictly correct for her to help entertain his guests before marriage. So Muryati came to live with her sister in Jogja, and before we left we saw her married to a young engineer. We felt a little guilty, but perhaps it was all for the best. The life of a *Ratu* would not suit a modern-minded girl; and cold winds were blowing round the *Kraton*.

Every now and then we would hear further scraps of news from our friends or the newspapers. The Sunan duly departed for Djakarta to study law at a private institution and the administration of the *Kraton* was taken over by his uncle, Prince Kusumoyudo, as Chairman of the Council of Regents. The following May the palace was the scene of democratic action for the first time in its history. The Palace Personnel Union staged a demonstration to demand bigger grants for the *Lebaran* holiday, and the figures revealed remarkable facts about royal economics. The grants had been fixed at one-sixth of the employee's monthly wage, and as some received only ten rupiahs a month, their bonus would be less than two rupiahs. This sounded shocking, but in fact crowds of families lived free at the Sunan's expense, provided with housing, clothing and food; in the old days palace posts were eagerly sought since all incidental expenses could simply be debited to the royal exchequer. Even now the numbers involved were such that the *Lebaran* grant cost 17,000 rupiahs, and the union's demands would add another 8,000. As we never heard of any strike, it seems that the demonstration had its effect.

Prince Kusumoyudo died in January 1956 and was buried at Imogiri; and shortly after he was followed to the grave by a nephew, Prince Mangkubumi, whom Coral had met at the little princess's puberty ceremony. The fate of these two princes illustrated the complications and dangers inherent in the Javanese dynastic system, for both were potential claimants to the throne. Kusumoyudo and the Sunan's father were both first sons of secondary wives, born within a month of each other, and as there was no son of the Queen, they were rivals for the succession. Kusumoyudo was his father's favourite and his partisans spread the story that he was a ten-months baby, so that, though born second, he was allegedly conceived first! The Dutch, however, appointed the first-born as Sunan Paku Buwono XI in 1939, leaving Kusumoyudo aggrieved; a success attributed by the people to the new Sunan's religious habits, as he often practised *tapa* in an ancestral cell still to be seen on the banks of the Solo river.

At Sunan XI's death in 1944 a different problem arose. He had had two successive first wives and both had borne sons. But the first of these wives had died before his accession and thus was never crowned *Ratu*; so her son Mangkubumi was passed over in favour of the son of the crowned Queen, that strong-minded lady who objected to the manner of our reception. The dominating personality that secured the appointment of her son as Paku Buwono XII perhaps also destroyed his chance of proving a leader when the testing time came; and the existence of a rival, living in the city and regarded by many as the rightful claimant, only made the young Sunan's position more invidious. It was easy to see how the fatal wars of succession arose, which left the monarch as a prisoner of his so-called allies.

But though the political history of Mataram was one of steady decline from the mid-seventeenth century, Solo reached the heights of cultural glory in the century of rich and peaceful impotence that followed the end of the Java War. With abundant resources and time the princes devoted themselves to the arts of Javanese poetry, dancing and drama, so that this period became known as the Javanese Renaissance. Not only did they patronise and encourage artists and poets; they practised poetry and music and choreography themselves. This was specially true of the secondary princes of Solo, who bore the title of Mangkunegoro, though the founder of the line was more famed for his prowess in war. Raden Mas Said had been leader of a second rebellion against the hapless Paku Buwono II, sometimes in alliance and sometimes in rivalry with his cousin Mangkubumi; and when the latter settled for a Sultanate, Said carried on until he too was awarded a semi-independent princedom in 1757. The artistic tradition was set up by the fourth Mangkunegoro, whose poems are still remembered and sung, sometimes to his own musical setting. He invented the speciality of the court of Mangkunegaran, a kind of danced opera known as *Langendriya*, while his

successor added a school of *Wayang Orang*. A spell of economy
under the sixth of the line enabled the seventh to indulge his all-
round artistic propensities in a renewed burst of splendour. A
quarter of a century's reign, lasting till the Second World War,
gave him time to develop to the full his tastes as choreographer,
musician, interior decorator, collector, orchid-fancier and so on.

We were specially pleased, therefore, to be invited to Mangkunegaran on a dance-practice day. The palace is not a *Kraton*
but a Javanese home on an extra large and splendid scale. The
pendopo in particular is famed for its size and perfection as a
dance-floor. But first we were received by Prince Mangkunegoro
VIII and his wife (the only *Ratu* in all the four princedoms)
in their private apartments. These were notable for their taste and
comfort, and evidently the royal couple were proud of their
home, for, after cigarettes on the wide verandah at the corner of a
cool garden court, bright with bougainvillaea, orchids and birdcages, they personally showed us round. We saw the princess's
bedroom, sunken bathroom and panelled octagonal dressing-
room, all designed by the prince's father; there were no tables or
chairs in these rooms, all was on floor level in the traditional way.
The reception rooms, corridors and the great *Dalam* or inner hall
were full of *objets d'art* and collections—sets of masks, puppets,
painted scrolls, *krisses*, coins, ancient jewellery; there was an
ivory tusk with the complete story of Ardjuna's wedding carved
inside; a golden betel-set with a thin conical handkerchief-cover
two feet tall; the gold crowns worn by the *Langendriya* dancers.
But for me the most striking item was the water-bottle of the
founder of the house, a half gourd with a chased gold spout and
fittings.

From the *Dalam* with its glassed-in nuptial couch (they spent
their first night there, said the princess, and everyone kept coming
with candles to peep!) we passed into the *Pringgitan*, where the
shadow plays would be performed. Here was a collection of
pictures, including the noble lions of Raden Saleh and some skilful family portraits by Basuki Abdullah. The prince had followed
the family's artistic tradition by taking up painting himself; but

he would not show us any specimens of his work, as his best pictures were away in Djakarta for exhibition. Down some steps and across a covered drive we came finally to the Great *Pendopo*, where seats and tables were set out for us at the edge of the lustrous marble floor, over a hundred feet square. Above us soared great wooden pillars thirty-three feet to the ceiling, decorated by Mangkunegoro VII with the symbols of the Javanese zodiac. To our right, in an unusual position at the side of the hall, was the famous *gamelan*, green with age, brought from Demak by the first prince, with its full complement of thirty-six musicians. The virtuosity of the seventh prince's taste had noted that the acoustic effects were best in that particular position. So we sat watching the dancing and sipping Coca-Cola from goblets designed by the poet-prince Mangkunegoro IV. It was too much to hope that they would be practising *Langendriya* that day, but a royal cousin in khaki trousers and a mauve sash gave a brilliant solo of Gatotkatja's love-dance.

When in May 1946 the revolutionaries had come to attack Mangkunegaran, they were driven off by the prince's own legion and thereafter left him alone. A judicious contribution of four million rupiahs to the library of the Hatta Foundation in Jogja placated the Republicans, yet left him rich enough to refuse a government subsidy and keep his independence and his collections. As we sat there, we could not help feeling that there was much to be said for wealth, when combined with talent and taste.

Since the Revolution, however, Solo had become more widely known, not for its courts and arts but for its Rehabilitation Centre. I am not a person who finds much pleasure in hospitals; but I had read and heard so much about the Solo Centre in American and United Nations publications and documentaries that I felt I must visit it when the chance arose to accompany a distinguished British pediatrician. This Centre, unique in Indonesia, was the creation of a single man with a vision, a surgeon named Suharso. He built it from nothing with his own efforts and, thanks to his enterprise in enlisting the support of international as well as

Q

national and local bodies, he was able to equip it in first-class style and continually extend the scope of its activities.

Dr. Suharso met us at the latest of his ventures, the Centre for Crippled Children, in a building that was completed in August 1954. A wide hall, already covered with plaques recording bene-factions from all over the world, led to the office of Mrs. Suharso, who encouraged and shared in her husband's enthusiasm. Out in the wide playground we were shown a shallow kidney-shaped swimming pool, where the children could forget their twisted, paralysed limbs and discard their crutches and leg-braces. The children were mostly polio cases, with a few spastics, and almost all seemed to have been affected in the legs. All round the court-yard stretched the wards, classrooms, gymnasium, special exer-cise rooms, playrooms; as at the main Rehabilitation Centre, where this children's branch was first set up, the mental and psychological side was cared for as much as the physical. The results, to judge from the expression of the children, as they hopped along on their crutches or banged the toys in their standing desks, were happy. Their minds would not become twisted like their limbs.

As we sipped orangeade in the sitting room, the doctor and his wife told us how all this started.

"It was in 1946 when I was a surgeon at the hospital here, that I began to think about the future of my patients after they left the hospital. I was doing many amputations as a result of the fighting, and I decided to make artificial limbs for the war-cripples. There were no facilities or proper materials, but with an engineer called Suroto we started work in the hospital garage. That garage was the germ of all this. We used scrap aluminium from crashed planes and the patients themselves helped us. Then in 1950 the British Council sent me to England with a year's scholarship to study the making of artificial limbs, and it was there that I realised what a lot more is involved in rehabilitation, training and helping them to start life again. So I came back here and tried to put into practice what I'd learnt. Fortunately I got support from our government and the United Nations, the

World Veterans Federation and the Colombo Plan. Now I have six foreign assistants and five distinct institutions—and we are still building.

"Then we found that there were many crippled children too, who needed equipment and training. So we started a branch for children in the Centre and some ladies of Solo set up a Foundation for the purpose. After a time they collected enough to build a special building, separate from the main Centre. We treat about eighty children here now, with some fifty living in—they come from all over Indonesia. We used to think there was no polio here, but we have cases from quite remote islands and I'm afraid it's increasing since the war. So we've set up branches in several cities, only for registration at present, but later, we hope, for treatment. Then we can turn the Solo Centre into a training school for branches all over Indonesia."

Dr. Suharso's plans were ambitious, his vision large. But when we moved on to the main Centre and saw how much he had already achieved—the orthopaedic hospital, the workshops, the artificial-limb factory, the training centres, recreation halls, office buildings and the rest, all built in the last five years—we felt they might well be fulfilled.

"This," he told us as we entered his ultra-modern air-conditioned operating theatre, "is an exact copy of the one I saw at Oswestry."

The doctor's success was due to his genuine readiness to seek and accept outside ideas and assistance; also to his understanding of the need for publicity to mobilise public sympathy. He had set an example of what modern Indonesian initiative and energy could achieve when they were not hampered by the lingering prejudice and inferiority complex that still bedevils the relations of so many with the West. By not being too proud to turn to the West for help, he had created something that he, and Indonesia, could be proud of.

12

THE RISE OF ISLAM

IN Jogja we could not help being conscious of history, but it was history with a hiatus. Borobudur and Prambanan on the one hand, the Sunan and the Sultan on the other, constantly reminded us of old and new Mataram. But somewhere in between there had appeared two highly important factors in the modern Indonesian scene, the memory of Modjopahit and the fact of Islam.

To fill in the picture it was necessary to go to East Java, to the basin of the river Brantas, whose almost circular course round a mountain massif and down into the marshy northern plains embraced most of the key sites in that vital period of change. Somewhere in that region was the seat of Sindok, the first king of East Java after the sudden desertion of Prambanan, traditionally dated 928. The capital of King Erlangga, Java's Alfred, was probably near modern Surabaya—near enough at any rate to justify the use of his name for the city's embryo university. Kediri, where his successors reigned, was still a small town where the river left the hills; and Singosari, that overthrew Kediri, was marked by a temple far upstream among the mountains, where the Brantas flowed south—yet not so far from the north coast where it eventually emerged after its vast detour. Modjopahit, built up by refugees from Singosari with the unintended aid of Kubla Khan, was down in the plains again; and it marked the apogee and end of the Hindu age. Long before its fall the Moslem traders of Gujerat were crowding the imperial port of Gresik, bringing their gospel together with their cloths from India; and there one could see the first Moslem grave in Java. Surabaya, then called Ampel, was the site of the first Islamic school; and the holy hill of Giri between the two ports became the seat of a line of prince-prelates so powerful that the first Dutch thought the Sunan of Giri a sort of 'Javanese Pope'.

I will not claim that it was pure historical enthusiasm that first drew me to Surabaya. We had heard that Western dancing was possible there and almost Western shopping. But while we were there we naturally made expeditions to the local antiquities, which in fact proved the more rewarding. The dancing was a disappointment. There was none at the dim rambling Oranje Hotel where we stayed; the once-exclusive Simpang Club was stiff without being smart; the Yacht Club was a damp deserted quay; and the pseudo-grottoes of the Tabarin were a bit too cheap and shady for more than one visit. The shopping was still more disillusioning. Whenever we turned up, it seemed to be a Moslem or Chinese or Christian holiday and everything was closed; or else the stores had run out of stocks and could not replenish them for lack of foreign exchange. Nor could Surabaya offer much in the way of alternative attractions, except the Komodo dragons in the zoo. Standing on the strait formed by the isle of Madura, where the Brantas—or rather one of its mouths, flatteringly called the Golden River—flowed muddily into the sea, it was a natural and ancient port. But it boasted no relics of history or romance; it was a prosaic business city with wide tramlined streets, graceless concrete blocks of shops, neat suburban housing estates and peeling nineteenth-century slums.

Yet it had had its moments of history, and recently too—so recently that the scars were not yet healed. In October 1945 the mob rose against the newly-landed British forces, when the rumour spread that Dutch transports were lurking just beyond the horizon. The Battle of Surabaya was the first and fiercest action of the whole war of independence, a tragedy of misplaced courage and patriotic fanaticism that got utterly out of control. From 28th October, when sudden and unexpected attacks were launched against both British and Indian troops, till the end of November, when the city was finally cleared and occupied by a full division with naval and air support, fighting went on street by street. The mob paid no attention to counsels of moderation, even though President Sukarno himself flew to Surabaya and arranged a truce and co-operation agreement. Within five hours of his departure the Indonesian attacks were resumed and Brigadier Mallaby was murdered when trying to parley. Outrages and horrors, the massacre of a convoy of Dutch women and children, the hacking to bits of prisoners, headless bodies floating down the river, were the terrible results of long repressed hatred of white domination. Irresponsible fanatics like 'Bung Tomo' (later a Minister) and 'Surabaya Sue' (a middle-aged lady from the Isle of Man) urged on their fury with radio calls to rise and kill. The Republican government's orders and rebukes went unheeded and only military action could restore order. The British command followed a strict policy of restraint in spite of Indonesian outrages and Dutch nagging; the terrorism of the Surabaya mob was not confused with the policy of the Republic and every attempt was made to avoid lasting bitterness and unnecessary destruction. For the Indonesians Surabaya became a legend of heroism, where the ill-armed patriots defied the full might of a modern army; but actually it was an outburst of undisciplined and hysterical folly that might, but for British patience, have jeopardised the whole struggle for freedom.

Perhaps we were affected by the recollection of that savage battle, for it seemed to us, as we went about among the strident *betja*-drivers, the bristling Madurese, the complex-ridden Eurasians, the half-naked beggars sleeping in the shop doorways, that there was a latent explosiveness in the place. The East Javanese were less inhibited than the people of Mid-Java, while the admixture from Madura added a more adventurous strain of sailors and wandering pedlars. Cities are apt to breed violence and Surabaya was often in the news with incidents like that at the Simpang Hotel, which was invaded by the mob when the Dutch manager tried to refuse accommodation to an Indonesian Minister. It was more pleasant as well as more picturesque to escape from modern Surabaya to the medieval sites that lay around it.

We had heard so much about Modjopahit, the Hindu-Javanese empire that was almost co-extensive with modern Indonesia. Naturally I expected some splendid ruins, yet my enquiries led nowhere; it seemed to be an intangible idea of glory rather than a historical site. My books asserted that the capital lay in the Surabaya area, but when I walked into a so-called Tourist Agency in that city, I might have been asking for the moon.

"You wish to travel to Europe?"

"No, to Modjopahit," I replied in my best Javanese accent.

"It is in India, perhaps? Will you fly by KLM?"

"I think a car would be better; it is somewhere near here."

"Oh, I suppose that is very difficult. But if you wish to go by boat or aeroplane . . ."

"But don't you run any trips there? After all, Modjopahit must surely be a tourist attraction."

"Ah, Modjopahit! Yes, it is near Modjokerto, I believe. Maybe if you went by train to Modjokerto and asked . . . . No, we do not know the train times, but you could find out, no doubt, at the station."

We thanked the travel experts politely and went off to make our own costly arrangements with a taxi.

The road led us for some forty miles along the banks of the Brantas, wide, golden with mud, and shallow enough for the punting of barges that looked like the primitive ancestors of gondolas. Down long avenues of tamarinds we sped through villages already, long before the elections, plastered with hammer-and-sickle signs. At last, seven miles beyond Modjokerto, we stopped at a beehive-shaped building with stones and statues scattered round. It was the Modjopahit Museum, but there was nothing of value on the dusty shelves: plentiful potsherds, some small worn stone figures, mouldy brass lamps, long-stemmed drinking vessels, clay waterpipes—the merest everyday relics.

The most interesting pieces were a tiny stone carving showing a pot-bellied Gadjah Mada and his master, King Hayam Wuruk, both defaced by their Moslem successors; and another worn little pottery head, heavy, ugly, jutting-jawed, that was the basis of the modern portraits of Gadjah Mada. From these vague scraps I got an impression of Johnsonian strength, uncouth, clumsy but full of personality. Obviously the great Prime Minister, whose first name means 'Elephant', had no use for flattery, about his looks at any rate.

A model of the city showed it stretching over a wide area on either side of the present road, but the only extensive remains seemed to be a bathing establishment. Raffles described this as a tank 1,000 feet long by 600 feet wide; but our explorations down the leafy, rutted *kampong* lanes failed to find it. What we did find was the great Gate of Gadjah Mada, said to have been the entrance to his residence, two tall crumbling pillars of brick flanking a stairway in the Balinese manner. That was all that remained of the physical glory of Modjopahit, about which the poet Prapantja enthused in his encomium on Hayam Wuruk, the *Nagarakertagama*. The mighty wall, the houses forty feet high, the decorated pavilions and heavenly palaces, were all made of wood and brick, and once the city was abandoned, they soon crumbled before the assault of nature. On our way home we saw a few pieces of statuary of better quality, collected in the little museum of Modjokerto; but the only striking piece, an elaborate group of Vishnu riding the Garuda bird, dated from the much earlier king Erlangga. The glory of Modjopahit lay in its proud memory, not its pitiful remains.

The empire lasted for some two centuries, starting with a refugee settlement in the riverside jungle and rising to rule almost the whole archipelago. Its name commemorated the romantic tale of the empire's birth. At the end of the thirteenth century King Kertonegoro of Singosari, famed for his martial and magical prowess, overreached himself. He had conquered the neighbouring islands and challenged the still formidable realm of Shrividjaya in Sumatra. Finally in his pride he insulted and mutilated the envoys of the mightiest emperor of the East, Kubla Khan himself, who was demanding tribute. But in his foreign preoccupations he had neglected the home front: while a Chinese punitive expedition was being prepared, the king was overthrown and slain in a revolution by the vassal ruler of Kediri. Kertonegoro's son-in-law, Raden Widjoyo, managed to escape and took refuge with his followers in the jungle of the Brantas plain. They halted by a big *modjo*-tree, whose fruit proved singularly bitter. Wryly Widjoyo chose a name appropriate to his fortunes, *Modjopahit*, 'Bitter Fruit', for his new settlement.

But the bitterness soon passed from all but the name. In 1294 the expedition of Kubla Khan at last arrived to punish the defiance of Kertonegoro, only to find the culprit already two years dead. Quickly Widjoyo allied himself with the Chinese against the usurper from Kediri and a great battle followed, which formed the theme of a Jogja mask-dance. But once Kediri had been taken and its king killed, the prince turned upon his now unwanted allies and drove them away. General Sih Pie, apprehensive of a big new campaign and further losses, decided that his punitive duties had been satisfied and re-embarked for China, leaving Widjoyo unmolested and undisputed as the chief power in East Java.

After Widjoyo's death in 1309 his realm faced its share of the usual troubles, plots and rebellions. But an extraordinary figure arose in the captain of the royal guard, Gadjah Mada, who first came to prominence by saving Widjoyo's successor from a plot against his life. Under the feminine regency that followed, Gadjah Mada was quickly promoted for his loyalty and character to the office of *Patih* or chief minister, a post he held from 1331 till he died in 1364. He set about reorganising the laws, taxes, trade, army and fleet, and made sure, unlike Kertonegoro, that the government's position at home was consolidated before embarking on his ambitious schemes of empire building. The result was unprecedented peace at home and power abroad. Bali was annexed, Shrividjaya got a puppet prince, the Moluccas, Celebes, south Borneo, even mainland Malaya came under the sway of

Gadjah Mada and the fabulous King Hayam Wuruk, the 'Young Cock' who succeeded his mother in 1350.

This monarch's reign was always held up as the Golden Age of Java's history, the exemplar and precursor of modern Indonesia; and it never seemed to strike the politicians as paradoxical to denounce imperialism and admire Gadjah Mada. Strangely, his only failure was in neighbouring West Java, where the kingdom of Padjadjaran held out in the face of every attack, military or diplomatic. Thus Java itself was never united until the Dutch times; and as West Irian (Dutch New Guinea) was well outside any medieval sphere of influence, Indonesia in practice bases her territorial pretensions on the boundaries of the Netherlands East Indies rather than on ancient history. But nationalist pride demands a native precedent and the importance of Modjopahit is that it provides reasonable justification for the new state's aspirations.

After the death of Gadjah Mada in 1364 and Hayam Wuruk in 1389 the empire steadily declined, weakened by complex dynastic intrigues and confused civil wars. But how Modjopahit actually fell is far from certain. Traditionally Raden Patah, one of the eight Apostles of Islam, led his Moslem hosts against Browidjoyo V and destroyed the Hindu capital and its king in 1478. But modern historians point out that Modjopahit still existed when the Portuguese arrived in the area forty years later, and in fact the Hindu king appealed to the newcomers for aid. If the year 1478 really represents any fatal event, they now believe it may mark the conquest of Modjopahit by another Hindu prince from Kediri; but its coincidence with the Saka year 1400, which by the back-to-front *Tjandra-Sengkala* system can be interpreted to read 'Lost and gone is the glory of the land', makes them very, very suspicious.

In any case Islam only took to the sword to administer the *coup de grâce* to the tottering empire. The confident tolerance of the Hindu rulers not only allowed but even assisted the infiltration and undermining of the state by the adherents of the new faith.

The earliest known Moslem tomb in Java, still to be seen at Gresik, was dated 1419. The wealth and Indian origin of the Moslem merchants made them acceptable as sons-in-law even to the nobles of Modjopahit and they proceeded to proselytise their new relations. The king himself took to wife a Moslem princess from Tjampa (Cambodia), whose grave was among the few relics preserved amid the ruins of the imperial city. Through her influence he even granted her nephew, Raden Rahmat, the land for an Islamic seminary at Ampel (Surabaya), from which missionaries set out to convert and subvert throughout the empire. One of them founded the mosque at Giri and his tomb there was still a focus of pious pilgrimage.

We found Gresik a fishing village, facing across the narrow strait to Madura, its quay crowded with brightly painted dhows and black-clad moustachioed Madurese sailors. But in the fourteenth and fifteenth centuries it was the main port of Modjopahit, the centre for the exchange of cloth and spices, the meeting place for traders from all over the East. The streets near the old Moslem cemetery had a suggestively Arabic look, quite different from the bamboo shacks and bungalows of the Javanese. White-walled houses and jutting iron-barred windows enclosed the narrow lanes, making us feel we were back in the Middle East. All the same the cemetery was protected by a holy banyan so vast that the screen of stems and cables, which had once been aerial roots, had had to be parted into a Gothic archway for the path to pass through. We noticed flowers and incense at its foot before we stepped through into the precincts of Islam. Among the little headstones the white marble tomb of Maulana Malik Ibrahim was conspicuous, elaborately engraved with decorative Arabic lettering that gave his name and the date. The marble was imported from Cambay, the great port of the Gujerati traders, and Malik Ibrahim was probably one of them—obviously he was rich, for his wife and child lay there under marble too. Pious tradition naturally claimed the faith's first grave as that of a learned missionary, but he was not one of the band of *Walis* or *Sunans*, as the apostles of Islam were called.

Not far away, however, lay another ancient tomb which was closely connected with one of the first apostles. A narrow lane opposite the railway station led through a tiled entrance so suggestive of a public convenience that I feared we had lost our way. But it opened into a shabby neglected graveyard. In a shack on the left a dingy lace canopy and some hideous mustard-colour tiles distinguished the tomb of Nyai Gede Pinatih, revered as the adoptive mother of Sunan Giri. The truth behind her story is problematical, for the history of the first Moslem missionaries and conquerors is confused, unreliable and largely legendary, especially as regards their family connections. Javanese respect for ancestry demanded that the new dynasties should somehow stem from the old and various ingenious genealogies served to link them. Nyai Gede Pinatih was a merchant's widow, rich and childless, who carried on her husband's shipping business about the time of Malik Ibrahim. One day one of her ships brought her a baby boy, found floating in the straits in a wooden chest, and she duly adopted him. As in all good legends, the foundling turned out to be a prince, son of a Moslem missionary and a daughter of the Hindu king of Balambangan at Java's eastern tip. Unfortunately the king resented his son-in-law's attempts to convert him and the missionary was expelled, leaving behind his pregnant wife. Balambangan was duly punished with a plague, but the king ascribed it to the anger of the Hindu gods and determined to get rid of the fruit of the impious union by launching his newborn grandson on the high seas. As with Perseus, this half-hearted measure only brought the results it sought to avoid. The child, rescued by the Moslem widow, was sent to the seminary at Ampel and rose to be the leading preacher of Islam and founder of the priestly dynasty of Giri.

Giri was quite near Gresik, a mile or two off the road to Surabaya, so on our way back we turned aside to visit the hallowed hill. It was reached by a long flight of steps, flanked by a row of cottages from which whole families of mendicants poured out, demanding holy charity regardless of whether they were halt, blind or whole. At the top a Hindu-style gateway led to the mosque, but we passed along the walls to a graveyard, where Sunan Giri lay in his mausoleum, surrounded by his descendants. A wide verandah sheltered the carved wooden walls and the gilded door; under the low lintel we stooped into the dark interior, where a green curtain stretched up to the roof all round the tomb; and through the opening of a smaller doorway we could just make out the shape of the Sunan's grave, its coverlet of embroidered Chinese silk glowing coral-red in the single shaft of light that penetrated from outside.

Back in the daylight I tried to identify the surrounding graves with the help of a pious booklet, which summarised the Sunan's life and miracles with a wealth of dubious dates and satisfied all possible requirements by tracing his ancestry not only to the first kings of Java on the female side but through his father to Fatima, the sister of the Prophet. Fortified by such illustrious forebears, the dynasty of Giri held its pre-eminence for two centuries until it unwisely pitted its influence against Mataram. In 1680 Mangkurat II stormed Giri and put its last Sunan and all his male relations to the sword.

The mosque of Giri, for all its antiquity, was not the oldest extant in Java, for the building we saw was the work of the first Sunan's grandson. Nor did the line, for all their spiritual authority, produce the first Moslem monarchs. Both these honours were claimed by Demak in the north of Mid-Java, where another more aggressive apostle, Raden Patah, set up his see. The mosque of Demak, built with stacked roofs like a pagoda, was famed for the eight pillars of its porch, believed to come from Modjopahit and said to commemorate the eight apostles who helped in its construction. One of the eight was the Sunan of the neighbouring Kudus, where the mosque was notable for the *tjandi*-like brick tower that held the great drum to summon the faithful to prayer. It was plain from these early mosques that Java's Islam was a local brand from the start—the Arab-style onion domes and minarets that one saw in some towns were modern and alien importations.

But Patah won the others' support not only for his building plans but for his political ones too. They acknowledged him as their leader and encouraged him to attack the infidels of Modjo-pahit with arms instead of sermons. Whether it was really Patah himself who overthrew the Hindu empire or his warlike son, it is certain that by the early sixteenth century Demak had replaced it as the leading power in Java. The Hindus retreated to the mountains of Balambangan or across the straits to Bali and there they held out. They had a close call when Patah's second son and successor, the Sultan Trenggana (the first prince of Java to be granted that title by Mecca), besieged their mountain fastness, but the siege was cut short by the Sultan's assassination. The assassin, strangely enough, was not an enemy but his own page, whom he had clipped over the ear for failing to attend to his request for betel-nut. To touch a Javanese on the head (as I was myself warned) is still regarded as offensive. But the page's reaction was rather extreme and led to the impalement not only of himself but of seventy-two of his relatives. It also saved Balambangan, for in the struggle for power that followed, Demak fell; and by the time Mataram established itself as paramount over the welter of petty Moslem princedoms, more urgent dangers were looming in the West.

It was in fact to the Dutch that Balambangan finally succumbed in 1767. After that Islam slowly spread over the area; but in the Tengger mountains the hillmen kept up the beliefs and customs of the old religion and once a year, at the full of the mid-year moon, an eerie and fantastic midnight festival was held in the crater of Mount Bromo. The name of the feast was *Kasada*, derived from the sweet *asada* flower that they offered to their ancestor Kusumo, the spirit of the volcano. The legend ran that as King Browidjoyo fled before the Moslems, his daughter fell in love with the son of a holy man in these mountains. But their marriage was childless until the old man advised them to pray to Bromo. The voice of the volcano replied that they should have many children, but at the end they must give one as a sacrifice to the gods. Only when their family had risen to twenty-five did the mountain make clear by thunderous roaring and flaming that the time had come. But who was to be the sacrifice? Bravely the youngest, Kusumo, stepped forward and offered himself to save the others. He jumped into the flaming crater, which soon subsided; and ever since the Tenggerese have venerated Kusumo as their protective deity, celebrating his sacrifice every May or June with moonlit offerings at his fiery shrine.

Kasada night sounded so romantic that we determined to try to see it one year despite the uncertainties of transport, lodging and dates in Java. It meant an expedition of three or four days and we planned to make the most of it by travelling via the mountain-lake of Sarangan and the historic sites along the Brantas valley. The journey started disastrously. At Madiun the car that was to take us up to Sarangan was requisitioned by an unexpected Minister and the cost of a taxi was so fabulous that we preferred the discomfort of a bus. The bus, cramped and rickety, stopped short of the lake and storm clouds forced us to spend the night as the sole occupants of a resthouse in the unpronounceable village of Ngerong. At dawn next day we scrambled up the hill on ponies (which looked a little less dangerous than the rough sedan chairs swaying on four coolies' shoulders), for a quick look at the misty lake cupped on the mountainside, before hastening back to Ngerong to catch the morning bus to town. Alas, no bus appeared for hours and by the time we were down again in Madiun we had missed our train to Blitar.

There was not much to look at in Madiun as we waited for the next train. A massive monument of a charging bull by Indonesia's only woman sculptor, Mrs. Tjokrosuharto, commemorated the Revolution. But in Madiun one thought rather of another revolution, for it was here that the Communists set up their abortive Soviet in September 1948. There was no monument to this peculiarly flagrant stab in the back. Though the Dutch were hemming in the shrunken Republic from the truce line and clearly preparing to attack, the Communists, as in occupied Europe, preferred to use their arms against their rivals at home.

But the government, forewarned, began to remove the Communist army leaders, forcing them to a premature outbreak of open resistance in Solo. The gaff was now blown and the senior officers in Madiun proclaimed the Red revolution, although the political bosses were away on a propaganda tour. Hastily they re-assembled and issued a radio call to rebellion. But Muso, just back from years in Moscow, was no match in popularity for Sukarno and Hatta, whom he rashly denounced as Japanese Fascist Quislings. The people looked on the rebels as traitors, and Madiun itself, bewildered at first, soon turned against them as their deeds—the arrest of other party leaders, the repression of free speech, the acts of brutality—belied their words. The students gathered in silent demonstrations of protest at the grave of a boy whose only misdeed was, as a sentry of the Students' Volunteer Force, to raise his rifle in salute to a passing troop of Reds. The friends of the People, too readily suspicious, bayoneted him through the mouth! After a fortnight, government troops recaptured the town, but the Communist resistance continued in the hills till early December. Ten days later the Dutch struck. Poor Madiun, once noted for its girls, was henceforward notorious for treachery and bloodshed.

The train that eventually took us to Blitar had nothing but second-class carriages of such a vintage that most of the window shutters were immovable and we had to sit in grimy semi-darkness. When darkness fell outside as well, the whole coach was served by only one small oil lamp. Here and there the evening was lit by the dance of myriads of fireflies over the glimmering ricefields; and here and there the hard flare of a pressure lamp showed up one corner of some wayside platform. One of them must have been Kediri, which I had wanted to see as a medieval capital, famed for its chivalry and its prophet-king Djoyoboyo. In his reign was composed the most celebrated of Javanese epics, the *Bratayuda*, a transposed version of the *Mahabharata*, that was the source of most of the shadow plays and dance-dramas we had seen; and the king himself made prophecies that not only came true but affected events in our own time. Despite confused chronology and varying details there is no doubt he foretold a period of subjection to a Western people (some versions said three centuries), who would be driven out by a yellow race from the north. The war was to start 'as soon as a wire should gird the earth, men be able to converse though widely separated, distance be annihilated and carriages move without horses'. To the Indonesians, therefore, the Japanese looked promising as potential liberators and the prediction of the twelfth-century king undoubtedly influenced them to welcome the yellow invaders, since their stay was to be short, and the freedom of Java would follow their departure—as indeed it proved. One can only hope that the conclusion of Djoyoboyo's prophecies—that 'a hundred years after the holy war Java shall be laid waste by volcanic eruptions, become partially submerged beneath the sea and return to its former condition of being eight islands'—will prove less accurate.

It was late evening when we at last reached Blitar, but from that moment our troubles ceased. This was entirely due to the kindness of the Regent, whose daughter was one of my students. A large car swept us to his residence, built in traditional style with a wide *pendopo*, marble-paved halls and high bare rooms. After supper he showed us round and pointed out a huge heavily carved table.

"They call that the Holy Table," he said, "because it has saved men's lives. In 1919 our volcano, Kelud, suddenly erupted and killed fifty thousand people. The lava rushed right in at the back door of this house—you can see the mark of its height on the doorpost there—and the then Regent and his family only saved themselves by climbing on top of this table. It is very solid, you see."

"But did they have no warning?"

"Kelud never gives warning, that is why it is so dangerous. There is a lake in the crater and nobody can tell when the weight of the water will make it collapse. It has broken out three times already in this century."

"So it might erupt at any time—even tonight?"

R

"Perhaps; the last time was in 1951, but it only killed some cows. And after 1919 they built a special refuge out there in the garden."

The refuge was comfortingly close, built on a high stone platform; and we slept soundly after our long day.

Next day the Regent's daughter took us to the ruins of Tjandi Penataran, the biggest Hindu temple in East Java. On the way she told us about her father and family; there had been ten boys and three girls, but some had died and one brother, Supriyadi, was missing. He had been an officer in the Jap-sponsored Home Guard, the PETA, but gradually they became disillusioned by Japan's selfish exploitation of the 'Co-Prosperity Sphere' and in February 1945 Supriyadi led a rising against the ever-growing oppression of the occupation. Unfortunately the Japanese secret police suspected something and the rebels were soon driven out to the foothills of Kelud. Six officers were captured and executed, but Supriyadi himself escaped into the jungle—and had never been seen again. The Regent was imprisoned and his family suffered house-arrest; but they were proud of one who, for all his failure, was remembered as a hero, the leader of the first nationalist rising, whose example gave courage to others to take up arms against all forms of imperialism, whether of East or West. Four years later the family were again in trouble for their stubborn nationalism. When the Dutch occupied Blitar during the Second Clash, they had to flee to the coastal hills, where they lived as refugees till the enemy withdrew.

After these reminiscences of modern violence Penataran seemed doubly serene in the clear cool sunlight of late afternoon. Nor was the atmosphere of peace too deceptive, for the temple dated from one of Java's most peaceful periods, the height of Modjopahit. Smooth lawns and carved grey stones against a backcloth of coconut palms made a pleasing general picture and closer inspection added artistic interest. In the middle stood a small restored temple with a steeply stacked roof; behind it another, notable for the great snakes undulating round the eaves; and behind that again the main temple rose in three terraces with wide platforms and relief-covered walls. The top was flat with a pit in the centre; but whether this was for royal ashes or a holy tree, or indeed whether Penataran at all resembled the earlier mausolea like Prambanan, was not clear. Its ground plan reminded us more of a modern Balinese temple than of the highly symmetrical pattern of Prambanan or Sewu, and there was also something Balinese in the flat *wayang*-like figures and vegetable whorls that filled the panels of reliefs. Penataran was typical of the later style of Hindu-Javanese architecture, when the rococo Javanese element prevailed, and it formed a clear link between the older monuments and modern Bali.

Not far away we came upon the so-called Pool of the Nymphs, which was really a pair of ancient stone bath-chambers in a deep hollow. Our approach disturbed some naked soapy youths at their evening ablutions under the flow of the monster-headed spouts. Gazing at these elegant showers with their permanent running water, where the Javanese had bathed perhaps every evening for the last six centuries, we could not help comparing the plumbing of Modjopahit with the rusty waterless apparatus at our hotel. . . .

The Regent's kindness did not stop at hospitality. He confirmed the date of Kasada night, booked us a room at the nearest resthouse to the volcano and lent us the indispensable jeep to reach it. So we drove off up the circling course of the Brantas and, perhaps because it was lovely weather and a holiday, the East Java countryside looked gayer and more colourful to me than the flat green sameness around Jogja. Deep ravines and steep hillsides gave variety to the scenery; the roads streamed with shining jingling dogcarts, gallant with banners and feathers; and the files of women in bright plain *kebayas* and scarlet shawls, proudly upright under loads that they carried Bali-wise on their heads, made a pleasing contrast to the dingy browns and bent backs of Mid-Java.

A few miles past the pleasant hill-town of Malang we turned down a side road in search of Tjandi Singosari, founded as a mausoleum for the proud king Kertonegoro. On we bumped till we came upon two guardian giants, sunk deep in the road and so colossal that two boys were playing on one gigantic hand. But they must have guarded some other shrine, for we found we had missed Singosari temple behind a thin screen of trees some way back. An old crone conducted us around and regaled us with fluent but dubious archaeology. Comparatively modest in size, the building looked slightly unfinished owing to the unwonted plainness of the monster faces over the four doorways. The cells were empty except for one, where a typical wise man with flowing beard and protruding belly was identified by our guide as the fabulous smith, Mpu Gandring, maker of the magic *kris* that played such a part in Singosari's brief and bloody history. Some other images were arrayed in the grounds, but I could hardly believe that a stout negroid figure squatting on his haunches portrayed King Kertonegoro himself, while Raden Widjoyo, the the founder of Modjopahit, was disappointingly represented by his lower half alone.

The rise of Singosari was a crime story of Elizabethan horror. At the beginning of the thirteenth century the district was ruled by a regent on behalf of the King of Kediri. But his wife conspired against him with a handsome but unscrupulous young adventurer called Ken Angrok, who employed Mpu Gandring, the most skilful of all the sacred caste of smiths, to make him a particularly holy and powerful *kris*. Angrok's thanks, however, were to try out the blade on the smith himself and the dying Gandring cursed the weapon, foretelling the death of seven princes of Singosari by this very blade. The first victim was Angrok's master, the husband of his mistress. With the ruthless cunning of Macbeth he lent the *kris* to a friend, then secretly took it back and left it in the murdered regent's body, so that his friend was executed for the murder while he won the queen and the throne. He then set about extending his power and conquered and slew his suzerain, the king of Kediri. But he could not escape the curse. Five years later his stepson Anusapati, learning like Hamlet the truth of his father's death, got an officer to assassinate him with the fatal *kris*—which was then used to execute the assassin! Anusapati in turn was murdered twenty years later by a genuine son of Angrok; but the latter was quickly despatched by his victim's son.

So far five rulers of the land had perished by the *kris*, and after a respite of one reign, the last two, Kertonegoro and the rebel who overthrew him, died violently in war. Legend does not make it clear whether they too fell to the cursed blade; but anyhow Gandring the smith's prophecy came near enough to the truth. Of Singosari's eight rulers only one died naturally.

From Singosari we sped down the main Surabaya road, but on reaching the north coast we veered eastward along endless avenues of tamarinds beside the reedy sea. At last we turned up into the mountains and by tea-time we reached Sukapura on the slopes of Bromo. Here a quadruple-bed awaited us and we took to it early in preparation for the midnight ordeals of Kasada. At 11 p.m. we dressed warmly and drove up the lonely road to Ngadisari, where the one-way track began. Here and there our headlamps lit up files of Tenggerese padding down the road with yokes of cabbages, leeks and onions for the markets in the plain far below. Many showed slanting Balinese eyes and fierce unusual moustaches, marks of a different type from the normal Javanese. Their isolation had also left them with different moral characteristics, according to Raffles, who reported that crime was almost unknown among them, so that they neither knew nor needed laws against theft, adultery, gambling, opium and other habits so deplorably common elsewhere.

At midnight the barrier at Ngadisari was lifted and we plunged into a maelstrom of bucking jeeps, skidding motor-cycles, shying horses, goggled Chinese and villagers loaded with live chickens, palm wreaths and even a *gamelan*, all pressing eagerly along the narrow muddy track. At last we emerged on a cliff-top where the brilliant full moon showed us a vast basin surrounded by sheer cliffs and in the middle two great grooved cones that were hills in themselves. This was the famous Sand Sea, so called from the mist that gathers in the basin, making it look, in moonlight or at dawn, like a wide silvery lake. Down a precipitous track our jeep slithered into the mists. In the blind and featureless sands of the flat floor we quickly got lost and it took some searching to find the foot of the lower, wider cone, Bromo itself.

Up on the volcano's summit torches and pan-pipes and weird shrieks like Redskin war-whoops made the moonlit scene still eerier. We joined a stream of people toiling up the damp sandy slopes, somewhat hampered by the need to be wrapped in a blanket. From inside we could already hear a roaring like the sea. At length Coral stopped, defeated by the slippery steep, though our guide offered to drag her up with a rope. But I persisted and five minutes' stiff clambering brought me to the narrow rim, three feet wide and uncomfortably crowded. Now the roar was thunderous like the rumble of a train in a long tunnel, and I could gaze down to the cavern of red-hot lava far below. But despite the menacing growl and the boiling vapour clouds the inner slopes were alive with small boys shouting and rushing about to catch the offerings of coins, cigarettes and sometimes live chickens that the pilgrims threw from the rim; while down near the lava a wandering torch indicated that a *dukun* was conducting the real sacrifice there.

Even on the volcano's edge it was cold. But we learnt how bitter the tropics can be when we returned to our jeep to wait till we should be allowed to go back along the one-way track—at 8 a.m. The chill mist curled round us and all our thick clothes, blankets, a flask of whisky and even a Highland Fling hardly kept us from freezing. At last, soon after 5 a.m., the light crept over the cliffs and the cones went through a dramatic succession of hues from purple to green. Bromo's ridged slopes grew quiet and deserted again, and by six o'clock we could wait no longer. In defiance of the regulations we fled from the frosty sands and dissolving vapours, luckily meeting no incoming traffic.

As we drove down the deep wooded valley towards the golden sheet of the sea, we began to thaw out and discuss our experiences. Coral told me how, as she sat waiting for me, she noticed a young guide moving from group to group of tourists with a pair of shoes in his hand. She pointed him out to a shoeless Chinese beside her and he gratefully reclaimed his footwear, which he had taken off to make a safer descent. In the crowds and darkness he had lost the guide carrying his shoes and never expected to see either again. It was good to find that even today the pristine virtues persisted in the unworldly realm of Kusumo of Bromo.

13

THE PRESIDENT

OUR visit to Blitar happened to coincide with the fifty-fourth birthday (in the Western sense) of President Sukarno. Knowing his mother lived there, we sought permission to call and give her our congratulations. I wondered in what state she lived, the mother of the man who had already been President of the Republic for ten years and looked a fixture for as long as he liked to remain—or at least till the Constituent Assembly, due to be elected in six months, should complete its laborious consultations. I half expected a grand new mansion and a crowd of obsequious well-wishers celebrating the day. But there was nothing of Madame Mère about Bu Sosrodihardjo; all we found was a simple old lady at home.

The house was a fair-sized place with a garden and a pavilion where the President stayed on his filial visits. This had been the family home since 1917, when her husband, a teacher, was posted to Blitar; and since his death, which occurred during the Japanese occupation, she had been living on his pension. We were received by the President's sister, Mrs. Wardoyo, a large forceful woman with the round Sukarno nostrils, who ran a bus service between Blitar and Malang. In a little while the old lady herself appeared, stout, white-haired and wrapped in a shawl, tottering along on the arm of another, who we learnt was the President's paternal aunt. Here were no celebrations or courtiers, as at Djakarta that day; just the family and ourselves. The mother was eighty-eight and only allowed up for two hours a day; but though deafness prevented her from taking much part in the conversation, she was lively and interested, with a jolly toothless smile and kindly eyes behind her steel-rimmed spectacles.

She herself was a Balinese, a niece of the last Radja of Singaradja, who was exiled by the Dutch. Her daughter had been born in Bali, but her son was born in Surabaya on 6th June 1901. I asked if his birthplace had perhaps been marked with a plaque, but they appeared surprised by the idea; it seems that only the graves of the great are commemorated in Java. The old lady was very proud of her son ("He speaks Dutch, French and English," she told Coral), but a little vague as to his status. Her old-fashioned notions did not comprehend Republics and Presidents —she only knew he was a Radja! On one point, however, she was quite clear: her own contribution to the liberation of her country. She was determined to be buried in the Heroes' Cemetery and kept asking the Mayor if her grave there was ready. And she was right. Without her son the Indonesian Revolution might never have succeeded.

The story of Sukarno was almost synonymous with the struggle for Indonesia's independence. He was not the first to rouse and organise the national consciousness, but it was he who fused the several groups into a mass movement, who insisted that the nationalist struggle must be all-Indonesian, who taught it to rely on the internal strength and inspiration of Indonesia herself instead of seeking outside help from Mecca or Moscow. The periods when he was active were times of advance, while the long years of his imprisonment were times of multiplying factions and confused counsels. It was not his ideas, however, nor his political flair, but his personality that made him the unchallenged leader of the revolutionary movement. He was a demagogue in the true sense of the word, a man who by his moving oratory and magnetic force of character stirred the common people in a way the intelligentsia could not. Not that his intellect was inferior; he was respected by the intellectuals as well and his conception of the Five Principles or Pillars of the Constitution, the *Pantja Sila*— belief in God; respect for all humanity; national unity; democracy;

social justice—became the accepted basis of the country's political philosophy. But his power was based on his ability to move the masses.

It was a dangerous power. The temptation to use it as President and interfere politically in the processes of parliamentary democracy was difficult to resist. One might almost say that he had reached his goal too soon and at the height of his powers found himself in a position where he could not constitutionally use them. His restless energy found it hard to be passive and neutral, an elder statesman in his fifties; and some arbitrary actions brought him into sharp collision with political and military leaders. His dynamic oratory still called for struggle, but now it was the less stirring struggle of reconstruction and hard work; he still called for unity, but party politics depend on division; he still denounced the Dutch, but his dramatic revelations of conspiracy and his demands for West Irian could not revive the fervour of the days when the colonial enemy was there for all to see. Through his very success he had put himself in a very difficult position.

Things were simpler in his early days, I reflected, as I sipped beer and talked to Mrs. Wardoyo. The objective was clear then and the only questions were about tactics: how and how far and how fast. The whole family backed his political aims; the whole nation shared his hopes. From his school days he was plunged in a nationalistic atmosphere, for as a boy at the Hooger Burger School in Surabaya he boarded with the family of Hadji Umar Said Tjokroaminoto, leader of the *Sarekat Islam* (Islamic Union), one of Indonesia's earliest nationalist organisations. Founded in Solo in 1911, it was more political than the first of them, called *Budi Utomo*, or the Sublime Endeavour, which was intended primarily as an educational and social movement. May 20th, the anniversary of the foundation of *Budi Utomo*, was observed as Indonesia's Day of National Awakening; but so recent were these developments that Sukarno was already seven years old when the nation awoke in 1908.

At fourteen Sukarno joined the newly formed 'Young Java'

association, one of the local youth organisations that rapidly sprang up in support of the national movement, and began writing fiery articles under the pseudonym of the tough *wayang* hero Bima. And when he moved on to the Technical College at Bandung he soon became known for his passionate oratory and ability to sway his audience. At one student rally the police chief became so alarmed that he was carried bodily from the platform; and his Professor pleaded with him not to jeopardise his prospects with politics. All Sukarno would grant was a promise not to neglect his studies, and in due time he gained his degree and the right to the title of Ingenieur. But Ir. Sukarno did not practise his engineering. Now he could devote all his time to politics and in July 1927 he founded his own party, the Indonesian National Party (PNI), with a programme of united mass action and the open aim of *Merdeka*, Indonesian independence.

Under his banner he gathered almost all the various national organisations except the Communists. The omission was not due to any particular disapproval of Communism *per se.* The Islamic Union had moved steadily to the Left, adding anti-capitalism to anti-imperialism, and though the older leaders, mindful of religion, resisted the Communists' attempts to infiltrate and control the party, they still believed that as fellow-revolutionaries they must be fellow-patriots and useful allies in the united front of nationalism—an illusion to which, in spite of repeated and violent disappointments, Sukarno always seemed wishfully liable. The reason for the Reds' absence was simply that their leaders were all languishing in concentration camps, following a premature and ill-organised rising in 1926. As usual they had jumped the gun, and the only result was to make things more difficult for their fellows. In Indonesia severe controls were imposed on the freedom of the Press, of meeting and of speech; while in Holland the police took an increasingly unfriendly interest in the activities of the Indonesian Students Union and especially its chairman, a brilliant young economist called Mohammed Hatta.

Thus by 1927 one of the two great stars of the Revolution was rising in Java among the masses and the other in Holland among the intellectuals. Hatta was the first to be arrested, thanks to his anti-Dutch line and his part in Communist-sponsored congresses of Asian students in Paris and elsewhere, where he openly demanded independence for Indonesia and incidentally made a lasting friendship with a young Indian agitator called Jawaharlal Nehru. In September 1927 the Dutch police seized him and his associates and though his brilliant defence won them acquittal in the end, they were kept in prison for six months before the trial took place. Sukarno's turn came two years later. His party, with its appeal to the peasants as well as to the intellectuals and town proletariat and its new self-reliant line, throwing off outside influences and calling on the Indonesians' own spiritual resources, went from strength to strength; and in October 1928 all the youth associations from the various islands united and adopted the three famous resolutions asserting their common Indonesian identity. His personal popularity was shown by the nickname *Bung Karno*, Brother Karno, the man of the people. In December 1929 the government, alarmed by his success, arrested the four leaders of the National Party on a charge of endangering peace and order. It took just a year to prepare and try the case, but the verdict was a foregone conclusion and Sukarno was sentenced to four years' imprisonment.

Without his dominating influence the party split and the nationalist movement came to a virtual standstill till 1932 when it was reinvigorated by the arrival from Holland of Hatta and another student leader named Sutan Sjahrir. Sukarno too reappeared soon after, as his sentence had caused indignation in Holland as well as the Indies and was remitted after only two years. But the colonial government soon struck again. In 1934 all three were arrested and exiled to remote islands, where they remained out of circulation for the next eight years. Again their movement was more or less paralysed. Under lesser leaders Sukarno's grand objective of national unity—unity of all Indonesians of all origins, all levels and all parties—became blurred and their sense of direction grew uncertain in the face of Dutch delaying tactics and the overriding threat of Fascism. New factions arose that remained mere fractions, new groupings that were only gropings. The solution was to come in 1942, but it was due to neither the Dutch nor the Indonesians.

The Japanese occupation forms the most controversial part of Sukarno's career—from the Western point of view. A traitor, a Quisling, a Jap puppet—these were among the epithets lavished on him by the shocked paternalists and echoed, as far as I remember (for I was busy elsewhere in 1945), by our own newspapers. A collaborator he certainly was; but why he should be supposed to owe loyalty to the Dutch, why he should now fight *for* those he had spent his life fighting *against*, why he should resist those who drove out the colonial rulers with the promise of national liberation and the slogan 'Asia for the Asians', is hard to prove. It was not the Dutch who released the nationalist leaders after their eight years' internment, but the invading Japanese. Their loyalty, however, was not given to Japan any more than to Holland; it was reserved for Indonesia and their actions were guided by the single consideration of Indonesia's independence. They were not blind to the imperialism behind the façade of the Co-Prosperity Sphere, and after consultations together they decided to come down on both sides of the fence. While Sukarno and Hatta would openly take part in Japanese-sponsored organisations, Sjahrir was to engage in underground resistance and maintain contact with America. In view of the ruthless power of the military occupation collaboration was a practical tactic, the best way to reap all possible advantage from the collapse of the Dutch administration. But it was patriotism, not servility, that dictated this course; the Japanese had no puppet in Sukarno.

There is no question that the Japanese made a vital contribution to the cause of Indonesian freedom, but it was not quite what they intended. Their eight-day conquest of the Indies shattered for ever Dutch prestige and the idea of white invincibility. The internment of the Dutch officials opened to the Indonesians hundreds of higher administrative posts that had been barred to

them before. Their encouragement of Indonesian writing, painting and language in the hope of assistance in their propaganda
spurred the development of the arts. The formation of the PETA
Home Guard gave the young men arms and military training.
Above all, as a young officer expressed it to me, the Japanese gave
'spirit' to the Indonesians, the self-confidence to fight and win,
not only by showing how Asians could beat Europeans but by
showing themselves more stupid than the people they ruled. The
Indonesian leaders and writers and officials, while eagerly avail-
ing themselves of every opportunity to gain experience, took
subtle pleasure in turning organisations meant to propagate pro-
Japanese feeling into vehicles of nationalism. For instance the
Putera (Concentration of the People's Power), a union of all
Java's nationalist groups, was set up to organise aid for Japan's
war effort and every village and city square was equipped with
radios to echo their propaganda, of which Sukarno's speeches
formed a major part. It is claimed that, though of course he had
to include a satisfactory amount of flattery and denunciation, 75
per cent of the content of his speeches was pure nationalism, anti-
Dutch but not anti-Allied, and so phrased that for his country-
men his attacks on imperialism clearly applied to Japan as well.
Through *Putera* he was enabled to contact the masses throughout the archipelago and awaken their national consciousness
in a way that would never have been possible under the
Dutch.

In return for this equivocal collaboration the Japanese promised self-government in due time and a certain degree of immediate responsibility. Thereupon Sukarno paid his celebrated visit
to Tokyo to express his people's thanks and to receive that decoration, the Order of the Sacred Treasure, 2nd Class, that has been
such a target for sneers ever since. Hatta too was decorated—by
mistake, it was said, as the secret police suspected his contact
with the underground and had meant to intern him. But the
Japanese could not be fooled all along the line. The military
government became more and more oppressive as the mask of
brotherhood slipped. My students, mere children at that time,

described to me the arrogant edicts and brutal punishments, the kidnapping and forced labour, the commandeering of crops and the dirty tricks (like offering schoolgirls scholarships in Japan and then shipping them to army brothels in the Moluccas), that they came to associate with the 'Leader, Protector and Light of Asia'. All this made the new yellow colonialism as much hated as the old white version. But while the looming shadow of defeat only made the military harsher, the politicians in Tokyo saw that concessions must be made. In March 1945 the Japanese authorised the setting-up of a Committee for the Preparation of Independence, and it was to this body that Sukarno propounded his Five Pillars of the Constitution, the principles that were to guide the new state. On 8th August Sukarno and Hatta were summoned to the Japanese G.H.Q. in Indo-China, where General Terauchi promised that independence would be granted to Indonesia within the month. They returned on August 14th to find the underground leaders determined to seize independence by force rather than accept it as a Japanese gift, with a national rising timed to coincide with the expected Allied invasion. But the next day Japan suddenly surrendered and the situation was officially frozen in the *status quo*.

All was confusion. Sjahrir and the fiery student leaders were still for seizing power by arms and declaring their independence at once. Sukarno and Hatta doubted their strength and hoped to avoid a bloody clash with the Japanese army, whose orders were now to preserve order till the Allies took over. On the 16th the students lost patience and kidnapped the two leaders at 4 a.m. in order to force them to make the declaration forthwith. Finding that the Japanese knew of their plans and would oppose them, the leaders now agreed that a bloodless revolution was impossible and immediate action was imperative; but they still wished to avoid provoking reprisals by too bellicose a tone in the proclamation. Finally at 10 a.m. next day a somewhat flat but quite definite Declaration of Independence was read by Sukarno to a small group on the porch of his residence at Pegangsaan Timur 56, Djakarta:

'We, the people of Indonesia, herewith declare the independence of Indonesia. Matters concerning the transfer of authority, etc., will be carried out effectively and in the shortest possible time.

'The deputies of the Indonesian People,

'SUKARNO.   HATTA.'

The red-and-white flag was hoisted; and the same flag, now an historic heirloom, was used again every year in the solemn re-enactment of the scene on its anniversary, the 17th of August, Indonesia's National Day.

The position of Sukarno, and of Hatta as his deputy, was unchallenged and remained so till after I left Indonesia. Universally acclaimed as President and Vice-President, they became known as the *Dwitunggal*, or Twin Pillars of the Revolution. They made a good combination, Sukarno the leader and Hatta the backroom boy, the inspiring fighter and the efficient negotiator, the Javanese and the Sumatran; and between them they guided the newly proclaimed Republic into a reality, backed by the devotion of many able lieutenants and a united people.

The Dutch were shocked to find the leaders of the pro-Allied underground like Sjahrir working in alliance with their bugbear, the 'Quisling' Sukarno. Sjahrir was Premier of the first three parliamentary cabinets and his presence, as well as his ability, was reassuring to the puzzled British, who preferred his reputation to that of Sukarno. Thus when the President and Vice-President, feeling their liberty of action compromised by the build-up of Dutch force in Djakarta, moved to Jogja on 4th January 1946, Sjahrir remained to negotiate with Dr. van Mook and the British. But Sukarno's retirement to the interior did not mean his withdrawal from the leading role. His progresses through the country, including a filial visit to Blitar, were triumphant demonstrations of popular backing, and it became clear, despite the occasional excesses of the fanatical youth gangs, that the people's comparative discipline depended on his personal authority. His removal to Jogja was an astute political and psychological move, for the new capital's tradition of nationalism and its position far from the Dutch-held areas made it a symbol of the Republic's refusal to compromise.

There followed the four heroic years of struggle to turn the Declaration of Independence into an internationally accepted fact. These were the great years of the so-called Jogja Republic, when this remote city was the heart and soul of a conflict of world significance between East and West, between the old and the new pattern of Asia. But the struggle was not in fact so much one of arms as of political manoeuvre, and actual open warfare only broke out twice. The details of the period are complex but the general development of events is clear enough—the Dutch, bent on reducing the extent of the Republic by force or finesse, splitting away the outer islands, setting up puppet states, wringing more and more concessions in bargaining backed by siege, finally losing patience and using their superior arms to seize still more; the Republicans desperately seeking to avoid open war, yet stubbornly clinging to the vital claim to complete independence and refusing to yield to force; the British, and later the United Nations, trying to hold the ring and the latter at last, after the second demonstration of Dutch intransigence, insisting on a final settlement.

There were relatively few spectacular incidents or names to remember—in 1946 the kidnapping of the Premier, Sjahrir, by the Communists, and the Linggadjati agreement, negotiated under the chairmanship of Lord Killearn, after which the British forces left Indonesia with relief and a clear conscience; in 1947 the 'First Clash' and another truce agreement, named after the U.S. warship Renville where it was signed; in 1948 the second Communist coup at Madiun and the second Dutch 'police action', when Sukarno and his whole government were captured and interned; and finally in 1949, when the guerillas made it clear that no quick settlement was to be obtained by military means, and the protests of the United Nations grew angry, yet another agreement under which the exiles were to be released and Jogja

s

restored, followed by a cease-fire and a Round-Table conference.

On 6th July Sukarno re-entered Jogja in triumph, and in August Hatta led the Indonesian delegation to the Hague. After months of hard bargaining a final agreement was reached and the Netherlands consented to transfer sovereignty to the Republic of the United States of Indonesia. The fight was won; two small points remained to save the face of the Dutch and cause more friction—a paper Netherlands-Indonesian Union (unilaterally repealed by the first elected Parliament) and the possession of Dutch New Guinea, called West Irian by the Indonesians. On 27th December 1949, the ceremony of the transfer of sovereignty was held in Amsterdam and Djakarta. But Sukarno with his usual sense of drama remained in Jogja, represented by Hatta in the Dutch capital and by the Sultan in Indonesia's.

Next day he left for Djakarta—and the great days of Jogja were over.

When we arrived in Java two and a half years later, Jogja had reverted to its status of a provincial capital. But the ' Jogja spirit ' still expressed all that was best in patriotic endeavour and the city held a special place in the memories and affections of the actors in its drama. Thus we often saw the President at University functions and mass meetings, at football matches and dance performances, at army conferences and antiquarian occasions. At our accidental first meeting in Bali I had been impressed by his magnetism and sure instinct for public relations, and every time I saw him I admired more the way he combined effortless domination with democratic gestures, singing or dancing or eating with the students and common people. It was easy to see how he had risen to such undisputed primacy, especially when we heard him speak; it was personality first and foremost, that dramatic quality which makes a great actor and also a great politician like Pitt the Elder or Churchill. His gift for simple but striking phrases was second to his emotional force, leaving a telling impression even on the half-understanding. When he was around, there was excitement in the air, for he was no ordinary man. Though his popular nickname proclaimed him 'Brother Karno', it was not surprising to find that the word *Bung* had become a sort of title of honour, practically confined to himself and Hatta. They were Indonesia's two 'Big Brothers'—but fortunately not like Orwell's.

It was interesting to compare the visits of the Vice-President to Jogja. Hatta came quite often for a week or so to give a course of lectures at the Faculty of Economics or inspect the big Oriental library he had inspired, the Hatta Foundation. But despite the wailing escort of motor-cycles he managed to slip unobtrusively in and out and I never caught a glimpse of him. Finally I determined to make a special effort to see this famous and respected man, who had not only been Vice-President from the beginning but twice Premier at critical moments as well as architect of the Round-Table Agreement. Worming myself into the front line of the crowd lining the route after a mass meeting at the local stadium, I was within inches of the car as it passed. But Hatta was sharing it with Sukarno; the plump little figure leaning back was almost hidden and quite overshadowed by the handsome waving figure leaning forward. In the end I was able to study him at my leisure during a public lecture on India's Five-Year Plan, which he had just been studying on a state visit to his old friend and fellow-rebel Nehru. Quiet, even, undramatic, his voice droned on, yet he held the packed audience of youth spellbound for two whole hours. His appearance was equally undramatic. Short, chubby and bespectacled, in a neat lounge suit, with a mischievous lurking smile, one would have guessed him to be a Professor or senior civil servant rather than a fiery revolutionary leader. Bung Hatta was the antithesis, and complement, of Bung Karno.

Their co-operation had worked wonders for Indonesia; but it was hardly surprising that with two such strong and diverse characters one often heard rumours of disagreement between the Twin Pillars, though the break did not come till after our time. In these rumours it was mostly the President who was criticised, for he was the more dramatic, more erratic personality, the one who roused strong feeling. Now that the dream had come true and the danger was past, his critics seemed to expect him to retire gracefully into the honoured and neutral obscurity of a constitutional President and leave the field for lesser politicians. For Hatta, the *éminence grise*, the role of elder statesman came more easily. But for Sukarno, the demagogue, to be content with the decorative functions and decorous pronouncements of his position was asking too much. It was all right when he went abroad and, speaking once more for the whole people of Indonesia, could use his powers to charm and at the same time enlighten the outside world with a few home truths. Then the whole country followed his progress with pride and (except for his brief encounters with a Honolulu beauty queen and Miss Marilyn Monroe) enthusiasm, mobbing the cinemas for the film of his U.S. tour in spite of torrential downpours. But at home, as politics grew tainted with faction and power with corruption, the President's words were not always so acceptable nor his person above criticism.

Every now and then, when the politicians were too flagrantly playing politics or lining their pockets, the army would lose patience and defy the government, though at the same time usually proclaiming their loyalty to the President himself. In other countries these military interventions would have been revolutions; but the Indonesians seemed genuinely devoted to the idea of democracy and their happy knack of dealing with the ensuing crisis was remarkable. There were conferences, consultations, compromises, but no decision or positive action till so much time had passed that everyone was bored with the business. After a time the offending government might fall and the search for a new coalition would begin, while the country and the army carried on as usual—for fifty-eight days on one occasion. There was never any bloodshed, and for us in the provinces very little perceptible effect.

There was the Affair of the 17th October, for instance, when the army chiefs shut down Parliament and trained guns on the Presidential palace, till the President dispersed them with a few moving words. For us it just meant the return of the Sultan, ousted from the Ministry of Defence in the subsequent reaction. Two and a half years later Jogja, as the home of national unity, was chosen as the scene of the officers' conference which officially healed the split and banned politics in the army. But the first result was another affair, when the government's choice for the new Chief of Staff was rejected as an unqualified political appointee. Even when the President, as Commander-in-Chief, insisted on his installation, the army leaders so completely boycotted the ceremony that the musical honours had to be provided by a police band. The Deputy Chief of Staff then kept the General locked out of his office, and this Gilbertian situation continued till the government fell a month later. The President wisely left on his previously arranged pilgrimage to Mecca, leaving Hatta to cope with the crisis; and finding the country still without a government on his return, he promptly took a holiday.

Such incidents inevitably tarnished his prestige. The new government criticised him for identifying himself too much with the previous National Party administration and its interests in the coming elections; the army criticised him for his support of the unlucky General; the students criticised him for undue loyalty to certain old comrades convicted of corruption—and the women criticised him for his second marriage. The last was perhaps the sorest point. There was nothing illegal, of course; as a Moslem he could have four wives. But the militant Women's Movements, fighting for their new marriage law, were furious at his failure to set an example of modern monogamy. What was worse, his new wife was notoriously pretty and gay, a divorcée with five children. Such was the cordiality at our visit to the President's mother that we dared to ask if she knew and approved of her new daughter-in-law. Yes, though she had not yet met her. The family defended the marriage with remarkable frankness on medical grounds and declared that if the public knew the full story, there would be no more criticism. Though I sympathised, I could not help doubting this; the opposition of the women's organisations was on social and general grounds, not personal ones; it was a matter of principle, a question not of Sukarno but the President. And a President, it seemed, should be inhuman.

Yet, for all the criticism and gossip, there was no suggestion of a rival on the horizon. And, for all the affairs and incidents, the state continued to advance with general support towards the goal of parliamentary democracy. Despite Dutch tales of rampant banditry, despite repeated postponements, despite the very real difficulties of geography and illiteracy, the first General Election in the history of Indonesia was duly held on 29th September 1955—just ten years after the Declaration of Independence and less than six from the recognition of Indonesia's sovereignty.

It was with some trepidation that we awaited the great day. For months houses, trees, street corners, highroads had been plastered with a growing number of party signs till they sprouted in small forests at every corner. The Communists as ever were particularly energetic and unscrupulous, proclaiming the Hammer and Sickle as the sign of the 'Communist and Non-Party' voters. No one could tell what would happen, all campaigning was forbidden for two days before the polling, police and army were on the alert. What struck us, however, was rather the lack of electioneering activity; each Sunday some party would hold a rally on the palace green, but there were no canvassers, no loudspeaker vans, no soap-box meetings to disturb our peace. Apathy seemed prevalent, and on the morning of the 29th our street was so quiet that I began to think that everyone must simply have taken the day for a nice holiday. Certainly the riotous mobs, predicted by some of our Western friends, showed no signs of activity, and I decided to take a walk round the nearby polling-stations.

I was amazed. The people were not visible on the streets because they were packed in the school yards in enormous sinuous queues, patiently waiting for their turn to vote. Evidently, like our own maids, they had all gone to the station early, before it opened at 8 a.m. There were all sorts from toothless old hags to young girl students, from smart westernised office workers to peasants from the *kampongs*, dressed in their best and complete with *kris*, as befitted a great occasion. Hundreds of babies, slung on their mothers' hips, suffered for democracy. Despite a staggering proportion of illiteracy Indonesia had universal suffrage over the age of eighteen, and here were the people, quiet, orderly but firmly determined to exercise their right to choose their own government at last. The arrangements were scrupulously fair and remarkably efficient, though the checking system meant slow progress and some voters had to wait as long as six hours. With no less than forty-eight parties in the field the voting papers were huge sheets covered with a bewildering array of emblems, since most of the voters could not read. The voter went into a booth, punctured a hole in the middle of the emblem he favoured, refolded the sheet and dropped it into a ballot-box, the emptiness of which had been publicly demonstrated beforehand. At 2 p.m. the gates were closed, but those waiting inside got their vote; and as soon as the station was clear, the counting began in public, watched by party scrutineers. It was the quietest election I have ever seen, but there was no doubt of its fairness and freedom. If this was not democracy, nothing was.

Later that evening we heard that the Communists were leading in Jogja. An American family spent all night packing in readiness for instant flight before the Red Terror. Anxiously we scanned the papers next day, but they contained only scattered and provisional results. (There was also a picture of the President waiting in the voters' queue in Djakarta like his fellow-citizens—a typical popular gesture.) In the next few days it became evident that four parties—the Nationalists, the Communists, and two Moslem groups—had swept the board between them, while the other three dozen or so had been more or less wiped out. The results, however, continued to trickle in from remote islands and all the ballots had to be checked in Djakarta; the caretaker government carried on from month to month, and the excitement died down long before the final results were published.

At last, on 26th March 1956, a full six months after the elections, Indonesia got its first elected government in history. The

National Party, the *Masjumi* (Liberal Moslems) and the *Nahdatul Ulama* (the dark-horse party of orthodox Moslems whose success in East Java was the surprise of the election) formed an overwhelming coalition under ex-Premier Sastroamidjoyo. The President, intent as ever on national unity, delayed his approval for two days while he sought the inclusion of some 'progressive' representation in the Cabinet; but the Moslems would have none of it, and the President bowed to the will of the majority.

Whether the experiment would work, whether the people were mature enough and the politicians responsible enough for parliamentary democracy, whether the army would bear with the government's blundering and the outer islands with its centralism, whether the President would let things take their course or step in with the theory of 'guided democracy', only the future could tell. But one thing was certain. Under Sukarno's leadership, which he might so easily have turned into dictatorship, Indonesia had won not only independence but real freedom, the chance to choose its own government.

14

GOING WEST

AT Christmastime we generally went to Bandung, the capital
of West Java, high in a plateau of the Priangan highlands.
This city has now acquired international fame as the seat
of the first Asian-African Conference, that historic demonstration of the resurgence of the East. But we used to go there—and
I fancy the conference was held there—not for its Asian but its
Western characteristics, first among which were the only two
comfortable modern hotels in Indonesia. To subject the delegates
of twenty-nine nations to the trials of a stay in Djakarta would
hardly have been a good advertisement or calculated to induce an
amiable frame of mind. For us Bandung's Christmas attractions
also included the visible signs of the Christian feast—shop windows
bright with trees and tinsel and cotton wool, dances and dinners,
sharkskin dinner jackets and long evening gowns—none of
which were to be found in Jogja, where the Christian population,
though not negligible in numbers, was nearly all Chinese or
Javanese.

Bandung was a Dutch-built city, just fifty years old on 1st
April 1956. There was, of course, a village there before and local
patriotism placed Pakuan, the capital of the shadowy medieval
kingdom of Padjadjaran, in the locality. But for all practical
purposes it was a Western city dumped amid the Sundanese hills
and it boasted itself as the 'Paris of Java'. We found this claim
rather exaggerated. Even the Braga, the vaunted shopping street,
could offer little of real quality, and its narrow length, obstructed
by cars, beggars and importunate hawkers of black sticks of

vanilla, bore no relation to the spacious boulevards. Of the celebrated beauty and gaiety of the ladies of Bandung we could not
really judge, for we went there to associate for a change with
Europeans, who formed a high proportion of its inhabitants.
Certainly the *kains* were gayer, greens and reds and mauves, with
kebayas of equal boldness; but few Javanese frequented the hotel
dances, whose non-European patrons were mostly Chinese,
deadly serious in their concentration on the most dashing evolutions of rumba or samba. And once the novelty (for us) of real
bars and Palm Court music wore off, there was not really so much
more to do. Paris, as we remembered it, was gayer than that.

Yet though it could boast no historic sites, Bandung's short
history was connected with some highly significant points in the
development of modern Indonesia—the rise of Sukarno, the fall
of the Dutch, the consolidation of the Republic and the new
state's entry onto the international stage. The Technical College
saw the start of Sukarno's political career and the Bandung Study
Club was the nucleus of the first National Party. The barracks
were the headquarters of General Ter Poorten, whose surrender
to the Japanese on 8th March 1942 marked the end of the Dutch
empire in the Indies. The seizure of the city by the private army
of 'Turk' Westerling on 23rd January 1950 brought such a
reaction against his federalist backers that the United States of
Indonesia soon merged themselves into a unitary Republic. And
the Bandung Conference of April 1955 made its name the symbol of the new spirit of the East and Indonesia's leading part in it.

The last was the only one of these events that took place during
our own time, but we caught the backwash of Westerling's
abortive coup through the imprisonment of Sultan Hamid II
of Pontianak (Borneo) in the gaol at Jogja. This handsome
playboy-prince had been one of the leading supporters of the
federal schemes of the Dutch, who hoped to set the outer islands
against the centre and thus retain indirect rule through division.
Sultan Hamid led the federalist delegation to the Round Table
Conference and was a Minister in the first government of the
United States of Indonesia that resulted. But apparently his

ambitions were not satisfied and with Westerling he concocted a wildcat scheme to liquidate the heads of the army (including the Minister of Defence, Hamengku Buwono, who was not only a fellow Sultan but had been his classmate in school at Jogja), kidnap Premier Hatta and force the President to appoint Hamid himself as chief minister. The Bandung coup was a bungle which served only to warn the government, and when Westerling moved on against Djakarta, their proper objective, his troops were easily driven off. The 'Turk' escaped to Singapore in a Dutch military plane and thence slipped off to Holland, having succeeded only in poisoning the accord just reached between Holland and the newly recognised Republic. Sultan Hamid was arrested, tried and gaoled in Jogja, where he languished in ignominious oblivion throughout our years there. Not unnaturally his old schoolfellow did not visit him.

Even the great A.A. Conference left us comparatively undisturbed. High hopes were entertained of seeing the distinguished guests among us at Jogja; programmes of dances were rehearsed; the Hotel Garuda was hastily redecorated and all the best rooms cleared. It appeared that large parties were expected as early as the second day of the conference. But the delegates proved strangely devoted to business, and in the end Jogja had to be content with the Iraqis, the Yemenis and King Norodom. A few days later we visited Bandung ourselves, staying at the hillside home of the British Council Representative, close to the villas which had sheltered Pandit Nehru, Premier Sastroamidjoyo and other leading figures. This house too had shared in the excitement, for the Gold Coast delegates, far from showing rabid anti-colonial bias, had sought the Council's help and borrowed the Representative's house for their official reception. It took place on 'Black Thursday', when Ceylon and others defied India's neutralist lead and denounced Communist imperialism as strongly as that of the West; the looks of Nehru, U Nu, Nasser and the rest had been grim, the atmosphere strained. But it was as a result of this clash that the final agreement was not merely a sterile and empty repetition of platitudes about colonialism and peace, and Chou En Lai made his offer to negotiate over Formosa instead of starting a war.

The Bandung Conference had positive results. Yet even without them it would have had world significance simply as a show of political maturity by the ex-colonies, a sign of the Renaissance of Asia.

The country round Bandung was much finer than Mid-Java, real mountain country. The most popular excursion was to the crater of Tangkuban Prahu, the Overturned Boat, whose flattened outline was easily distinguishable to the north. Clouds twice prevented us going there, but at last we picked a good day and were able to stand on the rim, gazing into the grey depths, streaked with sulphur green and viciously steaming, of the third largest crater in the world. The strange name was obviously suggested by its silhouette and various legends had been invented to fit it. One told that a lovely queen, desperate at finding her bridegroom-to-be was really her long-lost son, set him a seemingly impossible task to perform in a single night: to dam the river Tjitarum and turn the valley of Bandung into a lake, to fetch her in a boat big enough for his whole army and to prepare the marriage feast on board. As usual the suitor was on the point of success when the horrified mother sought the intervention of the gods. The dam was swept away, the huge boat capsized, and thereafter it lay stranded upside down, with the cooking fire still smouldering inside.

But mountains mean not only wilder scenery, but wilder conditions. Historically West Java had nothing to compare with the great Hindu civilisations of Central or East Java. We hear hints of a fifth-century kingdom of Taruma, and the Written Stone of Bogor gives evidence of the claims of Padjadjaran, contemporary with Modjopahit. But the area's history really began with the expansion of Moslem power in the sixteenth century, and then it was more or less confined to the northern plains and ports. The highlands of Priangan owed their development to the Western taste for coolness and tea, after the colonial power had been firmly established. But with the revolution the mountains once again became the stronghold of resistance to the rule of the centre. The fanatical *Darul Islam* was based on the hills south of Bandung, from which it waged its Holy War against the unfortunate peasants in the name of an Islamic Republic. Hardly a day passed without reports in the papers of villages looted, houses burnt and men killed by these ideological bandits. But though the government forces seemed incapable of finally cleaning up that remote corner of the hills, it was the only area of the island where security had not yet been re-established. No longer were bandits apt to hold up our friends in the suburbs of Bandung; our expeditions to the volcano or to local plantations were uninhibited; we safely risked the train to Jogja, though it passed through the worst area and once in a way might be derailed; and the road to Djakarta streamed with traffic.

When we drove down to the capital, we passed through rich, striking and varied hill country. Yet the suggestion, often voiced by our Indonesian friends and mutely supported by a pseudo-Swiss chalet on the saddle of the Puntjak pass, that the scenery rivalled the Alpine glories of Switzerland, was not appropriate. It was a different kind of beauty and appealed to a different taste. When Coral, in reply to President Sukarno's enquiry, replied too candidly that life was sometimes rather monotonous in Java, he protested, "But think of all the beauty of Nature!" She could hardly answer that for us this was one of the more monotonous items, too intensely, insistently green; the actual variety of trees and vegetation—the village clumps of bamboo and coconut and banana, the jungle ferns and foliage, the lonely scarecrows of kapok and the ranks of straight red teak or slashed silver rubber—all seemed overwhelmed by the universal tropicality. To expect the exhilarating grandeur of the Alps at the Puntjak was to court disappointment.

Further down the road at Bogor, tropic nature came into its own in the celebrated Botanic Gardens. In the heat of the afternoon we were able to stroll agreeably down long shady avenues of enormous trees, each one draped in a different creeper or parasite of exotic size or delicacy. There were flaring beds of cannas and astonishing orchids; there were terraces of fantastic cactus that put abstract art to shame; and there was a lake covered with vast Victoria Regia waterlilies, their five-foot leaves floating with turned-up rims like a set of old-fashioned tea-trays. In the midst of this riot of tropic exuberance we suddenly came on a quiet little Grecian temple, sheltering a marble urn on whose pedestal we read the following English inscription:

> Oh thou whom ne'er my constant heart
> One moment hath forgot
> Tho' Fate severe hath bid us part
> Yet still forget me not.

It was the memorial to Olivia, the first wife of Raffles, who died suddenly in the Governor's residence at Bogor on 26th November 1814. The verse was her own. Together with the Doric porticoes of what is now the President's summer palace, this monument brought me a sudden breath of England and the eighteenth century, as if I had been wandering in some unknown corner of Kew.

The palace at Bogor was Raffles' favourite home during the five years that he served as Lieutenant-Governor of Java. But though he was a great improver, he was not the founder of either the house or the gardens. The property was bought in 1745 by Governor-General van Imhoff for a country home, which he named *Buitenzorg*, the Dutch equivalent of *Sans Souci*. Soon it became the official palace of the Governors, as the climate was more refreshing and healthy than the miasmic mugginess of Batavia. The gardens were originally laid out in formal Dutch style, but in Raffles' time they were altered according to English landscape principles; and the idea of the Botanic Gardens may well have originated with him too, as his all-embracing interests included natural history and the biggest flower in the world was named after him. *Rafflesia arnoldi* was discovered in 1818 by an expedition that he sent to Central Sumatra, when he was Governor of Fort Marlborough (Bengkulu), after Java had been handed back to Holland; a gigantic parasite that measured more than a yard from the tips of the petals and weighed in all more than fifteen pounds.

The gardens were opened in 1817, the year after he left Java, and began with nine hundred varieties of forest trees. The second curator, a self-trained gardener called Teysman, turned to plants as well; and by now the plant collection was said to boast over half a million different kinds, while the tree specimens had risen to ten thousand. Gradually Buitenzorg became an organised scientific centre with laboratories and a zoological museum added to the old herbarium and library; and in the town there grew up related experimental stations for agriculture and forestry, institutes for chemical and rubber research, and what became the Veterinary Faculty of the University of Indonesia. Yet for all the comprehensiveness of the plant collection I could not find *Rafflesia*. A pity, perhaps; but it did not need a record-size flower to remind us of Raffles in that place. Even more than the rest of Java, Bogor was filled with memories of that astonishing Englishman.

There was another town in West Java that I always intended to visit for its English connections—Bantam (now Banten), the historic trading station of Elizabethan days, at the island's north-west corner. Most of our early descriptions of Java deal with the kingdom of Bantam, though the first two Englishmen to set foot on Javanese soil, Sir Francis Drake in 1579 and Thomas Cavendish in 1588, seem to have passed along the south coast, as they headed westward for the Cape of Good Hope. Their purpose, however, was raiding rather than trading. The first permanent 'factories' were set up by the East India Company in the first years of the seventeenth century, and in Java the chosen port was Bantam.

Originally the port of Padjadjaran, that obscure but obstinate Hindu kingdom that defied all the efforts of Gadjah Mada and in the end survived Modjopahit itself, Bantam gained independence and power as the spearhead of Islam. The Moslem traders, finding the Straits of Malacca blocked by the Portuguese, took to the Sunda straits instead, on which Bantam is strategically situated. Soon it became the chief port of call for the pepper trade; and as in East Java, religion followed hard on the heels of trade, and conquest on the heels of religion. In 1526 Sunan Gunung Djati, the Saint of Teak Hill, forestalled the Portuguese by seizing both Bantam and the neighbouring harbour of Sunda Kalapa for Islam. The Hindus of the interior of Padjadjaran were not subdued for another fifty years, and a mysterious and isolated remnant called the Badui has survived to this day. Sunda Kalapa was re-named Djayakerta, which was shortened to Djakarta.

Under the Saint's vigorous descendants Bantam quickly rose to supremacy in the west, rivalling the influence of Mataram in the east. The Portuguese were allowed to establish a trading station; but the union of Portugal with Spain under Philip II involved them in hostilities with the English and Dutch. The Protestants, aggressive and adventurous, began to poach on Spain's preserves. Drake and Cavendish sailed through the archipelago on their way home from raiding Spanish America; James Lancaster in 1592 reached Acheen (Atjeh) at the northern tip of Sumatra. But the Dutch were the first to undertake an organised venture with an expedition of four ships under Cornelis de Houtman, which succeeded in reaching Bantam in 1596. Both nations soon promoted their East India Companies, the English in 1600 and the Dutch in 1602, and both set up factories in Bantam and its dependency Jacatra (as the Europeans spelt Djakarta). The first English factor died quickly, but his successor, Edmund Scot, left a vivid account of the ways of the Javanese and the adventures of the westerners in the time of Shakespeare.

Once the Dutch had finally disposed of the Portuguese in a sea-fight in Bantam Bay, a collision between them and the English became inevitable despite the official alliance of the two countries. This rivalry, joined to the family quarrels of the Regent of Bantam and the prince of Jacatra, gave rise to some highly complex intrigues, which came to a crisis in 1619. The Dutch company was a national rather than a private enterprise and perhaps for this reason the cloven hoof of imperialism showed sooner in their case. Intent on the extremely profitable spice trade, they early decided to concentrate on the East Indies and in 1610 appointed a resident Governor-General with wide powers. The first Governor chose the Spice Islands (as they called the Moluccas) as his headquarters and he appointed as his deputy in Bantam a young man named Jan Pieterszoon Coen. Coen soon proved himself a character of wide vision and ruthless determination and in 1618 he succeeded to the Governorship-General. He decided that the Company must have a permanent fortified base and picked on Jacatra.

Meanwhile the English too had adopted a forward policy under Thomas Dale, ex-Governor of Virginia, and aimed to drive out their rivals with the aid of the Javanese, who found the English more liberal in their business dealings. A Dutch vessel was seized in Bantam harbour; Coen retorted with an attack on the English factory in Jacatra; and open warfare broke out. It was a very close thing. Only the disputes among the English and Javanese allies besieging the Dutch fort at Jacatra, as to the terms of surrender and division of the spoils, saved Coen's base—and perhaps changed the course of history. On 30th May 1619 Coen arrived from the Spice Islands with overwhelming naval reinforcements and forced the English to retire. He occupied the whole city in the name of the Company and renamed it Batavia, the town of the *Batavi* or Dutch. That date marked the foundation not only of the capital but of the Netherlands empire in the Far East.

It was the beginning of the end for the English. Four years later they were expelled from their foothold in the Spice Islands by Iron Curtain methods. The ten employees of the English Company in Ambon were arrested on a charge of conspiracy, tortured with water and the rack, and executed after forced confession—a scandal so notorious that Dryden used the story for a propaganda tragedy, *The Massacre of Amboyna*, during the Third Dutch War. Yet the English hung on in Batavia till 1628, Djapara till 1648 and Bantam until that kingdom's extinction in 1682. The

T

closing of Jacatra to all but Dutch shipping had meant that all the rival trading nations crowded Bantam, which thus rose to a peak of prosperity and power under its Great Sultan. But, as at Mataram, dynastic quarrels gave the Dutch the chance to intervene and expel the old Sultan, turning Bantam into a protectorate and their own monopoly.

The English factory was moved to Bengkulu in Sumatra, which remained in British hands till 1824, when it was exchanged for Malacca. It was Raffles who made this settlement, for he saw in Malaya a more promising field than Sumatra. With Malacca and his own creation of Singapore Britain held the keys of the Straits.

Certainly I intended to visit a place so closely connected with a romantic episode of English history. Besides, to judge from photographs, there were still several picturesque monuments in this now decayed port—the old mosque with its lighthouse-like minaret; the pilgrim-haunted tomb of Bantam's first priest-prince, Maulana Hassanuddin, son of Sunan Gunung Djati; and Ki Amuk, the Holy Cannon, related in legend to the married cannons of Solo and Djakarta—the third point, in fact, of an eternal ordnance triangle.

But a visit to Bantam meant a stay in Djakarta—and that was a thing I always avoided as far as possible. That sprawling, overcrowded, sweating, characterless conglomeration of ugly buildings, filthy canals and rowdy traffic had none of the features of a capital and hardly any of a city. With a population vaguely estimated as between two and three millions, it had been well described as 'the biggest shanty-town in the world'. For a newcomer it was a nightmare, the worst possible introduction to Indonesia; and even upon acquaintance it never seemed to improve. The same difficulties over accommodation, the same lack of transport, the same disobliging service, the same wrong information, the same hours wasted in getting anything done, the same clammy exhaustion—and in the end, in spite of all the help and hospitality of friends, the same desire to leave at the earliest possible moment.

Not that even that was easy. With planes and trains and hotels always booked to bursting, we were sometimes left in the dilemma of being unable to leave for lack of transport and unable to stay for lack of accommodation!

Only once did we go to Djakarta for pleasure, to see in the New Year in Western style. Our plans had been carefully laid; rooms booked by one friend, transport provided by another, all seemed watertight. But the Hotel Malvenuto was worse than anything our experience had taught us to expect. Our room— the best—was like an abandoned refugee camp, thick with dust, rickety furniture, holes in the walls and a wash-basin too grimy to allow any thought of washing. Frantic appeals to the other hotels brought the usual complacent negative; one even suggested that we might, with luck, find a room in Bogor, forty miles away! All our friends' houses were full, but one offered his from the next morning, when he was to leave on holiday. After a sleepless, dripping, flea-bitten night we fled from the hotel with the dawn. But our Jogjanese driver knew the way about the capital no better than we did. The elaborate system of one-way streets, diversions and roundabouts, devised to diminish the dangerous chaos of Djakarta's traffic, seemed to demand that we should always move in the opposite direction to our destination. Soon we were utterly lost and, after our driver got booked for a traffic violation, utterly demoralised. We gave up the house and made for the Embassy. Yes, we were lucky; there was a staff lodging whose occupant was on leave; true it was only a very damp garage, long condemned as unfit for human habitation— but at least it was a roof. Gratefully we accepted. But after that all the kindness of our friends, all the gaieties of the capital (such as they were) could not keep us longer than was imposed by circumstances.

All thought of Bantam was abandoned, and even of such few sights as the capital itself was said to offer. One or two eighteenth-century Dutch houses, an old Portuguese church, the Museum— why should these detain us? The old fort and city were long gone; the Amsterdam Gate was gone, quite recently; so was the grim wall where the plastered head of the Eurasian plotter, Pieter Eberfeld, had been fixed as a warning since 1722; even the Holy Cannon, Kyai Satomo, to which women had so long offered flowers and prayers for fertility, was now gone, removed to the cold impersonality of the Museum. Let us be gone, too. On the 2nd January we made at high speed for Jogja.

Djakarta, even more than most capitals, does not typify its country. It is neither East nor West; still less is it the desirable fusion of the two civilisations that must come. The form this fusion will take is the problem of the East, the achievement of modernisation without mongrelisation. The historic syncretism of the Indonesians, their quiet readiness to absorb and adapt, should ease this process; but the danger is that, given Djakarta as their model, they may aim at too low a standard and be satisfied with the third-rate. Two considerations, however, encourage me. First, as the opportunities of education and travel open wider horizons to them, the Indonesians are realising that Djakarta is far from representing the best in Western civilisation, on the material or any other plane. Secondly, though the capital may be the political centre of the country—rather too much so—it is not the spiritual centre.

As we rattled along the north coast road, through Tjirebon with its two titular Sultans descended from the Saint of Teak Hill; through Tegal, near which the sadistic Emperor of the Fragrant Earth lies buried; through Pekalongan with its *batik* factories; I could not help feeling that we were moving east spiritually as well as physically. At Semarang we turned south into the hills of Mid-Java and headed between the soaring cones of Sumbing and Merapi, towards Borobudur and Prambanan, Solo and Jogja, the land of the Slender Maiden and the Queen of the South Sea. We were weary, darkness was falling, and there was talk of bandits; but I found my spirits rising all the time. This was the real Java, and however little I might understand its ways, at least I could appreciate its quality.

INDEX